Programming with GNU Software

Programming with GNU Software

Mike Loukides and Andy Oram

O'REILLY®

Beijing · Cambridge · Farnham · Köln · Paris · Sebastopol · Taipei · Tokyo

Programming with GNU Software
by Mike Loukides and Andy Oram

Published by O'Reilly & Associates, Inc., 1005 Gravenstein Highway North,
Sebastopol, CA 95472.

Editor: Andy Oram

Production Editor: Ellen Siever

Printing History:

> January 1997:   First Edition.

ISBN: 1-56592-112-7
[M]

Table of Contents

Preface

In an age where computer software has become one of the most lucrative sources of income for both corporations and individuals, the willingness of many people to share their source code free is something of a miracle. How much more amazing is the success of the Free Software Foundation, along with numerous others around the world, in creating a complete programming environment that you can download across the Net.

This programming environment includes editors, compilers, source control software, debuggers, and numerous other utilities. And the tools are not toys or shaky houses of cards; some offer features that commercial products have been trying to emulate for years, and they are used daily in hundreds of corporations to do production work. The companies that provided the software for the accompanying CD-ROM, Cygnus Support, Inc. and Cyclic Software, have built quite a respectable business helping such corporations.

The tools in this book were developed for the UNIX operating system, although some of them have been ported to other systems, too. Many of the tools that began on UNIX (such as **make**, **lex**, and **yacc**—not to mention the C and C++ languages) have become standards on other systems. And the spirit of sharing and collaboration has been strongest in the UNIX community.

So it is natural that the most comprehensive set of free programming tools should arise on UNIX. In fact, the project that developed most of the tools (GNU, a project of the Free Software Foundation) is working on a complete clone of UNIX.

This book/CD-ROM collection is a complete starter kit for C programmers who want to work on UNIX systems. Binaries for six major platforms are included on the CD-ROM, along with complete sources. This book starts with the assumption that you know nothing about the software except how to program in C. But it takes you quite deep into the various tools and makes you a confident and competent user. So you'll find the book valuable even if your computer system already has the tools—if you're a student, for instance, trying to get programming projects done on your university's system.

If you don't have a UNIX system yet but would like to obtain one, you're in luck, because you can load up your computer with completely free software. Two versions of the Berkeley Software Distribution, FreeBSD and NetBSD, are available on the Net and on CD-ROM and run on a variety of hardware. It's also easy to get the popular Linux system, which currently runs on Intel x86 hardware and is being ported to the Alpha and other platforms. Most of the tools in this book usually come with these systems, and O'Reilly & Associates offers books about all of the systems. Finally, the Free Software Foundation is working on a UNIX-like operating system called HURD.

We hope that this book will unlock the doors to this powerful and enjoyable programming environment for engineers, students, and anyone else who finds himself or herself working on a UNIX system.

Organization of This Book

We've arranged the chapters to give you a gentle and enjoyable entry into UNIX and the tools on the disk. We start with basic utilities you'll use right away, like the Emacs text editor and the C compiler, and continue to more advanced tools that you'll be glad are there, such as **make** and RCS. The first two chapters are general and do not directly concern the software on the disk; later chapters are about particular tools on the disk.

Chapter 1, *Towards a Free Software Development Environment*, explains the benefits of using free software, why people developed it, and what restrictions the General Public License places on its use.

Chapter 2, *Introduction to the UNIX Operating System*, gets you started if you don't know its conventions and essential commands.

Chapter 3, *Editing Source Code with Emacs*, offers a special programmer's introduction to this incredible tool, which has interfaces to just about every other tool on the system.

Chapter 4, *Compiling and Linking with gcc*, explains the sequence of utilities that your C or C++ code passes through during compilation and the most important command options.

Chapter 5, *Libraries*, describes the most commonly used calls available from the libraries on the disk, including calls to handle errors, signals, and time.

Chapter 6, *Debugging C and C++ Programs*, offers a thorough introduction to **gdb**, the GNU debugger.

Chapter 7, *Automatic Compilation with make*, shows you a tool you'll want to use once you get beyond the smallest, most trivial programs. If you've worked on Microsoft systems, you'll already be familiar with **make**, but the GNU version offers a great deal more power.

Chapter 8, *Source Management with RCS*, shows you another tool that you might not think of using right away, but which is critical when you have a long-term project. RCS stores old versions of your files, which you can use to recreate previous releases, back out errors, and do other useful things.

Chapter 9, *Program Timing and Profiling*, shows you how to measure the system resources used by your program, with an emphasis on the profiler **gprof**.

Appendix A, *What Is Cygnus Support?*, briefly describes the company that supplied most of the software for the CD-ROM.

Appendix B, *Building GNU Software from Sources*, gives an overview of the configuration and build system used by the Free Software Foundation and Cygnus Support. This will help you understand what you need to do if you want to recompile any of the tools. However, it is not complete; you should also read the Cygnus documentation.

Appendix C, *Data Representations*, lists typical sizes for data types.

Appendix D, *The GNU General Public License*, reprints the text of the General Public License, which gives the rules under which the GNU software is distributed.

The enclosed CD-ROM contains all the software described in this book. Instructions for installing and setting up the tools can be found in the *read.me* file on the disk.

If You Have Problems with the Software

There's an enormous amount of very powerful software on the CD that comes with this book. O'Reilly & Associates will support the book like any other—we'll help you if you have trouble understanding the text, and give you any information that we can about installation. But we are not prepared to go beyond the text to give expert advice on how to use the tools.

If more expertise is what you need, you can buy a book that goes into more depth about each tool. We offer books about many of the tools:

Emacs	*Learning GNU Emacs*
RCS	*Applying RCS and SCCS*
make	*Managing Projects with make*
C language	*Practical C Programming*
C++ language	*Practical C++ Programming* and *C++: The Core Language*

Support is the whole business of Cygnus Support, Inc. and Cyclic Software. Cygnus offers help on Emacs, the C and C++ compilers, **gdb**, and **gprof**. They don't support RCS or **make**. Also be aware that they are set up to handle long-term relationships with large organizations, not one-time calls from individuals. Call 800-CYGNUS-1 or 415-903-1400 or send email to *support@cygnus.com* to get help from them. Cyclic Software provides a similar set of services for RCS and the CVS versioning system; for a description see its Web site at *http://www.cyclic.com/*.

If you think you have found an actual error in one of the programs on the CD, let us know, and we will make sure it is entered in Cygnus's bug database.

If you have a complicated question about building or using the software, and you aren't prepared to use Cygnus Support or Cyclic Software, where can you turn? Luckily, that is one of the great strengths of free software. Many newsgroups exist to help users support each other:

gnu.emacs.help
> For help using GNU Emacs

gnu.gcc.help
> For help using GNU C features and compiler

gnu.g++.help
> For help using GNU C++ features and compiler

Response from users of these newsgroups often comes within hours.

For each "help" group, there exists a corresponding "bug" group you can check if you think you've discovered a bona fide error in the utility. Since the other GNU utilities don't have "help" groups, people sometimes take their questions to the "bug" groups (even though the names suggest that they're only for reporting actual errors), such as:

gnu.gdb.bug
> Problems with **gdb**

gnu.utils.bug
> Problems with all other GNU utilities

Finally, *comp.software.config-mgmt* exists for discussing RCS and other version control tools.

Conventions Used in This Book

The following conventions are used:

Italic
> Represents file and directory names, function names, program variables, names of books and of chapters in this book, and general emphasis. In examples, it is used to insert comments that are not part of the text you type in.

Bold
> Represents command names, options, keyboard keys, user names, and C preprocessor directives such as **#if**.

`Constant Width`
> Represents programming language keywords such as `int` and `struct`. In examples, it is used to show program code, input or output files, and the output from commands and program runs.

`Constant Width Bold`
> Used in examples to show commands or input that you enter at the terminal.

`Constant Width Italic`
> Used in examples to show generic (variable) portions of a command that you should replace with specific words appropriate to your situation. For example:
>
> ```
>     rm filename
> ```
>
> means to type the command **rm**, followed by the name of a file.

$ Used to show the shell prompt. The default shell prompt is different for different shells and can be changed by the user.

Two different notations are used in this book to represent the use of control keys. One is more familiar to most readers: the notation **CTRL-X** means you must hold down the **Control** key while typing the character "x". When discussing Emacs, we use the notation that its documentation uses: **C-x** means the same as **CTRL-X**. The shift key is irrelevant when you type a letter along with the **Control** key.

We denote other keys similarly (e.g., **Return** indicates a carriage return).

All user input should be followed by a **Return**, unless otherwise indicated.

Acknowledgments

You can't write a book without something to write about, so we would like to offer a big round of applause to the Free Software Foundation and all the people who have put high-quality free software out to the public.

We also thank Cygnus Support, Inc. and Cyclic Software for making these tools attractive to corporations, for their bug-fixing and support, and for providing software on the CD-ROM. Roland Pesch at Cygnus drove the project forward at the beginning and has continuously provided a vision for it. Several engineers at Cygnus also reviewed the draft of this book. Michael Tiemann guided and coordinated the furnishing of the software and final checks on accuracy.

At Cyclic Software, Jim Kingdon provided RCS and CVS software and reviewed parts of the final draft of the book.

It took a lot of work to put a CD-ROM together. We thank O'Reilly system administrator Randi Simons for concerted and repeated work to put the files in the right form, and Jeff Moskow and Mike Raisbeck of Ready-to-Run Software, Inc. for careful testing.

Michael K. Johnson, an important figure in the Linux community, was particularly thorough and expert in his review of the book. He and Dr. Richard Brown at St. Olaf College also organized a contingent of new users to act as reviewers, including Damian Dela Huerta, Kevin T. Hedrick, and Dr. Steven McKelvey.

At O'Reilly & Associates, Ellen Siever was the production editor, Lenny Muellner and Erik Ray provided tools support, Sheryl Avruch and Nancy Kotary did quality control checks, Michael Deutsch entered edits, Chris Reilley created the figures, Seth Maislin produced the index, and Nancy Priest, Eden Reiner, and Mary Jane Walsh did the interior book design.

1

Towards a Free Software Development Environment

UNIX has long been known for its software development environment; the wealth of first-rate and innovative tools is one reason behind UNIX's commercial success.

Lately, however, good tools have gotten somewhat out of reach. Not that UNIX vendors haven't been doing their job, but nearly all of them have "unbundled" their development tools from the operating system itself, so that if you want to do any programming, you need to pay another $600 to $1000. That's not much for a large corporation, but it's a lot for a student or a home user.

This book introduces a set of software development tools that are parallel to the time-honored UNIX tools. They provide the same (or more) functionality and a high level of compatibility with the tools UNIX users have grown up with. These are the compilers and related development tools, often called the GNU tools, from the Free Software Foundation (FSF).

Unlike the UNIX tools—but displaying the same spirit as the early UNIX systems that were installed around college campuses—these tools are "free": they are available from many places without charge, they include source code, and you're encouraged to give these tools away to your friends. Instead of paying your UNIX vendor for a "development system," you can get the source code for the GNU tools from an FTP or UUCP archive.* That may tie up your phone for a few hours, but aside from the phone costs, it's completely free. For a few tens of dollars, you can buy this book/CD combination and get a complete, pre-compiled development environment; similar pre-compiled packages are available from other vendors.

---

* Unfortunately, the operating system sometimes requires features that GNU does not support. Currently, for instance, if you have the SGI Irix system, you need to buy SGI's development system in order to get some critical libraries.

There are a lot of advantages to the CD distribution—of which the most important is that the software has already been built and tested on several of the most commonly used computers and operating systems. If nothing else, that saves you a lot of time: although we'd all like to think that we can grab a software package from the Net, edit a few configuration files, type **make**, and forget about it, we know that real life is rarely this simple.

The CD distribution also solves a nagging "chicken and egg" problem. If you get source code for free software, you need a compiler (and related utilities) to build executables. If you have your vendor's development system, then you can get started, but if you don't, there's no point in loading up your disk with a few megabytes of free source code. By providing pre-built software for several common architectures, the CD gets you out of this bind.

This book is a fairly traditional user's guide to the GNU software development environment. We'll talk about what these tools are and how to use them: how they fit together. We won't go into esoterica; rather, we'll try to make you familiar and comfortable with the most common uses of these tools. So, while we'll spend some time discussing gcc -O (compile C code, with optimization), we'll barely mention gcc -mno-half-pic.

But first, we'll discuss what free software is, why it exists, and what it means for software developers.

UNIX, the Programmer's Playground

When it comes to the sophistication and flexibility of its tools, UNIX can compete with any programming environment on the market. Many tools that now see widespread use throughout the computer field started on UNIX. Just look at the C language.

But there's a hump to get over when you're beginning to use UNIX tools. One reason they're so fast and powerful is that you have to learn very brief commands, or even (in the case of Emacs) keystrokes. Many people try to avoid UNIX because few of its tools support graphics or point-and-click interfaces. But after a short period of getting used to the system, you will find that commands and keystrokes are faster than pointing and clicking. Even more important, you can combine and automate commands. Furthermore, don't forget the cost advantages: you can use the tools on a cheap terminal connected to a serial line.

So if you know what you're doing, the tools in this book help you get your job done a lot faster than a graphical user interface. As a programmer, what you need is a powerful interface to text—and the tools certainly offer that. Anyway, some movement in the direction of graphical interfaces can be seen. Emacs now supports menus and the mouse, for instance.

Integration is another strength of the free UNIX tools in this book. For instance, in the Emacs editor, you can issue a compile command, while making changes to a program. This compile command runs the **make** utility in order to build your program. If the source code is stored in the RCS source control system, **make** can automatically retrieve it. Throughout the discussions of tools, you will see ways to make them collaborate for your convenience.

Where the Power Lies

As we've said, free software tools are command-driven. Some of the commands can get quite powerful, too. For instance, in the **gdb** debugger, the **print** command can display any kind of variable from an integer scalar to an array of strings to a complicated data structure with members of different data types.

So the first stage of your learning is to find a set of commands that do most of the things you want. The next stage is to combine them. For instance, Emacs lets you combine a number of keystrokes into a package and execute it with a couple of keystrokes; this is called a macro. You can also put commands into a start-up file, and Emacs will execute them every time it begins. **gdb** offers a similar initialization file for debugging sessions.

What This Book Offers

If you're a student learning to program who happens to be on a UNIX system, or a programmer from another environment who has a project to do on UNIX, this book will make you comfortable with UNIX and its tools. The book won't teach you C or C++, but it will show you how to build, run, and debug programs.

If you're a more experienced UNIX user who wants a powerful set of tools, this book and CD combination will give you a one-stop programming kit. You might skip Chapter 2, *Introduction to the UNIX Operating System*, but even a UNIX-savvy programmer will find useful tips in the rest of the book.

When you begin to use a new operating system, you often feel like you want to learn everything at once. This book gives you the alternative of a saner step-by-step study plan.

First, after a whirlwind introduction to UNIX, you learn the text editor. Once you can write your programs, you learn about the compiler and some useful C and C++ library calls. Then come the more optional tools, such as the debugger and source control system.

Of course, we can't say everything about every tool in one book. But you won't need to consult other documentation too often; this book should satisfy 95 percent of your needs. We'll list other available documentation for each tool as we come to it. You can install the documentation online from the CD, or order it in hard-copy form from the Free Software Foundation (to be discussed next).

What Is Free Software?

Software developers have been trading their pet programs ever since computers were invented. Particularly in the university community, programmers have always felt free to share their tools with one another. And most computer vendors have, at one time or another, actively encouraged their users to share their software: for instance, DEC's user group (DECUS) maintains a free library of member-contributed software.

Of course, when networking became widespread (in the early 1980s for the university community and early 1990s for other users), it became much easier to share software: when you wrote something you thought useful, it was easy to send it to your friends through email or to post it in some FTP archive or (in the DOS world) on an electronic bulletin board, where others could pick it up. You could get the software "for free"; you could modify it and add your own features; and you could give your new versions to your friends.

So there has always been a lot of free software floating around. The sorts of programs that have been freely available haven't typically been large, substantial programs with significant commercial value—but that's not to say that the software hasn't been useful. We can't imagine someone selling a program like **sps** (which is a fancier version of the UNIX **ps** command), but you can't claim that **sps** isn't useful, either. In the early '80s, major pieces of free software with significant commercial value started appearing, a trend which has really blossomed in the late '80s and early '90s. Entire operating systems (like Linux, a UNIX-compatible operating system that is currently most popular on Intel X86 hardware), compilers (like **gcc** and **g++**), interpreted programming languages (like Perl and Tcl), editors (like Emacs), and other major tools are now freely available.

Different Kinds of Free Software

We can divide free software into three different classes. There are gray areas between each of these groups, but on the whole, most software falls into one category or the other.

Public domain software

Some software is truly and explicitly put into the public domain. This means that anyone can use the software for free and do anything they want to it. There are no restrictions of any kind.

Freely distributable software

A lot of free software, particularly software coming from the university community, is "owned" by the person or organization that developed it. The portions of BSD UNIX that were developed at Berkeley fall into this category, as does the X Window System, along with many, many smaller programs. In this context, "ownership" means that people redistributing the software as part of another project must credit the original owner; it (probably) also means that, while you can modify the software to your heart's content, you can't redistribute your changes under the same name as the original without permission. That is, if you modify BSD UNIX, you can't tell your friends that you're giving them a copy of BSD UNIX without the owner's (University of California's) permission.

General Public License (GPL) software

This means software that's covered by some version of the Free Software Foundation's General Public License (also called a "copyleft"), which is reprinted in Appendix D, *The GNU General Public License*. The GPL is designed to keep free software free. That is, it is crafted to guarantee that anyone receiving the software, no matter how they got it and how it has been modified, can continue to redistribute it under the same terms. We'll go into this in more detail in a minute.

By the way, some people think that GPL stands for "GNU Public License." It certainly originated with the people who started GNU, but it's used on a lot of other software (such as RCS and the Linux operating system). So "General" is the correct term.

In this book, the term "free software" generally means "software licensed under the GPL, or some relatively similar terms"—though many people use the term to include all three categories.

It's worth taking a few moments to understand why the GPL is necessary. The first two kinds of free software guarantee that the original program is, for the time being, free: i.e., you can get the code and modify it. However, they don't prevent one very common scenario. They don't prevent a commercial venture (say, Joe's Computers Inc.) from taking the free software from the Net, improving it significantly, and applying a restrictive license to it—perhaps preventing you from seeing the source code and requiring you to pay a large annual licensing fee for the right to use the software.

If you think that scenario sounds far-fetched, think about the networking code in most UNIX systems. Most UNIX network implementations are based on work done for BSD UNIX. That code is "freely distributable software"; you can get the original BSD network code over the net and do whatever you'd like to it. But would your UNIX vendor give you the source code for their improved version of this same software? Probably not, unless you were willing to pay a lot of money to them—and possibly not under any circumstances. Over time, this mechanism has caused a lot of software to evaporate from the public arena. The original code is usually still available, but the good code—the code you'd really like to have—is a commercial product, and it is not free at all.

The Free Software Foundation was created in the mid 1980s to foster the development of software that would always be free. Their General Public License is designed to prevent free software from evaporating, as corporations cull the best contributions, improve them, and remove them from circulation. It specifically states that anyone using the software has the right to redistribute it, with the source code, and that modifications to the software must also be redistributable. In practice, this means that you cannot apply a restrictive license to your modified version of free code.* In particular, the GPL states that software must always be distributed either with the source code, or with a promise to provide the source code upon asking.

The GPL (or a slightly limited version of it, called the LGPL) is applied to all software created by the FSF. It has also been applied to a lot of software that is not created or distributed by the FSF.

The software discussed in this book, and the software included on the CD-ROM, is all covered by the General Public License; most of it was developed by the Free Software Foundation, or in association with them.

Free but not cheap

It's a common misconception that "free software" means "software that doesn't cost anything." That's really not the case. There is nothing to prevent someone from selling you a disk containing free software, or even charging you for FTPing the software from their network archive. In fact, the General Public License explicitly states that selling the software is allowable—but that you cannot restrict others from reselling what you have sold to them. The CD-ROM that accompanies this book isn't free, for example; you also can buy copies of the software from the FSF itself, Cygnus Support, Cyclic Software, and other companies.

---

* It certainly does not mean that you are forced to distribute your modifications, even if you don't want to. You're free to keep your modifications to yourself—which, in many cases, is probably a good idea. But if you *do* decide to distribute your improved version, you must distribute it under the same terms as the original software.

The word "free" is used in a more political sense: it really means "liberated from licensing restrictions." That's a crucial part of the Free Software Foundation's vision: its goal is to create a complete set of software (an operating system, plus all necessary utilities) that can be circulated without restriction.

Free but not low-quality

Free software is one area in which the adage "You get what you pay for" doesn't apply. Sure, lots of public domain software and shareware is bug-laden and poorly maintained. However, the software distributed by the FSF is, on the whole, among the most well-maintained and up-to-date software available. As a rule, it is usually better than the best commercial equivalents. The **gcc** and **g++** compilers, which are discussed in Chapter 4, *Compiling and Linking with gcc*, are widely acclaimed and generally produce better code than most vendors' compilers. When bugs are discovered, as they are in any software, they are fixed very quickly; the FSF's response to bug reports should be the envy of any commercial software vendor.

Another concern that's often voiced about free software is security. The impression exists that free software is full of Trojan horses, viruses, and other noxious creatures that will disable your system as soon as you start using it. This may be true of some public domain software, but such behavior is (in the UNIX world, at least) fairly rare, though not unknown.*

You owe it to yourself to be cautious about true public domain software and shareware. However, the software that's distributed by the Free Software Foundation is completely trustworthy. Like any software, it may have bugs and security holes—no vendor, no matter what they charge, can guarantee that their software is "bug-free." But you can rest assured that there are *no* intentionally introduced hazards to plague you.

Finally, some users are concerned that free software is "not supported." As we've said, if commercial software vendors were as responsive to trouble reports as the FSF, our world would be a better place. However, that doesn't eliminate the need for traditional customer support services, to provide everything from "handholding" to bug fixes. Such support services are available for a fee, from Cygnus Support and other companies. Cygnus provides a level of technical support that's the equal of that provided with any commercial product. There are, we'll admit, a few people in the free software community who think that "support isn't necessary: you have the source code, so you can fix it yourself." However, you don't have to listen to them if you don't want to.

---

* Even in the DOS and Mac worlds, where viruses abound, it has been claimed that "free software" is actually safer than commercial software. We wouldn't stake our systems on that claim.

Free but usable in commercial applications

Several misunderstandings about the relationship between free and commercial software have discouraged their use together. The most common—though not particularly relevant to this book—is that software covered by the GPL can't be distributed with commercial products. This is just untrue. The General Public License requires that:

- The free software be distributed with source code or an offer to provide source code

- No additional restrictions be attached to the use or redistribution of the free software

Neither of these provisions means that you can't put free software on a distribution tape alongside your commercial product.

The next most common misunderstanding is that code that's "touched" by the GNU tools somehow becomes "free software" and can't be sold commercially—that is, that the General Public License requires output from the **gcc** compiler to be placed under the same license. Again, this just isn't true. While the Free Software Foundation hopes that **gcc** users will feel a sense of obligation to make their software freely available in one form or another, their license does not compel you to do so. Only if you incorporate source code from free software do you have to make your code freely available.

There are a couple of border areas that have contributed to this misperception, though. Because you cannot apply a typical software license to code covered by the GPL, you also cannot incorporate "free" code within a commercially licensed product. This means that libraries present a special problem. Incorporating code from a "free" software library (like **libg++** or the GNU version of **libc**) would create a program that had to be licensed under the GPL—since, by distributing this program, you would also be distributing the libraries.

There are several solutions to this problem. Most obviously, there's no requirement that you use GNU libraries when you compile; you can use commercial C or C++ libraries. If you want to use "free" libraries, however, the Free Software Foundation recognized that restrictions on the use of libraries was preventing people from using their software; free software that no one felt free to use was not helping their cause. To this end, the FSF created a special version of the GPL for libraries (the LGPL); the LGPL allows you to distribute software that includes the GNU libraries without requiring you to make your software freely redistributable or requiring you to ship the source code for your libraries.

This solution is not without its problems—and those problems lead to further solutions:

- Many programs require a parser to handle an input stream, a very difficult piece of software to write correctly. Programmers usually generate this part of their code through a "compiler-compiler" like **yacc**. Old versions of the **bison** parser generator would generate parsers that were under the GPL, thus preventing their use in non-GPL'd programs. This is not true of recent versions of **bison**, however. Nor has this ever been a problem with **byacc**, the parser generator included with this book.

- The LGPL still places too many requirements on the libraries that it covers. While you aren't required to apply the GPL to software that includes LGPL libraries, you *are* required to distribute your software in a way that allows the user to substitute updated libraries for the original ones. Depending on what you're doing, this can be a minor annoyance, or completely impractical: for example, if your software controls a microwave oven, you can bet that the users (a) have no way of relinking your program with a later library release, and (b) don't care.

  Cygnus Support provides their own version of the C libraries; these have a less restrictive license that only requires that you acknowledge use of their software. The CD supplied with this book includes these versions.

The GNU Project, the FSF, and Support Companies

Without a doubt, the GNU project is the world's premier free software factory. Its **gcc** and **g++** compilers set the standard for compilers on UNIX. They also made the development of Linux possible. Richard Stallman's Emacs editor not only boasts a fanatic following, but has been copied on other platforms.

We're not going to delve deeply into the purpose of the GNU project here (for an introduction, go to any site storing GNU software and get the file called *INTERVIEW*), but it goes beyond a set of tools; its goal is the creation of an entire UNIX-like operating system. The project was started by Richard M. Stallman, the developer of Emacs and a famous proponent of free software, around 1985. The Free Software Foundation coordinates and directs the GNU project.

Cygnus Support, Inc. and Cyclic Software put together the packages of free software on the CD-ROM included with this book. They were founded by free-software developers to promote the use of free software by large organizations that perhaps wouldn't consider it under normal circumstances.

The main role of Cygnus is to provide a level of support at least as reliable as that offered by software manufacturers for commercial software. In addition to solving customer problems, Cygnus creates some free software themselves (such as the GNATS bug-tracking system and the DejaGNU test platform), fixes bugs, and writes cross-compilers. They offer customer service for the most mission-critical GNU software, such as the compilers and related program-development tools.

Cygnus maintains close contact with the FSF, although the two are not affiliated. While no longer the only commercial company focused on free software, Cygnus is the largest and best known. A formal description of the company appears in Appendix A, *What Is Cygnus Support?*

The Software in This Book

This book discusses the Free Software development environment, specifically:

- Editor: the Emacs editor
- Compilers: **gcc** and **g++** for C and C++, respectively
- Libraries: **libc** and **libg++**. The libraries included on the CD are the Cygnus versions that are not subject to the LGPL.
- Assembler and linker: the **gas** assembler and **ld** linker
- Binary utilities: **size**, **nm**, **gprof**, and other tools that work with object files and executables. **gprof** does not run on all architectures.
- Debugger: **gdb**, the state-of-the art debugging tool
- Software build program: **make**, for automating the compilation process
- Source control program: the RCS package, for source file revision control

The CD-ROM includes source code for all these packages. The CD also includes **flex** and **byacc**, which aren't discussed in the book.* We've included them because they're needed to recompile several of the other tools.

The CD includes executables for SunOS 4.1.X (on SPARC processors only), Solaris 2.X (on SPARC processors only), HP-UX (on the HP 9000/700), AIX (on the IBM RS/6000), Irix (on the SGI Iris/Indigo), and Digital UNIX (on the Alpha). Linux executables are not on the disk, because Linux users already have binaries for most of the tools as part of their Linux distributions.

Although the CD contains executables only for the platforms listed above, it contains the source code for *all* platforms and cross-compilation environments that

---

* The best source of information on these packages is O'Reilly's Nutshell Handbook *lex & yacc*.

the Free Software Foundation knows about.[*] Thanks to the thoroughness of the Free Software Foundation, plus the loyalty shown by thousands of users who have ported the software to innumerable systems, an automated configuration procedure exists that can handle a huge variety of platforms. Check the configuration files provided with the software; you may be able to build the executables yourself. Appendix B, *Building GNU Software from Sources*, explains the basic procedure. A more extensive guide to building software on different platforms is available in the O'Reilly book *Porting UNIX Software*, by Greg Lehey.

Even if you have one of the platforms for which binaries are provided, you may find a reason to rebuild from sources. For instance, you may want to change the default pathnames stored in Emacs. Or you may hear of new versions of these tools (they are being upgraded all the time) and decide you want them. Since these platforms are so common, you should have no trouble rebuilding your software.

It's worth noting that the GNU tools are not only used under UNIX. Congruent Corporation has ported the GNU tools to Microsoft's Windows NT operating system, and many of the tools run under VAX/VMS. For some systems, the GNU tools are the *only* development environment: for example, they're the only tools available for Linux, 386BSD (another freely available operating system), and BSDI (a commercial operating system based on BSD UNIX).

Installing Binaries

Instructions for installing the binaries are on the CD-ROM, in a file named *read.me*.

These tools are not meant to run from your CD. We have compressed them so that we could fit more onto the CD. But you would probably choose to move the executables to a directory on your hard disk anyway. After all, you bought your CD player to hold a variety of disks, not just this one. Your editor, compiler, and debugger are pretty constant companions, and you won't want to unmount them just so you can load up the latest hot graphics CD.

Updating Your Tools

New features are being added to free software all the time; sometimes a radically different product results. For instance, Version 19 of Emacs (which is on the accompanying CD) introduced the pull-down menus that are so popular on graphics terminals. The most recent version of **gdb** supplies a graphical interface. So,

---

[*] Cygnus does *not* support all the tools or all the architectures; support is discussed in the section called "The Free Software Culture".

while you can be happy with the software on the CD for a long time, you will eventually want to get a new version of some tool.

One option is to get support from Cygnus (to cover the compiler tools) or Cyclic (to cover RCS and CVS). Neither company provides Emacs. If they can supply the binaries for your system, this is the simplest action. (They support a lot of platforms that aren't on this book's CD.) Their addresses are:

> Cygnus Support
> 1937 Landings Drive
> Mountain View, CA 94043
> USA
> WWW: *http://www.cygnus.com*
> Email: *info@cygnus.com*
> Telephone:+1-800-CYGNUS-1 or +1-415-903-1400
> FAX: +1-415-903-0122

> Cyclic Software
> 1701 16th St. NW #652
> Washington, DC 20009
> USA
> WWW: *http://www.cyclic.com/*
> Email: *info@cyclic.com*
> Telephone:+1-202-265-6119

You can also buy collections of products on tape from the Free Software Foundation. Only sources are provided. Their address is:

> Free Software Foundation, Inc.
> 59 Temple Place, Suite 330
> Boston, MA 02111-1307
> USA
> WWW: *http://www.gnu.ai.mit.edu*
> Email: *gnu@prep.ai.mit.edu*
> Telephone: +1-617-876-3296
> FAX: +1-617-492-9057
> FAX (in Japan): 0031-13-2473 (KDD)

When buying from Cygnus, Cyclic, or the FSF, you are helping to support free software.

But one of the attractions of free software is that it is free of charge—if you can take the trouble to obtain it over a network. A number of Internet sites have the sources for all the software in this book on FTP sites. One of the most popular is *ftp.uu.net.* Go to the directory */systems/gnu* on that site. The home site for the FSF is *prep.ai.mit.edu*, where the software is under */pub/gnu*, but that site is often overloaded and sometimes has to deny access to anonymous logins. If you want to **ftp** free software regularly, go to the */pub/gnu/GNUinfo* directory and get the file *FTP* for information on sites around the world that carry free software; you can then choose a site closer to you that is less well known. For people without Internet access, free software sources are also available on some BBS sites.

The Free Software Culture

As you have probably guessed, free software is based largely on volunteer efforts: although many people have contributed to the wealth of software that's available, the number of people who make their living (all or in part) from free software is very small, indeed.

The most important organization devoted to the proliferation of free software is the Free Software Foundation. They have made lots of software available on their own, and they're a good source for information about other programs. One of the FSF's goals is to develop a complete UNIX-like operating system; they have already developed many of the utilities for this operating system, including versions of **tar**, **more**, **vi**, and **sed** (plus the software described in this book).

The best way to find out what software is available from the Free Software Foundation is to **ftp** to *prep.ai.mit.edu* or one of the systems mirroring it, and look in the directory */pub/gnu*. It's also a good idea to look in the *gnu* Usenet newsgroups; this is where you'll find free software discussed most heavily. Particularly important newsgroups are:

gnu.announce
> For announcements of newly available free software, new releases, etc.

gnu.emacs.help
> For questions about the Emacs editor

gnu.g++.help
> For questions about the **g++** compiler

gnu.gcc.help
> For questions about the **gcc** compiler

gnu.misc.discuss
> For general discussion and questions

The last group, *gnu.misc.discuss*, is where to find out about the "feel" of the free software community; there's a lot of philosophical and legal discussion, in addition to questions about what software is (or should be) available (and if it doesn't exist, why not). This group is very sensitive to any mention of a commercial product, so be forewarned.

Another good source of information is the *GNU's Bulletin*, the Free Software Foundation's newsletter. This is published in January and June; you can get a copy by sending your name and address to:

> Free Software Foundation, Inc.
> 675 Massachusetts Avenue
> Cambridge, MA 02139
> USA

They ask you to send sufficient postage to return their reply, but this is not required. (The postage is $0.78 for someone in the U.S., and enough International Reply Coupons for a package of 100 grams to reach overseas correspondents.)

You can also send electronic mail to *gnu@prep.ai.mit.edu*; that's a good way to ask questions.

The Free Software Foundation is always in need of money, talent, and equipment. If you use the software described in this book, you should realize that they're giving away a package with a commercial value of several thousand dollars. You are encouraged to make a tax-deductible donation to the Foundation so they'll be able to continue providing this service. The donation allows them to do all the things that a software development environment has to do—rent space, pay staff, buy equipment, and so on.

We'll end the chapter by mentioning one other important organization. Although there is no formal connection between the Free Software Foundation and the League for Programming Freedom (LPF), most people who are interested in free software agree with the goals and aims of the LPF. The LPF is an advocacy group whose charter is to "protect the freedom to write software ... which is threatened by 'look and feel' interface copyright lawsuits and by software patents." Software patents, in particular, are increasingly being awarded to companies to cover common processes that many programmers use.

Many commercial software organizations support the LPF. Its purpose is quite different from the FSF. The LPF simply wants to make sure that the developers of all kinds of software—free and commercial—can live without fear of being sued because their software is vaguely "like" somebody else's. If you are interested in the LPF, send mail to *lpf@uunet.uu.net*.

2

Introduction to the UNIX Operating System

UNIX is an extremely versatile operating system with a wealth of program development tools, ranging from the mundane, like editors, to the esoteric, like compiler-compilers. For a new user, the heart of UNIX is its user interface: a program called the *shell*, which is a command interpreter that handles your keyboard input.

This chapter provides an introduction to the most basic features of UNIX: it introduces programmers to typical command syntax, describes the most commonly used commands, and describes the simplest way to manage input and output. It also provides an introduction to shell programming, or writing programs made from UNIX commands. Such programs are commonly called command files on other systems.

Finally, this chapter describes the organization of the standard UNIX documentation set, which is available online through the **man** command. Later chapters in this book move from the heart of UNIX to the fringes, discussing the powerful tools available for program development and management.

There are many sources for more information about UNIX. The documents "UNIX for Beginners" and "An Introduction to the C Shell," both in the UNIX *User's Supplementary Documents*, are useful. Many books provide more comprehensive introductions to the UNIX system. In particular, we recommend:

- *UNIX in a Nutshell* (O'Reilly & Associates), a desktop quick reference, with different versions for System V, SCO UNIX, and Linux.

- *The UNIX Programming Environment*, by Brian W. Kernighan and Rob Pike (Prentice-Hall), a standard work on UNIX and its tools.

Logging In to UNIX

To log in to a UNIX system, you must have a *username*, which your system administrator will assign. Typically, your username is your first name, your last name, or your initials. This name is public information. Others, who may not even be users of your system, will use this name to send you messages or mail. Your administrator may also assign a *password*. Always keep your password secret. You can change your password at any time by running the **passwd** program and answering its prompts.

When UNIX is waiting for you to log in, it displays the prompt "login:" at your terminal. Respond to this prompt by typing your username in lowercase letters, followed by a **Return**. If you have a password, UNIX displays the prompt "Password:". Respond to this by entering your password. Your password may have uppercase letters and special characters in it. For security reasons, UNIX does not display your password as you type it. If you are dialing in to the system over a telephone line, UNIX may also prompt you for a dial-up password. This is a special password that your system administrator may assign; it ensures that only authorized users can dial in over a telephone line. (Most versions of UNIX do not support dial-up passwords, but you should be aware of the possibility.)

On a dumb terminal, a typical login sequence looks like this:

```
login: joseph          Type your own username
Password:               UNIX doesn't echo the password

This is the message of the day.  It may contain useful
information, like scheduled downtime.  For example:

       system going down at 10 PM for maintenance

$                       UNIX prompt, indicating a successful login
```

If you log in successfully, UNIX goes through an initialization procedure in which it sets up your terminal and customizes your UNIX environment. This process may or may not require you to do anything; see your system administrator for details. Finally, UNIX displays a message of the day, which may contain useful information about your system's schedule. This is where your system administrator can tell users about any planned maintenance or downtime.

If you have a graphics terminal running the X Window System, you start by seeing the login and password prompts on the screen. After you log in, the system presents you with a collection of windows, including one or more terminal-emulation windows (controlled by the **xterm** program) showing prompts. You can enter UNIX commands in these windows.

After you have finished working, use the command **logout** to log out of the system. UNIX responds by displaying the "login:" prompt again:

```
$ logout

login:
```

On the X Window System, you may not be able to log out of your window, or logging out may not shut down the whole session. Try moving the pointer to the root window and pressing the buttons on your mouse to find a pop-up menu; it may have an "Exit" menu item.

UNIX Commands

When the shell expects you to enter a command on your terminal, it displays a prompt. In most cases, the prompt is either a % (percent sign) or a $ (dollar sign). This is a clue to the type of shell you are running, which sometimes determines the commands you enter. The prompt may contain other information too: your login name, the system's name, the directory you're in, etc. This can all be customized, but we won't go into that here.

A % indicates that you are running a version of the *C shell*. A $ indicates a version of the *Bourne shell*. Among free software users, a version of the Bourne shell known as *bash* (for "Bourne-again shell") is popular; it is created and maintained by the Free Software Foundation. The most significant differences between the C shell and the Bourne shell variants are the control structures they offer when you're doing shell programming (writing executable programs from shell commands). They also recognize different shell and environment variables to customize their behavior. Most of the commands discussed in this chapter are applicable to both shells.

When you see the shell prompt, you can enter a command by typing the command name, followed by **Return**. A UNIX command is simply the name of a file (i.e., the name of a program that the system will load and execute). For example, the command **date** is a program that prints the current date and time on the terminal:

```
$ date
Wed Jan 11 10:15:02 EST 1995
$
```

Many UNIX commands require *arguments*, which are placed after the command name. For example, the **date** command can optionally have the argument -u. In this case, it prints the Universal time (Greenwich Mean Time) rather than the time in your local time zone:

```
$ date -u
Wed Jan 11 15:15:02 GMT 1995
$
```

You may also wish to place a *directive* after the command's arguments; these allow you to redirect the program's terminal input and output. For example, the > (right angle bracket) lets you send output to a file that would normally be displayed on the terminal. Consider the command:

```
$ date -u > foo
$
```

This places the current universal time in the file *foo*, creating that file if it does not already exist and overwriting it if it does.

In general, the format of a UNIX command is:

```
$ filename arguments directives
```

Note that there are many variations in the way commands expect their arguments. Many of these arguments (such as the previous -u argument) are called *options*, or *flags*, indicating optional features of the program that you invoke; these typically begin with a – (hyphen). Many options require their own arguments. For example, the -o option to **gcc**, the GNU C compiler, lets you specify a filename for the compiled program. This requires an argument:

```
$ gcc -o outputfile program.c
```

In this command, the filename *outputfile* is part of the -o option, while the filename *program.c* is a separate argument specifying the source file for **gcc** to compile.

Many, but not all, programs let you combine flags. For example, the **ls** command, which lists the files in the current directory, considers the following two invocations equivalent:

```
$ ls -l -a
$ ls -la
```

If you make a mistake while typing a command, you can press the DELETE key or the BACKSPACE key to erase the last letter you typed. On your terminal, one (or both) of these characters should work correctly; if neither works, see your system administrator. To erase the entire line you have typed, hold down the **Control** key and type the letter "u". In the rest of this book, this action will be abbreviated CTRL-U.

The UNIX Filesystem

UNIX files are simpler than those on many other systems. You don't have to deal with drive names like C: or arbitrary restrictions on lengths of names (although some very old UNIX systems had a length restriction). If you learn the few simple rules in this section, you can move easily around the filesystem.

Files and Filenames

A file is a set of data that has been stored on the system's disk. A file is identified by a *filename*. Filenames generally include uppercase and lowercase letters, numbers, periods, underscores, and hyphens. UNIX is case-sensitive: the two filenames *Mine* and *mine* are *not* equivalent. Filenames may not include a / (slash); this is used to separate directories in a UNIX pathname (discussed later). Other punctuation marks, like an ! (exclamation point) and a ? (question mark), are technically legal, but will cause problems, because they have special meanings. There are ways to use these characters if you insist, but you are better off avoiding them. The following table shows some legal, illegal, and troublesome filenames:

Legal	Illegal	Questionable (not recommended)
more_data.dt	*more/data.dt*	*data?dt*
Program.C	*program/C*	*program!C*
2a,std		*2a*std*

In many systems, filename extensions (the part after the period) are considered distinct from the filename. The operating system knows about extensions and handles them separately. This is not true of UNIX. A period is just another character in the file's name. You may have as many or as few as you want. For instance, a common convention is to name a file something like *myprog.tar.gz.1*, meaning part 1 of a gzipped tar file.

The Filesystem's Structure

UNIX has a hierarchical, or tree-structured, filesystem. Each file can be found within a *directory*, as a leaf lives on a twig. Similarly, each directory can be found within a parent directory as a twig lives on a branch, as a branch lives on a bough, and as a bough lives on the trunk of a tree. At the top of this inverted tree is a special directory called *root*. The name of the *root* directory is represented by a / (slash). Figure 2-1 shows, schematically, a small part of a typical filesystem tree.

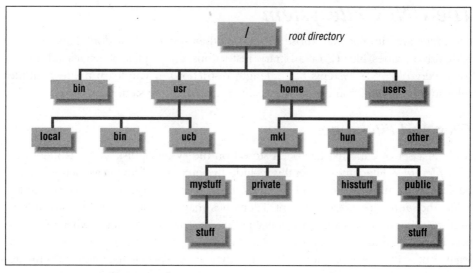

Figure 2–1: A UNIX filesystem tree

A directory usually contains files and subdirectories that somehow relate to each other. For example, on most UNIX systems, the directory */usr/local* contains generally used programs that have been developed at that particular site. For development projects currently under way, a directory should contain all the files and subdirectories needed for a given task or subtask. Organizing your files like this will make it easier to use some of the development tools in this book, like **make**.

As Figure 2-1 shows, there can be any number of directories between a given file and the root. To specify completely the name of any file or directory, you must enter a full *pathname*, beginning with the root and listing all the directories between your file and the root, separated by slashes. For example, the full pathname of *mystuff* is */home/mkl/mystuff*. Complete pathnames are long and cumbersome. Fortunately, they are rarely needed. At any point, you are within a current working directory. You can refer to files within this directory without giving a complete path; you only need the filename. When you log in, your current directory is initially the home directory that is assigned by your system administrator. You can change the working directory by using the **cd** command (which we will discuss later). To find out your working directory at any time, enter the present-working-directory command:

```
$ pwd
/home/hun/hisstuff
```

This shows that you are currently working in the directory */home/hun/hisstuff*.

The tree structure allows many files within the filesystem to have the same name. The files are completely distinct, as long as they are in different directories; remember that the file's complete name is a full path, beginning with a slash. For example, the files */home/mkl/private/stuff* and */home/hun/public/stuff* are different files. If your working directory is */home/mkl/private*, the name *stuff* refers to the file */home/mkl/private/stuff*. Similarly, if your working directory is */home/hun/public*, the name *stuff* refers to */home/hun/public/stuff*.

You almost never have to use a full pathname, starting with the root, to refer to a file. Instead of a full pathname, you can use a *relative pathname*. We have already seen that you can use a simple filename to refer to files in your current directory. In this case, the filename is technically a relative pathname: it is relative to your working directory. To refer to files in a subdirectory of your current directory, the relative path is just the subdirectory's name followed by a slash followed by the filename. For example, when the current directory is */home/hun*, you can refer to *stuff* underneath the *public* directory as *public/stuff*.

To refer to files that are further down the directory tree, add as many levels of subdirectories as you need. You can put the current directory in a pathname by specifying a . (dot); more often you'll find it useful to refer to the directory *above* the current one by entering .. (dot dot). For instance, if your current working directory is */home/mkl*, you can refer to */home/hun* as *../hun* where the double dot stands for the */home* parent directory.

The ~ (tilde) is another abbreviation to help you use short filenames. A ~ means your home directory; likewise, the abbreviation *~name* means the home directory of the user *name*. For example, if your home directory is */home/mkl*, then *~/private* means the same as */home/mkl/private*.

At this point, you may be wondering how UNIX finds commands. As we said previously, a command is nothing more than a filename. In most cases, you do not have to enter a complete pathname for the command. UNIX maintains a list of directories, called a PATH, in which it looks for files whenever you enter a command. This PATH is part of your UNIX *environment*. To find out what the current PATH is, enter:

```
$ printenv PATH
~/bin:/usr/ucb:/bin:/usr/bin:.
```

This reply means that when you enter a command, UNIX looks a directory called *bin* within your home directory, then directories */usr/ucb*, */bin*, and */usr/bin*, and finally the current directory (.). This is an example of a typical PATH. We'll show later how to modify it, in case you need access to another set of commands such as the ones in */usr/local*.

CAUTION   If you set the PATH variable incorrectly, UNIX will not be able to rec-
              ognize any commands without a complete pathname.

Simple Commands for Working with Files

So far, we have given little information about the commands used to work with the files and the filesystem. This section discusses some simple UNIX tools for working with files and directories.

Let's create a file or two in a crude way using the *echo* command. This just echoes the text you specify as arguments. If you use > you can create a file containing the text.

```
$ echo Lutes, lobsters, and limousines > foo1
```

This creates a completely new file, destroying the contents of *foo1* if it already exists. To display one or more short files on your terminal, use the command **cat**, followed by a filename. For example:

```
$ cat foo1
Lutes, lobsters, and limousines
$
```

cat is short for "con*cat*enate," which is what the command does: it concatenates a group of files and sends the output to the terminal. If, instead, you want to place the result in a file, *redirect* the output with a > (right angle bracket):

```
$ echo Make Jack a dull boy. > foo2
$cat foo1 foo2 > result
$ cat result
Lutes, lobsters, and limousines
Make Jack a dull boy.
$
```

This gives us a simple way to create a new file. If you don't enter any arguments, **cat** takes its input directly from the terminal. Remember that **> result** does not count as an argument. CTRL-D (end of file) terminates your input:

```
$ cat > newfile
Twas brillig and the slithy toves
```

```
Did gyre and gimble in the wabe
                  - Lewis Carroll
CTRL-D
$
```

Using >> instead of > (e.g., **>> oldfile**) adds the input to the end of the file, if it already exists.

We can copy the file, creating another new file using the copy command:

```
$ cp foo1 other
$
```

This creates a file called *other* that is identical to *foo1*. We can also rename the file with the move command, **mv**:

```
$ mv other movedfile
```

After this command, the file *other* no longer exists; a new file, *movedfile*, exists whose contents are identical to *other*.

We can now list the contents of all the files in this directory using the list command, **ls**:

```
$ ls
foo1     movedfile     result
foo2     newfile
$
```

ls can have a number of arguments. The most useful argument is the -l option, which produces a long listing. This lists each file's protection status (who can read, write, or execute the file), its owner, length in bytes, and its creation date, in addition to showing the filenames:

```
$ ls -l
-rw-r--r-- 1 loukides 31 Jun 5 13:38 foo1
-rw-r--r-- 1 loukides 20 Jun 5 13:38 foo2
 .
 .
 .
$
```

The letters on the left side of the report show the file's protection status; we will discuss this topic in the section "File Access Permission" later in this chapter. **ls** can also be given the name of a directory or the names of a group of files within a directory. For example, to list the files in your home directory, you can enter the command **ls ˜**, where the ˜ (tilde) is a shell abbreviation for your home directory.

If you no longer need a file, delete it by using the remove command, **rm**. For example, to delete the file *foo1*, enter the command:

```
$ rm foo1
$ ls
foo2      newfile
movedfile result
$
```

The **ls** command verifies that *foo1* has disappeared from the current directory.

Remember that all the commands discussed here can have any kind of filename as an argument: complete pathnames, files in the current directory, relative path-names, and abbreviated pathnames. If you try to do something illegal (e.g., if you try to **cat** a file you are not allowed to read), UNIX prints an error message. But be forewarned: UNIX will let you do many destructive or unpleasant things, such as **cat** to an important data file, without any warning.

If you want to be safe, use the commands **rm –i** and **mv –i**. **rm –i** asks for permission before deleting each file, giving you one last chance to change your mind. **mv –i** asks you for permission if renaming a file requires destroying a file that already exists. In either case, typing **y** says "go ahead," while **n** means "STOP".

You can also keep the shell from accidentally overwriting a file when you use > to redirect output; this requires setting the **noclobber** variable. See the section "Shell Customization" later in this chapter.

Simple Commands for Working with Directories

To create a new directory, use the make-directory command, **mkdir**, followed by the directory name:

```
$ mkdir newdirectory
$ ls
foo2        newdirectory      result
movedfile   newfile
$ ls newdirectory
$
```

When you list the contents of *newdirectory*, you find out that UNIX always creates empty directories (i.e., directories without any files in them). If you try to create a directory that already exists, the command will complain by printing the message "mkdir: *name*: File exists."

If you finish with a directory and want to delete it, use **rm** to delete all the files within the directory, then use the remove-directory command, **rmdir**, to delete the directory itself:

```
$ rmdir newdirectory
$
```

If there are some files remaining in the directory, the command complains "Directory not empty". If the name you give does not refer to a directory, the command complains "Not a directory" or "No such file or directory". You can also use **rm -r** to delete the directory. This automatically deletes all files and directories with it. You won't get unwanted complaints, but you also won't get any warnings either.

The **ls** command does not normally list files whose names begin with a period (e.g., *.bashrc*). Several UNIX customization files have names of this form, as do some scratch files created by UNIX programs. Therefore, a directory may appear empty and still have some files in it. To list all files, enter the command **ls -a**.

```
$ ls -aF
./              .bashrc         gensched.c
../             .newsrc         update/
$
```

Now you can see *.bashrc* (a start-up file for the **bash** shell) and *.newsrc* (a start-up file for news programs). In addition, you see two strange directories named with a single dot and a double dot. These mean the same thing that we described before: a single dot represents the current directory, while a double dot represents its parent. UNIX needs these entries in every directory so it can move up the directory hierarchy and find other directories.

Another useful variation is **ls -F**. This appends a / (slash) to all directory names and an * (asterisk) to all executables. It lets you easily distinguish between files and directories. For instance, in the following display, the slash indicates that *RCS* is a directory, while the asterisk shows that *gensched* is an executable file. This makes sense, because we compiled the C code *gensched.c* to produce *gensched*.

```
$ ls -F
Makefile        RCS/            gensched*       gensched.c
$
```

To move from one directory to another, use the change-directory command, **cd**. In most cases, you will follow this command with the name of the directory you wish to enter. If you do not enter any arguments, **cd** will move you to your home directory. The following sequence of commands uses **cd** to move between directories:

```
$ mkdir newdir
$ cd newdir
$ ls
$ pwd
/home/mkl/newdir
$ cd
$ pwd
```

```
/home/mkl
$
```

Remember that you can use abbreviations like .. (dot dot) to mean the parent of the current directory and ˜ (tilde) to mean your home directory.

Wildcards

You will often wish to refer to a group of files, and from time to time, you will want to abbreviate long filenames. To do this, the shell allows you to use *wildcards* in filenames. The wildcards are:

*   The asterisk matches zero or more characters (including numbers and special characters).

?   The question mark matches any single character (including numbers and special characters).

[]   The sequence [`selection`] matches any character appearing in `selection`. A group of consecutive letters or numbers can be expressed with a – (hyphen); for example, **[a–z]** means all English lowercase letters.

The name * means "absolutely everything" (except files beginning with . (dot), which are a special case). Remember that UNIX doesn't consider extensions separate; you don't need to say *.* . The name *my*file.c* means "all filenames beginning with *my* and ending in *file.c*" (with or without something in between), the name *myfile.?* means "all filenames beginning with *myfile.* and followed by exactly one character", and the name *myfile.[co]* means "*myfile.c*, *myfile.o*, or both." You can use as many wildcards as you need. For example, the filename *.?* is perfectly legal and means "all filenames that end with a period followed by one character." Wildcards can be used in directory names too.

It is legal to use a wildcarded filename in a command that requires a single argument, provided that the filename matches only a single file. If it matches several files, UNIX prints the error message "filename: Ambiguous".

File Access Permission

The group of 10 characters on the left side of an **ls -l** report show the file's protection status, more commonly known as the *access mode* or *mode bits*. Here is a sample report:

```
$ ls -lg
total 11
-rw-r----- 1 mkl staff  344 Jun 14 14:45 complex.txt
-rw-rw-rw- 1 mkl staff 1715 Jun 14 14:45 datarep.txt
-rwxrwxrwx 1 mkl staff 2345 Jun 14 14:45 program
drwx------ 1 mkl staff 3522 Jun 19 10:33 mail
```

The far-left character on each line of the report shows whether the entry represents a file or a directory. A – (hyphen) indicates a file; the **d** indicates a directory. In the listing above, *mail* is a directory; the other entries show regular files. You may occasionally see **b**, **c**, or **s** in this field. These letters stand for *b*lock devices, *c*haracter devices, and *s*ockets, all of which are beyond the scope of this book.

The remaining nine letters are one-bit flags that control file access. A - indicates that the flag is not set, while any other letter indicates it is. To make the display more readable, *ls* uses an **r** to show that a bit allowing read access is set, a **w** to show that a bit allowing write access is set, and an **x** to show that a bit allowing execution access (i.e., permission to execute a program) is set. You may also see **s** or **S** in fields where you expect an **x**. These encode some high-order bits (e.g., the "setuid," "setgid," and "sticky" bits), which are also beyond the scope of this book.

These flags are divided into three sets. One set controls access for the file's owner (the three bits to the immediate right of the directory bit). Thus, the sample report shows that the owner has read and write access to all three files. The owner has permission to execute only the file named *program*. The other two files look like simple text files, which we wouldn't want to execute anyway. The access bits have slightly different meanings for directories, which we'll discuss later.

The next three bits control access for members of the file's group. Each file belongs to a group, as does each user. When a file is created, it belongs to the same group as its creator, although you can change a file's group membership with the **chgrp** command. All the files in the previous report belong to the group **staff**. Thus, in our sample report, *complex.txt* can be read (but not written) by **staff** members, *datarep.txt* can be read or written by members of the group, and *program* can be read, written, or executed.

The rightmost three bits control access for all others. Only the owner and group members can read *complex.txt*; others have no access to it. Anyone who can log on has both read and write access to *datarep.txt* and is also allowed to execute *program*.

Earlier, we mentioned that the bits have special meanings for directories. You can understand the read and write bits by realizing that the directory is also a file. Listing the contents of a directory means reading the directory and requires "read" access. Writing a directory means adding or deleting a file from the directory and requires "write" access. You can modify a file in a directory without write access, because modifying a file doesn't require any changes to the directory itself. The execute bits mean something completely different. For directories, execute access means permission to "search" a directory for a file. In other words, execute access means you are allowed to look up and access files within the directory. If you do not have execute access to a directory, you can't do anything to it. On the other hand, if you have only execute access, you can do quite a lot. You can't list the files in the directory (so you can't do anything with a file unless you know its name); you can't add or delete files, but if you know the name of a file, you can read, modify, or execute it, depending on what permissions you have for the file.

The change-mode command, **chmod**, lets you change file-access permissions. It is used like this:

    $ **chmod** *who op perm files*

where:

who

> Indicates whose access you want to change and is optional, but usually present. The **u** (user) indicates the file's owner, **g** indicates the file's group, **o** indicates others, and **a** indicates all (i.e., user, group, and others). If *who* is omitted, it defaults to **a**.

op Is + (plus) to allow access, – (minus) to restrict access, or = to allow the indicated access and disallow all others.

perm

> Indicates which permission you want to change. The **r** indicates read access, **w** indicates write access, and **x** indicates execute access.

files

> One or more files affected by the command, separated by spaces. Directories and wildcards can appear here, too.

For example, the command:

    $ **chmod g+w complex.txt**

allows group write access for the file *complex.txt*. Formerly, group members were not allowed to write the file. You can set multiple permissions in one command. For instance, to allow read and write permission to both the user and the group, enter:

    $ **chmod ug+rw complex.txt**

Online Documentation

The standard UNIX documentation is a set of online files (often published as a set of manuals, too) that you can read through the **man** command. The traditional "man page" is the ultimate authority on any command. Every UNIX system comes with manual pages online, and most also have them as hardcopy documentation. Being reference documentation, manual pages are hard to understand until you have some experience with UNIX. But once you know what you're looking for, you'll use them regularly. We'll start referring you to manual pages later in this very chapter.

On many systems (including BSD, Linux, and older versions of System V) the documentation is divided into the following eight parts:

1. Commands and utilities, giving a summary of each command and all its optional flags

2. System calls, giving a summary of every operating system call

3. Library routines, summarizing every routine in libraries available to programs running under UNIX

4. Special files which are the basis for low-level UNIX I/O

5. File formats, describing the formats of different UNIX files. This includes the formats of various system database files, different kinds of executable files, initialization files, etc.

6. Games, describing game programs that are part of the UNIX system

7. Miscellaneous, describing the ASCII character set, typesetting macro packages, and other features that don't fit elsewhere

8. Special commands for system administration, describing how to perform tasks like accounting, filesystem management, disk quota management, etc.

Newer versions of System V use a different numbering system, but the principle of sections is the same. You can read manual pages through the **man** command, which you enter as follows:

```
$ man part topic
```

where *part* is a number between 1 and 8 (broken down further on some systems into combinations such as 3F, 3M, 3N, 3S, etc.) and *topic* is the name of a topic discussed in the manual (e.g., a command name or a filename). In most cases, you can omit *part*, and you can certainly omit *part* if you are interested in section 1 of the manual.

The command **apropos** serves as an online index to the manual pages Typing **apropos** *keyphrase* produces a list of manual entries, section numbers, and summary descriptions that contain *keyphrase* in its entirety. For example, the following is the report you might get if you are looking for information about the *sine* function:

```
$ apropos sin
awk (1-ucb)                     - pattern scanning and processing language
mailaddr (7-ucb)                - mail addressing description
moo (6-ucb)                     - guessing game
rcsintro (1-ucb)                - introduction to RCS commands
sin, cos, tan, asin, acos, atan, atan2 (3M-ucb)
                                - trigonometric functions
sinh, cosh, tanh (3M-ucb) - hyperbolic functions
$
```

Some of this material is extraneous; for example, the entry "moo" appears because the letters "sin" occur in the word "guessing". However, this report does have the information you want: the trigonometric and hyperbolic sine functions are discussed in Section 3M. The commands **man 3m sin** and **man 3m sinh** will produce detailed descriptions of these functions.

In Emacs, you can display a manual page right in the editor by executing **ESC-x man**. (This will make more sense after you read the next chapter.)

Most of the tools described in the following chapters have their own complete online help in a different format: *info files*. Info files can be read by entering the command **info**, or in Emacs by pressing **C-h i**. Info files are a classic form of hypertext and quite enjoyable (as well as rewarding) to use, even though they may seem clunky nowadays in the age of graphical Web browsers and help files.

Standard Input and Output

On occasion we have mentioned redirecting input and output. Now it's time to expand on what this means. Most UNIX commands read their data from *standard input*, write any data they produce to *standard output*, and send error reports to *standard error*. By default, standard input is taken from your terminal's keyboard, and standard output and standard error are both sent to your terminal's screen. You can redirect any of these three to read input from a file, write output to a file, or send data directly from the output of one program to the input of another.

To send the output of a program to a file, use the > (right angle bracket):

```
$ cat foo > outputfile
```

This is similar to entering **cp foo outputfile**. To redirect standard output and standard error to a file, use the command sequence:

```
$ cat foop >& errfile
$ cat errfile
cat: foop: no such file or directory
```

In this example, we redirected the error message "No such file or directory" to the file *errfile*. Therefore, no error message appears on the terminal until we list the contents of *errfile* with another **cat** command.

On some Bourne shells, instead of using the >& construct, you have to enter:

```
$ cat foop > errfile 2>&1
```

The group of characters at the end may look mysterious. Just understand that the shell always uses 1 to refer to the standard output and 2 to refer to the standard error (internally, these are the file descriptors opened). The 2>&1 construct means "Send anything meant for file descriptor 2 to the same place you send things meant for file descriptor 1."

To redirect standard output and standard error to different files in Bourne shells, enter the command:

```
$ cat foop > outputfile 2> errfile
```

This time it's the C shell that has trouble. It doesn't let you redirect the standard error by itself, so you have to use the following workaround:

```
$ ( cat foop > outputfile ) >& errfile
```

Both the command and the standard output directive must be placed within () (parentheses). The standard error directive appears outside of the parentheses.

If **outputfile** or **errfile** already exists, using > and >& to redirect output destroys the data that are already there. To redirect output to the end of a file without touching anything you have put there already, use the sequences >> and (C shell only) >>&.

To take the input of a program from a file, use the < (left angle bracket):

```
$ dc < script.dc
```

dc is a desk calculator program that normally takes its input directly from the terminal. However, you can place a series of **dc** commands in a file and then send the file to **dc** through standard input. The ability to read standard input from a file, rather than from the keyboard, lets you use **dc** and many other UNIX utilities as simple programming languages.

You may often wish to redirect both standard input and standard output. For example, consider the **spell** program, which produces a list of misspelled words. To check the spelling in a file named *text*, we can invoke **spell**:

```
$ spell < text > spelling
```

Pipes

The UNIX standard I/O facility lets you connect one program's output directly to another's input. This is called a *pipe* and is represented by a | (vertical bar). For example, if we wanted to find out if the user **johnson** is logged in, we could use the command **who** to list all current users and pipe the result to the **grep** program, which reads standard input and outputs a list of all lines containing some pattern:

```
$ who | grep johnson
johnson tty2 Jun 3 09:21
$
```

The **troff** typesetting system presents a more notable use of pipes. **troff** has several preprocessors for producing pictures, equations, and tables. These three programs, **pic**, **eqn**, and **tbl**, all read from standard input and write to standard output. They must all process the input file before **troff** gets it. Therefore, to send the text file *typeset.ms* through this chain, enter the command:

```
$ pic < typeset.ms | eqn | tbl | troff -ms > typeset.out
```

pic reads *typeset.ms* as its standard input, sends its output to **eqn**, which sends its output to **tbl**, etc. Finally, this command redirects **troff**'s standard output to *typeset.out*, a printable file which can be sent to a typesetter. (By the way, the Free Software Foundation offers an excellent version of **troff**—it's called **groff**.)

Programs of this type are called *filters*. UNIX programmers typically use many filters, which are small programs that can be debugged independently, but combined through pipes and other mechanisms to perform larger tasks. For example, imagine four signal analysis programs: one that gathers data from an input device, one that reads a file of data to produce a Fourier transform, one that strips the high-frequency components from a Fourier transform, and one that produces a graphical representation of a waveform from a Fourier transform. In most cases, writing these four smaller programs independently would have been simpler than writing and debugging one large program that performed all four tasks together. When the smaller programs are working correctly, they can be connected through pipes to perform the larger task simply:

```
$ sample | fourier | filter | plotfourier > output.plot
```

Controlling Execution

At the beginning of this chapter, we described how to use a UNIX command to run a program. This section describes some additional tools you can use to control a program.

Stopping Programs

To stop a program, press CTRL-C. Under most circumstances, this forces the program to terminate. If it doesn't, any of a number of things may have happened. For example, the program may have sent a strange sequence of special characters to your terminal that managed to confuse it.

On an X Window System, just remove the window containing the runaway process. (Usually the window manager provides a menu option with a name like "kill" or "close" to do this.) If you are running on a text-only terminal, do the following:

1. Log in at another terminal.

2. Enter the **ps** command. This displays a list of the programs you are running, in a form like the following:

```
$ ps
PID     TTY   STAT  TIME    COMMAND
163     i26   I     0:41    -bash (bash-1.14.2)
8532    i26   TW    2:17    emacs ts.ms
22202   i26   S     12:50   emacs UNIXintro.ms
8963    pb    R     0:00    ps
24077   pb    S     0:05    -bin/bash (bash-1.14.2)
$
```

On some systems (because they use a **ps** derived from BSD) you have to add an **-x** option to the command.

3. Search through this list to find the command that has backfired. Note the process identification (PID) number for this command. It may help you to check the TTY column. In the preceding display, the **ps** command is running on the terminal named *pb*. This means that the command you want to kill is running on the other terminal, named *i26*.

4. Enter the command **kill** *PID*, where *PID* is the identification number from the previous step.

5. If the UNIX prompt ($ or %) has appeared at your original terminal, things are back to normal. If it hasn't, find the shell associated with that terminal (identified by a TTY number) and **kill** it. The command name to look for is **bash** if you are using the Bourne-again shell, **csh** or **tcsh** if you are using the C shell, and **ksh** if you are using the Korn shell (another popular variant of the Bourne shell). Killing the shell will also destroy any other commands running from your terminal. Be sure to **kill** the shell on your own terminal, not the terminal you borrowed to enter these commands.

6. Check **ps** to ensure that your shell has died. If it is still there, take more drastic action with the command **kill –KILL** *PID*.

7. At this point, you should be able to log in again from your own terminal.

The **ps** command, which lists all the programs you are running, also gives you useful information about the status of each program and the amount of CPU time it has consumed. Note that **ps** lists everything you are running, including many programs you may not know about (e.g., programs that other programs execute automatically). For more information, see the manual page for **ps**.

Foreground and Background

UNIX distinguishes between background and foreground programs. This feature allows you to run several programs simultaneously from your terminal.

When a program is running in the foreground, anything you type at the keyboard is sent to the program's standard input unless you have redirected it. As a result, you can't do anything until the program finishes. When you run a program in the background, it is disconnected from the keyboard. Anything you type reaches the UNIX shell and is interpreted as a command. Therefore, you can run many programs simultaneously in the background. You can run only one program at a time in the foreground.

To run a program in the background, type an & (ampersand) at the end of the command line. For example:

```
$ gcc program.c &
[1] 9145
$
```

This runs a compilation in the background, letting you continue other work while the compilation proceeds. The shell responds by printing a job number in [ ] (brackets), followed by the process identification (PID) number for the command. It then prompts you for a new command. Entering the command **jobs** produces a short report describing all the programs you are executing in the background. For example:

```
$ gcc program.c &
[1] 9145
$ jobs
[1]+ Running        gcc program.c &
$
```

To bring a program from the background into the foreground, use the foreground command, **fg**. If you have more than one background job, follow **fg** with a job identifier: a % (percent sign) followed by the job number.

```
$ jobs
[1]+ Running          gcc program.c
[2]- Stopped          emacs sinus.c
$ fg %1
```

The + (plus) in the report from **jobs** indicates which job will return to the foreground by default.

To suspend a job running in the foreground, press CTRL-Z. This stops the program but does *not* terminate it. Entering the background command, **bg**, lets this program continue execution in the background. The foreground command, **fg**, restores the program to execution in the foreground. For example:

```
$ gcc -o program program.c
CTRL-Z
[1]+ Stopped              gcc -o program program.c
$
bg
[1]+ gcc -o program program.c &
$
```

There is no prompt after the **gcc** command because the compiler is running in the foreground. After you press CTRL-Z, the shell prints the word "Stopped," to indicate that it has stopped execution. At this point, you can enter any command. The **bg** command lets the job continue executing in the background. This feature is useful if you forget to type an & at the end of the command line.

To terminate a background job, you can use the command's job number rather than its process identification (PID) number, as follows:

```
$ kill %1
```

Remember to include the % (percent sign) before the job number! If you omit it, the kill command interprets the job number as a process number. This will probably be the process number of an operating system function. UNIX will not let you make such a mistake unless you are superuser (a user with special privileges). If you are superuser, the command is fatal. You may be a superuser from time to time and therefore should not develop sloppy habits.

A program running in the background cannot read input from a terminal. If a background job needs terminal input, it stops; the **jobs** command prints the message "Stopped (tty input)". Before the program can continue, you must bring it into the foreground with the **fg** command and type the required input. You can save yourself this trouble by redirecting the program's input so that it reads all its data from a file. You may also want to redirect standard output and standard error. If you don't, any output the program produces will appear on your terminal. Since you will probably be running other commands, having miscellaneous data and other messages flying across your terminal may be confusing.

Running a Job at a Later Time

To run a job at a later time (e.g., at night), use the command **at**, followed by a list of commands, as follows:

```
$ at 1pm
perl ~/bin/gensched
lpr ~/log/96Sep01
CTRL-D
warning: commands will be executed using /usr/local/bin/bash
job 839955600.a at Tue Aug 13 13:00:00 1996
$
```

The arguments to **at** specify the time at which you wish to execute the commands on the following lines. The time can be specified as one, two, three, or four digits. If it is one or two digits, UNIX interprets it as a time in hours (for instance, 11 for 11:00 a.m.); if it is three or four digits, UNIX interprets it as hours and minutes (for instance, 11:30). The time can also be followed by the letters **am** or **pm**, specifying whether the time is before noon or after noon; two other modifiers, **n** and **m**, specify whether the time 1200 refers to noon or midnight. **a** and **p** are legal abbreviations for a.m. and p.m. If no modifiers are present, **at** interprets the time in terms of a 24-hour clock (e.g., 2300 is the same as 1100pm and 0000 is the same as 1200m).

Check the manual page for other interesting and convenient ways to specify the time, such as:

```
$ at now + 2 hours
```

The list of commands can be as long as you want. A CTRL-D, which must appear on a separate line, terminates this list.

Alternatively, you can place the commands you want to execute in a file and invoke **at** as follows:

```
$ at time filename
$
```

Like programs running in the background, programs run through **at** cannot read any data from a terminal. If these programs read standard input, you must take standard input from a file. You might consider redirecting the standard output and error of each command, too. If you do not, any data the commands produce are mailed to you. Note that the command:

```
$ at 9am commands <inputfile > outputfile
```

does not redirect standard input or standard output successfully. It redirects standard input and output for the **at** command itself, not for the commands you wish to run at 9 a.m.

If you want to run a command regularly (for instance, to clean up some files every night) use the **cron** facility. Read the manual page for **crontab**. (The **cron** manual page is very short and uninformative; the interesting information involves the format of the **crontab** file.)

Shell Programs

The UNIX shell can be used as an interpreted programming language. Within the shell, you can create variables, read arguments, loop, branch, do I/O, etc. Shell programming allows you to break large programming tasks into many smaller tasks. You can take a group of small programs, each of which is written in the language most suitable for accomplishing its subtask, and connect them in very flexible ways through a *shell script*. This kind of modularity simplifies large development projects, since each portion of the task can be developed and debugged separately. Furthermore, careful design may leave you with a whole that is more useful than the sum of its parts. Some of the subprograms in this larger project may come in handy for another development project later.

This section discusses how to write simple shell scripts using the Bourne shell. For further information on Bourne shell programming, read the O'Reilly books *Learning the Korn Shell* by Bill Rosenblatt or *Learning the Bash Shell* by Cameron Newham and Bill Rosenblatt. Programming for the C shell is significantly different. Even though the C shell was originally developed for its programming features, it has fallen into disfavor because of bugs and the awkward techniques required. If you come across a C shell script or have some other reason to be interested in programming it, see the manual page for the C shell (**csh**).

The simplest shell script is nothing more than an executable file containing one or more commands. For example, consider the following task: We want to format two versions of a file called *shoplist*, one version for a line printer and another for a laser printer. To write a shell script for this task, place the commands needed to create these two versions in a file with a convenient name (e.g., *format*):

```
# use nroff and troff to format shoplist
troff < shoplist > shoplist.tr
nroff < shoplist > shoplist.nr
```

The first line is a comment, since the shell interprets lines beginning with a # (pound sign) as comment lines and ignores them. The second line uses the UNIX program **troff** to format *shoplist* and produce an output file named *shoplist.tr*. The third line uses **nroff**, a similar program for formatting line printer documents, to produce the output file *shoplist.nr*.

Before using this script, you must make it executable: you must tell UNIX that you intend to use the filename *format* as a command. To do this, use the **chmod** command:

```
$ chmod +x format
```

The **chmod** command with the **+x** option makes a file executable. Sometimes you must also enter the command **rehash** to tell the shell to rebuild its table of command locations.

After making the file executable with the **chmod** command, you can type the filename to execute the commands listed in the file. That is, the command:

```
$ format
```

executes the commands in the file *format*—in this case, producing the two formatted versions of *shoplist*. If you try to run your shell script before you've made it executable, UNIX prints the error message "Permission denied." Note that there is no difference between invoking a shell script (such as *format*) and invoking a compiled binary program (such as **troff**). UNIX knows the difference between shell scripts and binary executables and acts appropriately.

Some people don't have the PATH environment variable set to search their current directory. If you try to execute your script and get a message saying "not found," that's your problem. Just specify a fuller path:

```
$ ./format
```

By default, UNIX uses the Bourne shell to execute shell scripts. On most modern systems, you can specify any tool you want as the executing utility. To indicate your choice, put a special comment (a line beginning with #) as the first line of the file. Thus, the line:

```
#!/bin/csh
```

forces the script to run with the C shell (assuming that it is available on your system and is located in */bin*). You can similarly force the script to use the Bourne-again shell or Korn shell, if you want to exploit the extensions these shells offer. Use the **which** command to find out the full pathname of your shell, for instance:

```
$ which bash
/usr/local/bin/bash
```

Now you can put the following line at the top of the script:

```
#!/usr/local/bin/bash
```

We recommend that you put a #! line at the beginning of every script you write—unless your system is one of the few that does not interpret the line—to ensure that the right shell is used. If you begin the script with the line:

```
#!/bin/sh -x
```

UNIX uses the Bourne shell and prints each line in the shell script as it executes. This is useful for debugging.

Several powerful command languages have emerged recently to do the tasks for which people used to use shell scripts. In many cases, the languages are doing jobs that C programs used to do. If you find yourself doing complicated text processing or system administration, you should consider learning one of them. The most popular of the new scripting languages are:

- Perl, a useful language for text filtering and report generation. It is described in two books, *Learning Perl*, by Randal Schwartz, and *Programming Perl*, second edition, by Larry Wall, Tom Christiansen, and Randal Schwartz, from O'Reilly & Associates.

- Tcl, a command interpreter. It is most popular in conjunction with the Tk extension, which lets you easily create and manipulate windows on the X Window System. These tools are described in *Tcl and the Tk Toolkit*, by John K. Ousterhout, published by Addison-Wesley Publishing Co.

Command-Line Arguments

The previous simple shell script is not particularly useful. Unless it is modified, it can only process a single source file named *shoplist*. To make this program more useful, we'll modify it so that it can read the name of a file from the command line, then process this file to produce two appropriately named output files.

To read arguments from the command line, a shell program uses special symbols of the form $n, where n is an integer number. **$0** refers to the command itself, **$1** refers to the first argument on the command line, **$2** refers to the second, etc. We can use these symbols to rewrite the commands in *format* so that they take their arguments from the UNIX command line:

```
# format: a shell script to format a file with troff and nroff
troff < $1 > $1.tr
nroff < $1 > $1.nr
```

The second line tells **troff** to process the first name appearing after the command *format*. To generate a name for the output file, it adds the extension *.tr* to the name of the input file. The third line works similarly. For example, consider the command:

```
$ format shoplist
```

During execution, the value of **$1** is *shoplist*. Therefore, this command reads the source file *shoplist* and produces the output files *shoplist.tr* and *shoplist.nr*.

Shell Variables

Within a shell script, you can use *shell variables* to hold values. Following is a
shell assignment statement:

```
name=value
```

This assigns *value*, which is interpreted as a character string, to the variable *name*.
Do not insert a space before or after the = (equal sign). To use the variable *name*
in a statement, precede it with a $ (dollar sign), as follows: $*name*. For example,
we might know that all shopping lists are in the directory */usr/lib/shoplist*. To save
the user the trouble of typing the entire pathname as an argument, we could write
the script as follows:

```
name=/usr/lib/shoplist
troff < $name/$1 > $name/$1.tr
```

It is often useful to set a shell variable to hold the output from a UNIX command.
To do this, enclose the command within ` ` (left single quotation marks), as follows:

```
name=`ls`
```

When the assignment statement is processed, the **ls** command is executed and its
output is assigned to the variable *name*.

Loops

What if we want to format a large group of files? The shell has a loop facility that
lets you iterate through a set of arguments. The general form of a loop is:

```
for i in list
do
        ...Loop commands...
done
```

where *i* is a shell variable, like *name* in the previous example; it can have any
string value. The shell executes the loop once for each value in *list*. On each iteration, it assigns the next value in *list* to the iteration variable *i*. If in *list* is omitted,
the shell forms a default *list* from the command-line arguments. For example,
let's write a shell script to format a series of texts. We can do that by adding a loop
to *format*:

```
# a simple do loop to pass several files through
# the formatter
for i
do
        troff < $i > $i.tr
        nroff < $i > $i.nr
done
```

With this modification, the command **format list1 list2 list3** produces the files
list1.tr, *list1.nr*, *list2.tr*, *list2.nr*, etc. Note that the variable **i** is specified within
commands as **$i**. This tells the shell to substitute the value of **i** when it executes
this line.

The shell expands any wildcards in *list*; the statement **for i in *** sets **$i**, in succes-
sion, to the name of each file in the current directory. Consequently, the command:

```
$ format *
```

formats each file in the current directory, producing a series of *.tr* and *.nr* files.

Conditionals

The shell has several kinds of conditional statements. We'll describe the shell's **if**
statement here, for it is one of the most useful. For information about the **case**
statement and other control structures, refer to the manual pages for the Bourne
shell (**sh**).

Many UNIX commands return a value to the shell upon completion. During normal
interactive operation, this value is ignored: as a user, you never see it. However,
an **if** statement in a shell script can test this returned value and take action accordingly. A shell **if** statement has the following form:

```
if command
then
      Commands to execute if command returns true

else
      Commands to execute if command returns false
fi
```

command can be any valid UNIX command or command sequence. If the return
value from *command* is 0 (or true), the shell executes the commands following
the **then** statement. If the return value is nonzero (or false), the shell executes the
commands following the **else** statement. The **fi** statement terminates the **if** structure
and must always appear on a separate line.

For most UNIX commands, the returned value is true if the command executes
without incurring any system errors and false otherwise. Some commands use the
returned value to encode the result of execution; for example, the compare command, **cmp**, which compares two files, returns true if the files are identical and
false if they are not. The manual page describing the command tells you if a particular command uses the returned value in any significant way.

Your own programs can return any value they wish by calling the function *exit* with an argument; this terminates the program and returns the value of the argument to the shell. Similarly, your shell scripts can exit with any value you choose, as in:

```
exit 1
```

The **test** command is one of the most useful features for shell programmers. It provides an easy way to write conditionals for **if** statements. It evaluates a conditional expression and returns 0 (true) or 1 (false) accordingly. To make programming easier, **test** can be abbreviated [*args*]. Note that you must have a space before and after the arguments. In an **if** statement, using **test** looks like this:

```
if [ args ]
then
        ...Commands...
else
        ...Commands...
fi
```

where *args* is an expression. Here are the basic building blocks for expressions:

str1 = *str2*	True if	*str1* equals *str2*
str1 != *str2*	True if	*str1* does not equal *str2*
-r *file*	True if	*file* exists and is readable
-w *file*	True if	*file* exists and is writable
-d *file*	True if	*file* exists and is a directory
-f *file*	True if	*file* exists and is not a directory
-s *file*	True if	*file* exists and has nonzero length
expr1 -a *expr2*	True if	Both *expr1* and *expr2* are true
expr1 -o *expr2*	True if	Either *expr1* or *expr2* is true

Here are some examples showing how basic **test** expressions can be combined:

```
if [ "$1" = "foo" ]               # if the first argument
                                  # matches the string "foo"
if [ -r file.txt ]               # if "file.txt" is readable
if [ "$1" = "foo" -a -r file.txt ] # if both are true
```

You might want to use the –r or –s operator to find out whether the input file for a program exists; if it doesn't, you can print an error message or take some default action. You can use the string comparison tests to handle command arguments.

Remember that this is a very basic introduction to shell programming. The shell allows more complicated control structures, including a **case** statement that is useful for testing command-line flags, an **else if** structure, a **while** statement, and many other features. The manual pages for the Bourne shell (**sh**) and the C shell (**csh**) give much more complete information, as do the books listed at the beginning of this section.

Shell Customization

All UNIX shells allow you to customize them: you can define your own abbreviations for commands (aliases) and set a number of variables (shell and environment variables) that control the shell's behavior.

Two files are used for *bash* customization: *.bashrc*, executed whenever UNIX starts a new shell, and *.bash_profile*, which is executed when you log in to the system. *.bashrc* runs first.

When does a new shell start without your logging in? One example is when you run commands using **at**, as described earlier in this chapter. Another is when you create a new window running the **xterm** terminal emulator on the X Window System. Under these circumstances, *.bashrc* runs, but not *.bash_profile*. (If you want your **xterm** to run both files, start it up with a –ls option.)

The corresponding files for the C shell are *.cshrc*, which is executed when a new shell starts, and *.login*, which is executed when you log in. The Korn shell offers only one start-up file, named *.profile*, and it runs only when you log in.

Your system administrator should put default versions of the proper start-up files in your home directory when creating your account. On most systems, the default versions of these files are satisfactory. However, don't be afraid to edit them to your own satisfaction.

Environment Variables

PATH is an example of an environment variable—one used not just by the shell, but by programs started by the shell. Another important environment variable is TERM, which indicates what type of terminal you have. Many programs check that variable so they can execute correctly on different types of terminals. In general, environment variables are used by both the shell and the programs it runs in order to customize their behavior for your environment.

To define an environment variable in Bourne shells, use the command:

```
$ export VARNAME=value
```

where *VARNAME* is the name of the new environment variable and *value* is the definition you want to give it. The corresponding command in C shells is:

```
% setenv VARNAME value
```

These commands are very popular for inclusion in shell customization files, because usually people want environment variables to be set automatically when they log in.

By convention, environment variable names are uppercase. To see the defined environment variables at any time, enter the command **printenv**:

```
$ printenv
HOME=/home/los/mikel
SHELL=/bin/csh
TERM=sun
USER=mikel
PATH=.:~/bin:/usr/local/bin:/usr/ucb:/bin:/usr/bin
LOGNAME=mikel
PWD=/home/los/mikel/sunview
PRINTER=ps
EDITOR=/usr/local/bin/emacs
```

You can give environment variables any name you want. However, the shell and other programs recognize some special environment variables and use them to control their behavior. These variables are:

PATH

Determines the search path for commands (i.e., it specifies where the shell looks to find the commands you execute). Its value is a list of directory names separated by colons. For example, the previous **PATH** variable displayed says "to find commands, look first in the current directory, then in the user's *bin* directory, then in */usr/local/bin*, and so on." Nonexistent directories along the path are ignored.

Whenever you change the path or add a new command to any directory on the path, some shells require you to use the command **rehash**. This command rebuilds the hash tables the shell uses to look up new commands. The shell automatically executes a **rehash** at startup, so you don't need to add it to your customization files.

Be careful about changing your path. If you make a mistake, the shell may not be able to find any commands. You will have to add a complete pathname for every command you type until you get a correctly defined path. Change **PATH** as you would any other environment variable. Usually, what you need to do is add one or more directories to your path. In most Bourne shells, you can do this easily by referring to your current path when you reset it, for instance:

```
$ export PATH=$PATH:/usr/local/bin
```

In the C shell, another syntax also works:

```
% set path = ( $PATH /usr/local/bin )
```

TERM

Tells the shell what type of terminal you are using. Terminal types are defined in a database named */etc/termcap*. Here is a typical entry:

```
ye|w50|wyse50|wyse-50|Wyse 50 in Wyse mode:\
        :al=\EE:am:bs:bt=\EI:cd=\EY:ce=\ET:\ :cl=^Z:cm=\E=%+ %+
        :co#80:\ :da:db:dc=\EW:dl=\ER:ei=\Er:\
        :im=\Eq:is=\E'\072\200\EC\EDF\E'\E(:\
        :kd=^J:kl=^H:kr=^L:ku=^K:li#24:nd=^L:\ :up=^K:us=\EG8:ue=\EG0:\
        :so=\EG4:se=\EG0:sg#1:sr=\Ej:ho=^^:ug#1:\
        :if=/usr/share/lib/tabset/stdcrt:
```

The first line of this entry—the only one you care about now—defines a number of different names for this terminal type. You can use any of these names, except for the last, to define the TERM variable. For example, the command **setenv TERM wyse50** tells the shell to use this entry for information about your terminal.

Setting the TERM variable by itself has no effect. In your *.bash_profile* file, you should follow the **setenv** command with a **tset** command. **tset** forces the shell to read the **termcap** entry for your terminal, telling the shell what features the terminal has and how to use them. Many UNIX users use a bit of additional code to detect whether they are using a remote login, dialing in through a modem, or directly connected. Once they figure this out, they set TERM appropriately for their situation. We won't discuss this here; if you look at a few *.bash_profile* or *.cshrc* files at your site, you should see how to do this.

Here is an example for Bourne-compatible shells one author actually uses. He's usually either working on a graphics terminal running **xterm** windows at work, or dialing up from home on a personal computer that emulates a VT100 terminal. He's on the graphics terminal if the DISPLAY variable is set, so the script bases its actions on a test for that variable.

```
if [ "$DISPLAY" != "" ]
then
        # Yes, DISPLAY is set--I'm on a graphics terminal
        set noglob
        eval `tset -s -Q xterm`
        unset noglob
else
        # Set up for VT100 emulation on home computer
        set noglob
        eval `tset -s -Q vt100`
        unset noglob
fi
```

Here's the same operation written for the C shell:

```
if ( ${?DISPLAY} ) then
        # Yes, DISPLAY is set--I'm on a graphics terminal
        set noglob
        eval `tset -s -Q xterm`
        unset noglob
else
        # Set up for VT100 emulation on home computer
        set noglob
        eval `tset -s -Q vt100`
        unset noglob
endif
```

The only magic here is the *tset* incantation. This sets the terminal type based on the *etc/ttytype* (or */etc/ttys*) file, which your system administrator should maintain. If you are dialed in over a modem, the command as we've written it will assume you are using a VT100 terminal. In these days of networked systems, this may not be adequate. You can make this part of the script as complex as you like, checking baud rates, hostnames, system architectures, or anything you wish to set. For a thorough discussion of *tset*, see the Nutshell Handbook *termcap & terminfo*.

EDITOR

Defines a default editor. Its value should simply be the name of your favorite editor—after reading this book, this will supposedly be **emacs**. Several programs that ask you to edit files read this variable to decide which editor to invoke. If you don't set it, you get the standard editor, **vi**.

PRINTER

Defines a default printer. Its value should be the name the system administrator has assigned to the printer you use most often. The UNIX print spooler, **lpr**, reads this variable and uses this printer unless you specify a different one.

There are a number of other environment variables, some automatically defined, that have special purposes. For more information, see the manual page for your shell.

Shell Variables

Shells check several variables to control their own behavior. In this section we won't refer to environment variables, but to variables that are meaningful only to the shell. In Bourne shells, you set them through:

```
$ varname=value
```

and in the C shell, you use the syntax:

```
% set varname=value
```

where *varname* is the name of the variable and *value* is the value assigned to it. Some variables, like the **noglob** shown earlier under the discussion of TERM, are binary (either they're set or unset—they don't take a value). Handle these variables by leaving off the *=value*. This sets the variable; use **unset** to reverse the operation. The command **set** by itself displays all currently defined shell variables.

Unlike environment variables, shell variables are not inherited by subshells. Every time you start a new shell, you start with a clean slate. There are many (two dozen or so) significant shell variables. The most important of these are:

ignoreeof

> If set, pressing CTRL-D does not terminate the shell (possibly logging you off of the system). You have to enter the **logout** or **exit** command explicitly. This is a safeguard if you happen to press CTRL-D accidentally.

noclobber

> If set, standard output redirection is not allowed to destroy existing files by accident. For example, if **noclobber** is set, the command **ls > foo** fails if the file *foo* already exists.

HISTSIZE (*bash*)

> This variable is named **history** in the C shell. It represents the number of commands saved in the shell's history list. For example, if you set this variable to 100, the shell remembers the most recent one hundred commands. You can retrieve and execute these commands with the notation !*n*, where *n* is the number of a command, and you can display the history list with the command **history**. There are many more complicated ways to invoke the history feature; see the manual pages for *bash* and *csh* for more information.

A portion of a *.bash_profile* file setting these shell variables might look like this:

```
noclobber=      # don't let standard output destroy files
ignoreeof=      # don't let CTRL-D terminate the shell
HISTSIZE=100    # remember the last 100 commands
```

The corresponding *.cshrc* file would be:

```
set noclobber    # don't let standard output destroy files
set ignoreeof    # don't let CTRL-D terminate the shell
set history=100  # remember the last 100 commands
```

Aliases

Aliases let you define your own commands and abbreviations for commands. To define one in *bash* or the Korn shell, enter the command:

    $ **alias** *newname='command'*

where *newname* is the name of the command you are defining and *command* is what you want *newname* to do. If the *command* contains any spaces, enclose the entire *command* string within double or single quotation marks as shown.

The corresponding command for the C shell is:

    % **alias** *newname 'command'*

In either syntax, you can use double quotes instead of the single quotes shown here.

As an example, assume that you want to define the command **clean** to delete all core dumps and all files whose names begin with the # (pound sign) in the current directory. Enter the command:

    $ alias clean='rm -f core \#*'

The backslash is needed in *bash* and the Korn shell because otherwise the # is interpreted as the start of a comment. After the shell has executed this command, entering **clean** is the same as entering the more complicated **rm** command.

If your command contains quotes, enclose it in a different set of quotes. If that sounds confusing, look at this example:

    $ alias gsharp='grep "BSD UNIX"'

This **bash** version of the **alias** command defines a new command that searches files for the string BSD UNIX. Because the string contains a space, we put it in quotes. So a different set of quotes was needed to go around the entire **grep** command. Now we can enter commands like:

    $ gsharp README*

to search files for the string.

One common use of the alias feature is to redefine commands that you commonly mistype. For example, if you find you often type **mroe** when you mean **more**, adding the line:

    alias mroe=more

to your *.bash_profile* will take care of the problem. This isn't a good practice, but we admit to doing it.

Another common use of aliases is to make UNIX look like some other operating system. For example, if you are accustomed to typing **dir** to find out the contents of the directory, add the line:

```
alias dir=ls
```

to your *.bash_profile*. We're not sympathetic to this usage. You are using UNIX and will be better off in the long run if you don't pretend that it is DOS, VAX/VMS, TOPS-20, or some other operating system.

One final important usage of command aliasing is to make commonly used commands safe. Earlier we mentioned that **rm** will gladly destroy all of your files, no questions asked, but that **rm -i** will ask for permission before deleting anything. To ensure that you never make any mistakes, add the line:

```
alias rm="rm -i"
```

to your *.bash_profile*. You have now redefined the pure **rm** command as **rm -i**; this means that you will always have to confirm that you want to delete a file. You may find this annoying, but at least it's safe.

It is not uncommon to see users with several dozen aliases defined in their start-up files. Virtually every command given is an alias of one sort or another. You can work this way if you want, but it does cause a problem: the longer the file is, the longer it takes to start a new shell. It is preferable to use a few aliases for the most commonly used commands and misspellings.

Other Basic Tools

The UNIX system has more than 300 standard programs covering an extremely wide range of applications. It would be impossible to discuss more than a few of them in this book. Often they are not free software, but they exist on most UNIX systems. Here are a few of the tools that will be most useful to you in developing software. For more information about any of them, see their manual pages.

grep

Finds all occurrences of a pattern within a file or a group of files. One of the many applications for this command is to look for strings when you're not sure how you've used them. For instance, suppose you want to see quickly every place that you've referred to the variable *num_iterations* in the file *grif.c.*[*] Enter the command:

```
$ grep num_iterations grif.c
```

This lists all the lines containing the string "num_iterations" in the file *grif.c* on your terminal (standard output). **grep** can use wildcards in the filename to search multiple files. For example:

```
$ grep num_iterations *.c
```

searches all C source files in the current directory. In this case, **grep** reports both the name of the file and the line in which it finds "num_iterations". The string for which **grep** searches may contain wildcards, although these wildcards differ from the shell wildcards discussed in this chapter. They form a system called "regular expressions" (**grep** stands for "global regular expression print"). **egrep** and **fgrep** are two important variations of **grep**. **egrep** has an extended wildcard mechanism that lets you make very general searches. **fgrep** searches for a fixed string; it does not accept wildcards. For more information, see the manual page for **grep** (and for **egrep** and **fgrep**).

more

Allows you to page through a file that is too long to fit on your screen. It lets you search for strings and page through the file. The popular alternatives **less** and **pg** exist on many systems.

sort

Puts a set of input lines into a new order, usually based on the ASCII character set, but optionally alphabetic or numeric.

diff

Takes two files as arguments, and produces a list of differences between them. There are many circumstances in which this is useful. For example, you may have forgotten which is the most recent version of a file, or you may need to integrate two different versions of a program that have branched from a common development tree.

cmp

Like **diff** but more useful for binary files. It reports the first location at which the two files differ. For example, the command:

```
$ cmp foo1 foo2
foo1 foo2 differ: char 5, line 4
$
```

tells you that the files *foo1* and *foo2* are identical until the fifth character in the fourth line.

---

[*] By the way, to learn about a much more powerful and convenient tool for tracking variables, look at the section "Tags" in Chapter 3, *Editing Source Code with Emacs*.

spell

> Reads a file and produces a list of misspelled words in the file. Its dictionary is built in to UNIX.

strip

> Removes symbolic information from an executable or object file to make it smaller.

In this section, we have only included relatively simple tools that are not discussed elsewhere in this book. We have devoted chapters to the more complex and more important tools, like **make** and RCS.

3

Editing Source Code with Emacs

Emacs is undoubtedly the preferred editor for serious programmers. It has also been, for many years, the "flagship" free software application; it's by far the most widely used and most popular. For many of us, Emacs was the first piece of free software we ever used; for many people, it is the only piece of free software they use; and we'd have to say that it's the only piece of free software we absolutely couldn't get along without.

Historically, Emacs goes back to the mid-70s, when Richard Stallman wrote a set of "editing macros"* for the TECO editor: a powerful, but incredibly obscure piece of software. Most people have been happy to say good-bye to TECO; Emacs has since been rewritten independently. Like TECO, Emacs is highly customizable: it includes its own programming language (a form of Lisp), which means that you can generally add any features you want. In fact, many basic Emacs commands are written in Lisp rather than C.

Emacs's most important "feature" isn't any single thing that it does (though it can do almost anything), but the integration it brings to different development activities. Without leaving Emacs, you can edit source code and compile it, issue UNIX shell commands, read and write email and Usenet news, etc. You could argue that Emacs provides a complete operating-system interface, complete with a menu-oriented approach to filing. Because it's window-oriented, all these activities can go on concurrently: you can paste a function that's giving you trouble into a posting to the *comp.unix.c* newsgroup, for example, without leaving the editor. This may not seem like a big deal in the days of X, but remember that Emacs preceded X by about a decade. Furthermore, at least as far as we're concerned, Emacs gives you all you need from a window system—except that you don't need to deal with

---

* Hence the name Emacs.

a mouse (though you can, if you want to). Everything you need can be done from the keyboard.

Although Emacs does absolutely everything you need your system to do—someone has even written a "spreadsheet mode" for it—this chapter looks at it only from a C programmer's point of view. We assume that you're editing C or C++ source code, and (hence) that you will be using Emacs's C mode, which provides many special features for editing programs. In fact, Emacs in some ways is a language-sensitive editor, although it doesn't have as many features as some of these editors do.

If you want to learn more about what you can do with Emacs, we recommend the Nutshell Handbook *Learning GNU Emacs* or the Free Software Foundation's *GNU Emacs Manual*. If you want to learn how to customize Emacs, we recommend *Learning GNU Emacs* for a brief introduction, the Nutshell Handbook *Writing GNU Emacs Extensions* for an in-depth guide, and the FSF's *GNU Emacs Lisp Reference Manual* for the gory details. Like all FSF documentation, the Lisp manual exists both online and on paper.

In this chapter, we won't be saying much about how Emacs works on the X Window System. Emacs has been enhanced to provide a powerful set of mouse commands, a scroll bar, and other X features. But 99 percent of the time you'll be using Emacs the same way whether you're on X or a text-only terminal.

Getting Emacs Started

Let's start at the beginning. As you'd probably guess, you start Emacs by typing the command **emacs**, followed by a filename:

```
% emacs source.c
```

You'll see something like this:

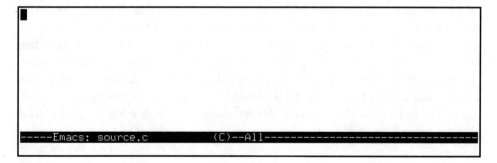

The upper part of the screen is a "window" onto the file you're editing, which (so far) is empty. Beneath the window is a status line that tells you the name of the buffer you're editing (usually the same as the filename), the mode you're in (C mode), and the portion of the file that you're looking at (currently, all of it). The line below the status line is called the "minibuffer"; it's used mostly for typing filenames, and other commands that require some kind of text input, but it's also where Emacs prints error and warning messages. Right now, the minibuffer is telling you that *source.c* is a new file. The cursor is in the upper-left corner of the screen; it shows you where any characters you type will be placed.

On the X Window System, Emacs runs in its own window and displays a menu bar at the top of the window. You can explore the menu options on your own; virtually all of them offer commands that you can enter more quickly using the keyboard, but they may be useful when you're using a command with which you're not familiar and for which you don't remember the keystrokes.

If you don't specify a file on the command line, you'll see a copyright notice and an invitation to enter the built-in help system or a tutorial. It's worth exploring the "help" system sometime—but let's not do it now.

Stopping Emacs

Most Emacs commands involve holding down the **Control** key while pressing another key. For instance, to exit from Emacs, hold down the **Control** key and press **x** followed by **c**. We'll follow the conventions used in the Free Software Foundation's manuals and call this combination **C-x C-c**.

If you have no "unsaved" files, then **C-x C-c** puts you back in the shell. If you have modified a file without saving it, Emacs asks you whether you want to save the file, as in the following example:

```
I've done a little typing, but now it's time to
quit.




--**-Emacs: source.c          (C)--All-------------------------------
Save file /home/andyo/source.c? (y, n, !, ., q, C-r or C-h) █
```

If you type **y**, Emacs saves the file and exits. If you type **n**, Emacs asks another question in the minibuffer:

```
Modified buffers exist; exit anyway? (yes or no) ▮
```

If you answer **yes** (followed by a **Return**), Emacs quits, without saving your changes. If you type **no**, Emacs does *not* quit; instead, it cancels the exit command and you can continue editing.

Of course, there are better ways to save files, which we'll discuss later. While you're getting used to Emacs, though, you can just type **C-x C-c** and answer the questions accordingly.

If we're not getting too far ahead of ourselves, it's worth noting that you can also "pause" Emacs (e.g., stop Emacs, putting it in the background) by typing **C-z**. You can then work on the command line, and resume editing where you left off by giving the UNIX command **fg**. (On the X Window System, **C-z** doesn't suspend Emacs, but iconifies its window.) However, don't get the idea that you need to pause Emacs before you can do "normal" shell work. There's a shell mode for running interactive shell sessions within Emacs; we'll discuss that later in the chapter.

Preliminaries: Avoiding Customization

Before going on to basic editing, we'd like to touch on some background information. Emacs may be the most customizable editor in the world. That's both a great feature and a great burden. It's a burden because almost every Emacs user takes the opportunity and customizes it—with the result that no two users' versions of Emacs are ever alike. On top of that, many administrators think it's a great idea to inflict their local customs on new users. Which means that, before we can tell you how Emacs works, we'll have to tell you how to undo any "improvements" that will prevent Emacs from doing what we say.

First, look in your home directory and see if there is a file named *.emacs*. That's where users generally keep their private customizations—your system administrator may have given you one as a favor. If the file exists, rename it. (It's probably better not to delete it; you might want to experiment later.) Now you have to get rid of any system-wide customizations. To do so, use any editor (or even the **cat** command) to create the following one-line *.emacs* file:

```
(setq inhibit-default-init t) ; disable global customization
```

Now you're OK, as long as you only use Emacs from your account. If you sit down at someone else's workstation to help with a problem, you may still be facing an unfamiliar Emacs. You can solve this problem by starting Emacs with the command **emacs -u** *yourname* followed by the name of the file you want to edit. That tells Emacs to use the initialization file in your home directory.

Like the other language-specific modes, C mode tries to enforce a certain coding style. Unfortunately, we don't like this style very much; we prefer the "Kernighan and Ritchie" style. So we're going to break our own rule and ask you to add the following customizations to your *.emacs* file:[*]

```
;; customizations for K&R style
(setq c-indent-level 5)
(setq c-continued-statement-offset 5)
(setq c-argdecl-indent 0)
(setq c-brace-offset -5)
(setq c-label-offset -5)
```

If you don't do this, C mode will still work as described—but what you see on your screen won't match the examples in the book exactly. Indentations, and indentation style, will differ.

Basic Editing in C Mode

Editing in Emacs is fundamentally simple. Basically, you just type your text. All commands begin with a control character or the **Escape** key; anything else goes into the buffer you're editing. The cursor on the screen shows you where the next character will appear. Emacs documentation refers to the location just to the left of the cursor (i.e., between the cursor and the character to its left) as *point*, meaning the current position. So we could also say that when you type new characters, they are inserted at point.

Here's a short function that we typed:

```
void gen_and_sort(numels, genstyle)
int numels;
int genstyle;
{
     if (genstyle == TYPE1) {
          init_type1(numels);
     } else {
          init_random(numels);
     }
}█
--**-Emacs: gen.c            (C)--All----------------------------------
```

Here are a few things to watch for as you type this function:

* The two asterisks on the left end of the status line tell you that this buffer has been modified since the last time it was saved. They appear as soon as you start typing and disappear when you save the file.

---

[*] All Emacs users probably think that most customizations, aside from the ones they use, are evil.

- If you start each line with a **TAB**, Emacs automatically positions you at the right place on the line, given your current nesting level. You shouldn't have to do anything special to get the nesting shown above; just type a single **TAB** at the beginning of every line.

- When you type a right brace (}), Emacs briefly moves the cursor to the matching left brace ({). This makes it easier for you see whether your opening and closing braces match properly. The same is true of square brackets and parentheses.

- Emacs often adjusts the position of a brace after you type it, to match the code style that it's trying to enforce. For example, after typing the line `init_type1(numels);`, a **TAB** aligns the cursor under the "i" in "init"—after all, Emacs expects you to type another statement in the code block. When you type a right brace instead, Emacs realizes that the code block has ended, and moves the brace back to line up with the "i" in "if."

Moving Around

Now that you can enter text, how do you edit it? Emacs's commands for moving around on the screen have been called obscure, but we find them reasonably mnemonic. First of all, most keyboards have arrow keys that work under Emacs. If you don't have them, or they don't work (this is a problem with your terminal initialization that an Emacs expert can fix), then use control keys. To move to the previous line, type **C-p** (previous); for the next line, **C-n** (next). To move backwards on the line, type **C-b** (back); to move forward, use **C-f** (forward). Figure 3-1 shows **C-p** in action.

Of course, you often need to move larger distances. This is also easy. To execute any command four times, precede it with **C-u**; for example, **C-u C-p** moves four lines "up." You can stack up multipliers; **C-u C-u C-p** moves 16 lines, and so on, as shown in Figure 3-2.

You can also move around by words or sentences. A word is any combination of uppercase and lowercase letters, numerals, and dollar signs. **ESC b** brings you to the start of the word to the left of the cursor; **ESC f** brings you to the end of the word to the right of the cursor. It's worth noting that these are very similar to **C-b** and **C-f**; using the **Escape** key instead of **Control** often changes character-oriented commands to word-oriented commands.

On any line, **C-a** moves to the beginning of the line; **C-e** (end) moves to the end. Their "escape" counterparts move to the beginning or end of the current "sentence." This might not be meaningful while you're editing code—in C code, these commands usually move you to the previous (or next) blank line. But they are

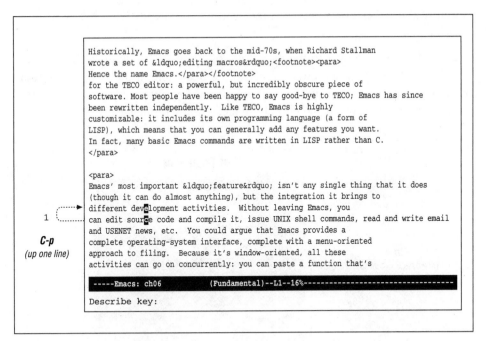

```
           Historically, Emacs goes back to the mid-70s, when Richard Stallman
           wrote a set of &ldquo;editing macros&rdquo;<footnote><para>
           Hence the name Emacs.</para></footnote>
           for the TECO editor: a powerful, but incredibly obscure piece of
           software. Most people have been happy to say good-bye to TECO; Emacs has since
           been rewritten independently.  Like TECO, Emacs is highly
           customizable: it includes its own programming language (a form of
           LISP), which means that you can generally add any features you want.
           In fact, many basic Emacs commands are written in LISP rather than C.
           </para>

           <para>
           Emacs' most important &ldquo;feature&rdquo; isn't any single thing that it does
           (though it can do almost anything), but the integration it brings to
       1   different development activities.  Without leaving Emacs, you
           can edit source code and compile it, issue UNIX shell commands, read and write email
           and USENET news, etc.  You could argue that Emacs provides a
    C-p    complete operating-system interface, complete with a menu-oriented
(up one line) approach to filing.  Because it's window-oriented, all these
           activities can go on concurrently: you can paste a function that's
           -----Emacs: ch06          (Fundamental)--L1--16%-------------------------------
           Describe key:
```

Figure 3–1: Moving back one line

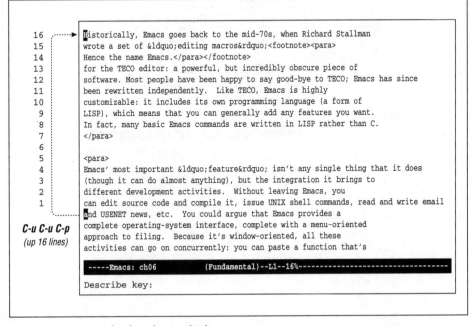

```
    16     Historically, Emacs goes back to the mid-70s, when Richard Stallman
    15     wrote a set of &ldquo;editing macros&rdquo;<footnote><para>
    14     Hence the name Emacs.</para></footnote>
    13     for the TECO editor: a powerful, but incredibly obscure piece of
    12     software. Most people have been happy to say good-bye to TECO; Emacs has since
    11     been rewritten independently.  Like TECO, Emacs is highly
    10     customizable: it includes its own programming language (a form of
     9     LISP), which means that you can generally add any features you want.
     8     In fact, many basic Emacs commands are written in LISP rather than C.
     7     </para>
     6
     5     <para>
     4     Emacs' most important &ldquo;feature&rdquo; isn't any single thing that it does
     3     (though it can do almost anything), but the integration it brings to
     2     different development activities.  Without leaving Emacs, you
     1     can edit source code and compile it, issue UNIX shell commands, read and write email
           and USENET news, etc.  You could argue that Emacs provides a
C-u C-u C-p complete operating-system interface, complete with a menu-oriented
(up 16 lines) approach to filing.  Because it's window-oriented, all these
           activities can go on concurrently: you can paste a function that's
           -----Emacs: ch06          (Fundamental)--L1--16%-------------------------------
           Describe key:
```

Figure 3–2: Moving back with a multiplier

helpful within block comments, and they can be very handy when you start using Emacs for other purposes.

Within a file, ESC > moves to the end of the file (you can think of ">" as an arrow pointing to the end), while ESC < moves to the beginning. If the file is longer than one screen, ESC v moves "up" one screenful and C-v moves "down" a screenful,* that is, one screen towards the end of the file, as shown in Figure 3-3.

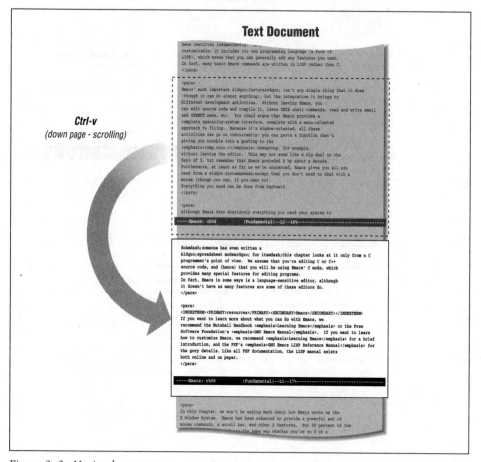

Figure 3–3: Moving by screens

---

* Emacs documentation calls this "up," because any given line on your screen moves "up." We find it easier to think in terms of moving "down" in the file. To each his own, though.

Some commands are provided especially for editing programs, such as ESC C-a. (Press and release the **Escape** key and then **C-a**. Or if you are good at parallel processing, press the ALT key, the **Control** key, and **a** all at once.) This command goes backward to the bracket that starts the function that you're in. ESC C-e goes to the closing bracket. ESC **a** goes to the beginning of a statement, and ESC **e** to the end.

Note that many commands use the ESC key, sometimes in conjunction with the **Control** key. On most modern keyboards, you can replace the **Escape** key with the ALT key. Hold down ALT just as you hold down the **Control** key, while pressing the proper letter or other character to invoke a command. Some people find this difficult (and long-term use may hurt your wrist) so we'll stick to ESC in this book. On the keyboards that were around when Emacs was invented, the same effect was produced by a key called **Meta**, and the Emacs documentation still refers to these keystrokes by names like **M-a** and **M-e**.

Here's a summary of the commands we've discussed so far:

Table 3–1: Basic Motion Commands

Command	Meaning
C-b	Move back one character
C-f	Move forward one character
C-p	Move to previous line
C-n	Move to next line
ESC b	Move back one word
ESC f	Move forward one word
C-a	Move to the beginning of the current line
C-e	Move to the end of the current line
C-v	Move "down" one page (towards the end) of the file
ESC v	Move "up" one page (towards the beginning) of the file
ESC >	Move to the end of the file
ESC <	Move to the beginning of the file
ESC a	Move to the beginning of a statement
ESC e	Move to the end of a statement
ESC C-a	Move to the beginning of a function
ESC C-e	Move to the end of a function
C-u	Multiply the previous command by four

Deleting Text

Now that you can move around in a file, what about deleting text? The most basic command for deleting text is DEL, which deletes the character before the cursor. It has the interesting behavior that it "understands" tabs; rather than deleting a tab character, it turns a tab into the proper number of spaces, and then deletes the rightmost space.

You should be warned that DEL doesn't work right on many terminals. This is because these terminals don't transmit a true delete (ASCII code 127), but a backspace (ASCII code 8) instead. And it so happens that Emacs uses the backspace as the help key. The symptom you'll see is that when you press DEL you will be prompted with a little **C-h** at the bottom of the screen.

If you have this problem, restore DEL to its original purpose by putting this in your *.emacs* file:

```
(keyboard-translate ?\C-h ?\C-?)
```

The syntax of this Lisp command is rather mysterious. The first question mark is needed to say "The name of a key follows." The **\C-h** refers to the help key, and the **\C-?** to the delete key. So the effect of this tangled code is to make DEL work like a true delete.

But you probably want a help key, too. So put in the following command. We have arbitrarily chosen the Control-backslash key (**C-**) as the help key, because people rarely use it for anything else.

```
(keyboard-translate ?\C-\\ ?\C-h)
```

If you are running the X Window System, there's another solution to the delete key problem that lets you keep **C-h** as your help key. Since there's no completely portable solution, we're going to have to refer you to the **xmodmap** and **xev** manual pages. The basic idea is to run **xev** and press the backspace key in its window to find out what key code is transmitted by your backspace key. Then you can use **xmodmap** to bind this code to Delete instead of Backspace. In addition to requiring some research, this solution has the potential problem of causing keys to misbehave in other X programs, particularly those based on the Motif programming kit.

The other basic deletion command in Emacs is **C-d**, which deletes the character under the cursor (to the right of "point"). Once you become fluent with Emacs, you'll find yourself relying on both of these; you'll know instinctively which is more convenient in any situation.

```
void gen_and_s█t(numels, genstyle)
int numels;
int genstyle;
{
     if (genstyle == TYPE1) {
          init_type1(numels);
     } else {
          init_random(numels);
     }
}
--**-Emacs: gen.c              (C)--All----------------------------------
```

As you might expect, you can precede both **DEL** and **C-d** by the "multiplier," **C-u**: this deletes four characters to the left or to the right, respectively. You also shouldn't be surprised to hear that **ESC DEL** deletes the previous word (i.e., left from the cursor to the beginning of the word), while **ESC d** deletes the "next" word (right from the cursor to the end of a word). Here's the result of deleting a word:

```
void gen_and_s█numels, genstyle)
int numels;
int genstyle;
{
     if (genstyle == TYPE1) {
          init_type1(numels);
     } else {
          init_random(numels);
     }
}
--**-Emacs: gen.c              (C)--All----------------------------------
```

Another way to delete text is to "kill" an entire line with **C-k**. The "kill" command deletes from the cursor to the end of the line:[*]

```
void gen_and_s█
int numels;
int genstyle;
{
     if (genstyle == TYPE1) {
          init_type1(numels);
     } else {
          init_random(numels);
     }
}
--**-Emacs: gen.c              (C)--All----------------------------------
```

---

[*] One peculiarity is that a single **C-k** deletes the line itself, but not the "newline" at the end of the line. If you use **C-k C-k** you'll get the newline, too. However, if you precede **C-k** by a multiplier, it does delete the newline. So **C-u C-k** deletes four lines.

You can also delete any size region of text by using the "wipe" command, **C-w**. Here is what you do:

1. Mark the start of the region by pressing **C-@**. (On many keyboards, **C-SPACE** is equivalent, and more convenient.) This is called "setting the mark."

2. Move the cursor to the first character past the end of the region.

3. Press **C-w**.

Emacs doesn't highlight a region the way many word processors do. (There is a way to do it if you are on the X Window System, but it's complicated.) The command **C-x C-x** switches the positions of the mark and the cursor; this is a good way to find out where the mark is located.

If you want to copy a region without cutting it, use **ESC w** instead of **C-w**.

More about marks

Emacs's C mode provides some additional help with marks. You often want to mark a function—for example, to delete it entirely, to move it somewhere else, or to help you look at it more easily. You can do this with the command **ESC C-h**. This puts the cursor at the beginning of the function, and sets the mark at the end.

(If you have mapped your **Backspace** key to the **Delete** key as described earlier in this chapter, you can't use **C-h** in this way. Later in this chapter you will learn how to bind another key to the desired function, which is called **mark-defun**.)

ESC C-h gives you a "shortcut" for moving to the beginning of the function. It's easy to get confused while you're working with a large chunk of code and lose track of what function you're editing. By taking you to the first line, **ESC C-h** makes it easy for you to see what you're doing.

Recalling Deleted Text

Of course, you often want to recall text that you have deleted—either because you didn't mean to delete it,[*] or because you want to move it somewhere else. In Emacs, this is called "yanking" text, and the corresponding command is **C-y**. You use "yank" most often to retrieve lines that you "killed," or regions that you "wiped": you will often use **C-k** or **C-w**, move somewhere else, and use **C-y**.

You can also use **C-y** to recall words that you deleted (**ESC DEL**, **ESC D**), or sentences, or groups of individual characters (**C-u DEL** or **C-u C-d**). In fact, single character deletions are about the only thing that **C-y** won't recall.

---

[*] Though in this situation, the "undo" command (**C-x u**) might be more appropriate.

Try performing several kill commands in a row: remove a few lines with **C-k**, then a few words with **ESC d**, and so on. Now press **C-y**. All the deleted text comes back in one block. Emacs keeps adding successive kills to one region, so long as you don't intersperse other commands, like inserting text or moving the cursor.

Even if you do put other commands between kill commands, you can get back previous deletions. Follow a **C-y** with **ESC y**. That deletes what you just yanked, and substitutes the *next previous* deletion. This might sound difficult, but it's easy to get used to—and very useful. To get successive prior deletions, just continue to type **ESC y**. Emacs saves your last 30 deletions (more than you'll ever need) in a buffer called the "kill ring."

Here's a summary of the commands available for deleting and recalling text:

Table 3–2: Deleting and Recalling Text

Command	Meaning
DEL	Delete character to the left of cursor
C-d	Delete character under cursor (to the right of "point")
ESC DEL	Delete word to the left of cursor
ESC d	Delete word to the right of cursor
C-k	Delete the line to the right of cursor
C-SHIFT-2	Mark one end of a region
C-w	Delete the region between the mark and the cursor
C-y	Retrieve the last chunk of text deleted (doesn't work for single characters)
ESC y	Retrieve the next-last chunk of text (use after C-y)
C-u	Repeat the next command four times
C-x u	Undo the last command (works for many things besides deletions)

Searching and Replacing

Search-and-replace functionality is basic to any editor; Emacs is no exception. It supports many different ways of searching and replacing; we'll only go over the most common techniques here.

The standard Emacs search is a case-insensitive incremental search. This means that Emacs doesn't distinguish between uppercase and lowercase letters and that it

searches for each character as you type it. Let's search for the third occurrence of
"numels" in our sample program. Assume that the cursor is in the upper-left corner
of your screen and that you start an incremental search by typing **C-s**:

```
void gen_and_sort(numels, genstyle)
int numels;
int genstyle;
{
    if (genstyle == TYPE1) {
        init_type1(numels);
    } else {
        init_random(numels);
    }
}


-----Emacs: source.c            (C Isearch)--All--------------------
I-search:
```

You're prompted for the search character in the minibuffer. If you type the letter **n**,
Emacs moves the cursor to the **_**, the space after the "n." If this doesn't make
sense, think in terms of "point," the true current location. It is just to the left of the
cursor, and to the right of the "n," which is where you want it to be.

Of course, that's not what you want yet. So you type a **u**, the next letter in the
word you want. Now you have:

```
void gen_and_sort(numels, genstyle)
int numels;
int genstyle;
{
    if (genstyle == TYPE1) {
        init_type1(numels);
    } else {
        init_random(numels);
    }
}


-----Emacs: source.c            (C Isearch)--All--------------------
I-search: nu
```

You've found the word you want—but not the right occurrence of the word. To
go to the next occurrence of the search string, type **C-s** again; that brings you to
the word "numels" on the second line—which is where you want to be. To get to
the third occurrence, type **C-s** again:

```
void gen_and_sort(numels, genstyle)
int numels;
int genstyle;
{
    if (genstyle == TYPE1) {
        init_type1(numels);
    } else {
        init_random(numels);
    }
}

-----Emacs: source.c        (C Isearch)--All---------------------
I-search: nu
```

When you've found what you want, terminate your search by pressing **Return**. Don't forget to terminate the search; until you do, any further characters you type will be added to your search string—and, if you're unlucky enough to find them, you'll end up in some random part of the file. Press the **Delete** key to remove characters from your search string and go back to an earlier match in the file.

Incremental searches also end whenever you type any control character, in which case Emacs stops searching and executes the control command. However you end the search, Emacs puts the "mark" on the current location—often a convenient feature.

If you don't find the string you're searching far, Emacs beeps and prints the message "Failing I-search" in the minibuffer:

```
void gen_and_sort(numels, genstyle)
int numels;
int genstyle;
{
    if (genstyle == TYPE1) {
        init_type1(numels);
    } else {
        init_random(numels);
    }
}

-----Emacs: source.c        (C Isearch)--All---------------------
Failing I-search: nul
```

At this point, you can type ESC to terminate the search; or you can type DEL to delete the last character in the search string and try again. If you want to go back to where you started and forget about searching altogether, press **C-g**.

Incremental searches "wrap" around a file; that is, if the search fails to find something between the current location and the end of the file, it starts searching again from the beginning of the file. There's a trick, though. When Emacs reaches the end of the file, the search fails; you'll see the "Failing I-search" message in the minibuffer. If you type C-s again, the message changes to "Wrapped I-search," and the search begins from the beginning of the buffer.

If you want to search from your current position back towards the beginning of the file, use C-r instead of C-s. You can also use C-r in the middle of an incremental search to "reverse" its direction (look for the next prior occurrence of the current search string).

Incremental searches are popular and convenient because they tend to minimize the amount you have to type. They can be annoying, but once you're used to them, they usually do what you want.

While we won't describe them here, Emacs also supports:

- Case-sensitive searches
- Regular-expression searches
- "Simple" (i.e., non-incremental, non-regular expression) searches
- Word searches (multiline matches of entire words or phrases)

The next logical step past "search" operations is "search and replace." Emacs provides an unadorned "replace-string" command, which unconditionally replaces all occurrences of one string with another. However, this command usually isn't used from the keyboard. A more useful replacement operation is "query-replace," which is bound to the keyboard command ESC %.

Here's how to use query-replace. In our sample program, let's say we've changed the name of the *init* module to *startup*. Now we want to change the prefix *init_* to *startup_*. So we move the cursor to the beginning of the file and type ESC %:

```
void init_type1();
void init_random();

void gen_and_sort(numels, genstyle)
int numels;
int genstyle;
{
    if (genstyle == TYPE1) {
        init_type1(numels);
    } else {
        init_random(numels);
    }
}

-----Emacs: source.c          (C)--All----------------------------------
Query replace: █
```

It's easy enough. Type your search string (*init_*), followed by **Return**. Emacs then prompts you for the replacement string, again in the minibuffer: type *start_*, followed by another **Return**. Emacs moves the cursor to the first occurrence of *init_*:

```
void init_type1();
void init_random();

void gen_and_sort(numels, genstyle)
int numels;
int genstyle;
{
    if (genstyle == TYPE1) {
        init_type1(numels);
    } else {
        init_random(numels);
    }
}

-----Emacs: source.c          (C)--All----------------------------
Query replacing init_ with start_: (? for help)
```

The text in the minibuffer is asking you to tell Emacs what to do with the string it has found:

- Type SPACE or **y** to make the substitution and go to the next occurrence of *init_*.

- Type **!** to make a global replacement (replace all future occurrences of *init_* without asking).

- Type DEL or **n** to skip to the next occurrence of *init_*, without replacing the current occurrence.

- Type ESC or **q** (or almost any control character) to quit the search/replace operation, without replacing the text at the current location.

- Type **.** to make the replacement at the current location and terminate the operation (i.e., don't go on to the next location).

- Type **^** to go back to the previous match.

- Type **C-r** to enter a recursive edit, which allows you to do any other editing you'd like (type ESC C-C to leave the recursive edit and return to the query-replace).

- Type **C-h** to get a help message.

There are a few other options, but these cover 99 percent of what you'll need. Remember that **^**, followed by a recursive edit, is *very* useful if you accidentally make a replacement where you shouldn't.

Other kinds of search-and-replace are available. Emacs provides:

- Queried regular expression search-and-replace (query-replace-regexp)
- Unconditional regular expression search-and-replace (replace-regexp), which is only for the brave

These searches are beyond the scope of the book, because getting the most out of them requires a thorough understanding of Emacs's regular expressions. They can be very effective, but for the time being, put them on a list of things to learn later.

Table 3-3 summarizes the commands you can use while searching and replacing.

Table 3-3: Searching and Replacing (Including Subcommands)

Command	Meaning
C-s	Incremental search forward; repeat search forward
C-r	Incremental search backward; repeat search backward
ESC	Terminate incremental search (after you've started it)
DEL	Delete last character from the search in progress
ESC %	Query replace
!	Make all replacements without asking (within a query-replace)
n	Skip to next occurrence of search string
ESC	Quit query replace without making further replacements
.	Make replacement at current location and quit
^	Go back to previous match

Saving and Visiting Files

As with any reasonable editor, Emacs distinguishes between its internal buffer that stores the file you're editing and the actual contents of the file on the disk. What you see on the screen is a portion of Emacs's buffer. Pushing the changes you've made from the buffer back to the "real" file on disk is called "saving" the file.[*] Saving files is easy. Type **C-x C-s** to save the file that you're currently editing:

---

[*] You should know that buffers aren't necessarily connected to files; Emacs often creates buffers for special purposes that have no "file" underneath them. You can also create fileless buffers, which you can use as scratch areas. Just enter a "filename" that begins with an asterisk (*).

```
void init_type1();
void init_random();

void gen_and_sort(numels, genstyle)
int numels;
int genstyle;
{
    if (genstyle == TYPE1) {
        init_type1(numels);
-----Emacs: source.c          (C)--Top-----------------------------
Wrote /work/nutshell/gtools/screens/source.c
```

The message in the minibuffer reports that the file has been saved successfully. If you want to save the file under another name, type **C-x C-w**; this prompts you, in the minibuffer, for a pathname:

> Write file: ~/cuser/█

Emacs supplies the directory component of the filename, assuming that you want the new file to be in the same directory as the file you're editing. If this is OK, just type the new filename, followed by **Return**. If it isn't, you can edit the pathname, using normal Emacs editing commands.

Sometimes things get a bit more complicated. If Emacs notices that the file you're saving has been changed on the disk without its knowledge, the minibuffer prompts you:

> Disk file has changed since visited or saved. Save anyway? (yes or no) █

It's time to be careful; two people may be editing the file simultaneously, or you may have accidentally started another Emacs session to work on it. But assuming that you want to save the file, type **yes**.[*] Then you'll see another message:

> File has changed on disk; really want to edit the buffer? (y, n, or C-h) █

Again, type **y** to save the file and continue editing, **n** if you want to figure out what's going on before committing yourself.

Emacs always keeps backup copies that reflect the state of your files before you started an editing session. When you first save a file, it renames the old version by adding a tilde to its filename. For example, the first time you save the file *qsort2.c*, Emacs saves the old version as *qsort2.c~*. You can use that file if you want to "back out" of the changes you made during an editing session. Note that backup files aren't deleted automatically when you end an editing session; from time to time, you may want to clean them out by hand.

---

[*] Emacs is very fussy with these prompts. You must type one of the choices it gives you. Unfortunately, it doesn't always want the same thing; sometimes it wants "yes," and sometimes it wants "y" by itself.

In addition to backup files, Emacs keeps "auto-save" save files, in which it stores the state of the file periodically, based on the number of keystrokes (300, by default). These may be useful if the system you're using crashes during an editing session. If you try to edit a file, and the auto-save version is newer than the "actual" file, Emacs prints the following message in the minibuffer:

```
Auto save file is newer; consider M-x recover-file
```

M-x or **ESC x** is a special command that we haven't discussed yet; it lets you execute Emacs commands by name. The **M** stands for Meta, which exists on many modern keyboards as the **ALT** key. So you can hold down the **ALT** key while pressing **x**, or (as most people find easier) just press the **ESC** key and then **x**.

When you type **ESC x**, Emacs prompts you in the minibuffer with M-x, and waits for you to type a command:

```
void init_type1();
void init_random();

void gen_and_sort(numels, genstyle)
int numels;
int genstyle;
{
    if (genstyle == TYPE1) {
        init_type1(numels);
------Emacs: source.c            (C)--Top--------------------------------
M-x
```

Type **recover-file** followed by a **Return**. (You don't even have to type the whole string **recover-file**; a few characters that uniquely identify the command are enough.) Emacs now asks you for a filename. Type the name of the file you want to edit, and Emacs fetches the auto-saved version, rather than the original.

Auto-save files are deleted whenever you save the file, so you rarely need to clean them up by hand.

Emacs lets you work on different files (i.e., different buffers) without starting a new editing session. To edit a different file, use the command **C-x C-f**. You'll be prompted for a pathname in the minibuffer:

```
Find file: ~/cuser/
```

Again, Emacs provides the directory; you can supply the filename and edit the directory.

The command **C-x C-r** is very similar, but it finds a file "read only": it puts it in a "read-only" buffer, so you can look through the file, do searches, etc., but you'll get an error if you try to modify the file. This command is good for inspecting files that you don't want to change, like global header files. This feature is very useful for preventing you from making accidental changes. Emacs sticks the marker "%%" on the left side of the status line to show that this file is read-only. Note that this marker is used for *all* read-only files: that includes files you've read with **C-x C-r**, and "ordinary" files that you don't have permission to write.

Finally, **C-x C-q** makes a "read-only" file writable, and vice versa. You can use this command even on a file that somebody else owns, where you don't have write permission. This behavior makes sense, if you think about the distinction between files and buffers. **C-x C-q** changes the buffer's status (from read-only to writable, or vice versa), and even lets you edit the buffer, but doesn't do anything to the underlying file. When you try to save the modified file, you'll find that you can't. But you can always use **C-x C-w** to save the buffer to a different file.

Multiple Windows

One of the most useful features of Emacs is its ability to split its screen into multiple windows. Sure, that's commonplace now that we have window systems—and a modern windowing system is certainly a lot more elegant than Emacs windows on an ASCII terminal or an X-terminal emulator. However, we have to admit that we're retrogrades and prefer Emacs. You can manipulate Emacs windows from the keyboard, without bothering with a mouse.

When you want to edit or inspect another file, it's a lot easier (and faster) to open another window in Emacs than it is to start a new window on your workstation. It's particularly handy if you want to copy text from one file and paste it into another. You can also use Emacs windows when you don't have your fancy graphics workstation or X terminal, or when you're logged into some other system over a slow serial line.

To split the Emacs screen into two windows, use the command **C-x 2**. You'll see something like this:

```
void init_type1();
void init_random();

void gen_and_sort(numels, genstyle)
-----Emacs: source.c          (C)--Top-------------------------------
void init_type1();
void init_random();

void gen_and_sort(numels, genstyle)
-----Emacs: source.c          (C)--Top-------------------------------
```

The cursor's position remains unchanged, but the screen splits into two windows displaying the same buffer. The command **C-X o** moves you to the "other" window. You can move around and edit these windows independently. Of course, since there is only one buffer, changes that you make to one appear in the other.

Two windows displaying the same file can be handy, particularly if you need to look at two functions at different ends of a large file. But that's usually not what you really want: you're really interested in seeing two files on the screen at the same time. To get another file into your current window, use the **find-file** (**C-x C-f**) command; you might see something like this:

```
#ifndef _mytypes_h
#define _mytypes_h
#include <sys/stdtypes.h>
#endif
--**-Emacs: mytypes.h           (C)--Top----------------------------
void init_type1();
void init_random();

void gen_and_sort(numels, genstyle)
-----Emacs: source.c            (C)--Top----------------------------
```

To combine the two activities—splitting the window and finding a new file—use the command **find-file-other-window**, which you execute by typing **C-x 4 C-f**:[*]

```
#ifndef _mytypes_h
#define _mytypes_h
#include <sys/stdtypes.h>
#endif
--**-Emacs: mytypes.h           (C)--Top----------------------------
/*        @(#)stdtypes.h 1.6 90/01/04 SMI */

/*
 * Suppose you have an ANSI C or POSIX thingy that needs a typedef
--%%-Emacs: stdtypes.h          (C)--Top----------------------------
```

You can further subdivide windows until Emacs runs out of room on your screen. On screens with multiple windows, **C-x o** moves you "down" the screen. You can move up the screen by giving **C-x o** a "negative argument," but we find this inconvenient (you need to type **ESC -1 C-x o**).[†]

---

[*] This command is so basic it should be more accessible. To bind it to **C-x v**, put the following line in your *.emacs* file:

```
(define-key global-map "\C-xv" 'find-file-other-window)
```

[†] One solution is to create two custom key-bindings. The following line, when added to your *.emacs* file, defines the sequence **C-x p** as "move to the previous window." It's not the most profound example of customization, but we find it essential.

```
(define-key global-map "\C-xp"
    (function (lambda () "" (interactive) (other-window -1))))
```

Emacs also lets you split windows horizontally (**C-x 3**). In our experience, horizontally split windows aren't used frequently, probably because they're really useful only if you have a very wide screen; but you should know it's there. (We find the typical workstation screen to be just a bit too narrow.) It might be very helpful if you want to make a line-by-line comparison between two files.

Of course, now that you can create windows, you need to be able to make them go away. To delete the window you're currently in, type **C-x 0** (that's a zero, not an "oh"). The other windows are resized accordingly. To make the window you're currently in the only window on the screen, deleting all the others on the screen, type **C-x 1**.

When you delete a window, you should realize that you *aren't* deleting the buffer you're editing, or losing the changes you have made, even if you haven't saved them. Emacs still keeps track of the buffer. If you "visit" the file at some later time, Emacs will give you the edited buffer, assuming you want to continue with the changes you've made; if you try to exit Emacs, it realizes that you have made unsaved changes and asks whether or not you want to save the corresponding files—even if these files aren't displayed on the screen. (There are commands for deleting buffers, but we won't discuss them.)

You can open a new window on an X terminal while staying within a single Emacs session. Since Emacs was using the term "window" long before the X Window System existed, a new X window is called a frame. Type **C-x 5 2** to open a new frame onto the same buffer. **C-x 5 f** opens a new file in a new frame. **C-x 5 0** closes a frame. Be careful to remember that you're editing multiple frames. If you press **C-x C-c** to remove a frame, you'll end up removing all the open frames; your editing session will come to an end.

Help with Indentation and Comments

For a programmer, one important feature of Emacs is its ability to help you conform to a programming style. Not only does your code look more consistent, but when you type a bracket or parenthesis and its placement doesn't look right, it could clue you in that you've forgotten a quotation mark or something else to mess up your syntax.

We've already said that if you begin each line with a single TAB, Emacs automatically indents the remainder of the line correctly. Ending the previous line with a C-j (newline, or linefeed) rather than the customary **Return** also positions you in the right place to type the next line. As we mentioned earlier, Emacs often "adjusts" your position when you type the first character, and it can determine what kind of statement you're typing.

If a line of code is indented incorrectly, you can put the cursor anywhere on that line and type TAB, and Emacs adjusts the line's indentation for you. It doesn't matter where the cursor is; the TAB you type won't open up new space on the line. (It's worth trying this a few times to get a feel for how it works.)

That's it for code; what about comments? If you type ESC ; Emacs inserts a set of "comment markers" (/* */ in C, // in C++) for you after the end of the line and conveniently leaves the cursor between these markers. Here's how it looks in C:

```
void gen_and_sort(numels, genstyle)
int numels;
int genstyle;
{
    if (genstyle == TYPE1) {   /* █*/
        init_type1(numels);
    } else {
        init_random(numels);
    }
}



--**-Emacs: gen.c              (C)--All----------------------------------
```

You're now ready to start typing your comment. The comment normally begins in the column given by the Emacs variable **comment-column** (by default, 32), so your comments throughout the file will be aligned. However, if your line extends past column 32, Emacs just picks a point past the end of the line.

If you type long comments that cover many lines, you may want to turn on auto-fill mode. This mode is normally used in text files, where it does several nice things like wrap lines automatically as you type. It can be convenient in C mode, too, where it understands C syntax. Look at what auto-fill mode does to a long comment as you reach the end of one line:

```
/* Two calls to get_text are nested within a call to the insert function so
```

Emacs ends a line with the */ string and inserts a /* string to start a new comment on a new line:

```
/* Two calls to get_text are nested within a call to the insert */
/* function so
```

It also indents C statements intelligently, if you type beyond the end of a line.

To turn on auto-fill in a single buffer, just type ESC **x auto-fill-mode**. To make it the default for your C files (not a common practice), put this in your *.emacs* file:

```
(setq c-mode-hook '(lambda () (auto-fill-mode 1)))
```

The idea of a *hook* is that it executes a command automatically whenever certain things happen. In this case, c-mode-hook is invoked by Emacs whenever you find a file that ends in *.c*. So the above command says, "Whenever I enter a file of C code, turn on auto-fill."

Compiling Without Leaving Emacs

The command ESC **x compile** builds your program automatically; it allows you to repeatedly build your code while you're editing. Emacs asks you for the actual compilation command. The default is **make -k**, which requires you to have a makefile in the same directory (see Chapter 7, *Automatic Compilation with make*).

```
void gen_and_sort(numels, genstyle)
int numels;
int genstyle;
{
    if (genstyle == TYPE1) {
        init_type1(numels);
    } else {
        init_random(numels);
    }
}
-----Emacs: gen.c            (C)--All-----------------------------------
Compile command: make -k
```

If you want to accept this default, type **Return**. Otherwise, edit the command; remember that the minibuffer is just like any other buffer, except that it's only one line high. This new command, whatever it is, becomes the default compilation command for the rest of the editing session; if **make -k** isn't satisfactory, you should have to change it only once.

After you give a compilation command and type **Return**, Emacs takes the following steps:

- It checks whether you have any unsaved files; if so, it asks whether or not you want to save them. Obviously, you want to make sure that the sources you'll be compiling have been saved.

- It splits the screen into two buffers; the second buffer displays any output that your compilation generates (i.e., all messages sent to standard input or standard output), plus a few annotations from Emacs itself (the compilation command executed and the time of the compilation).

- It runs the compilation command.

Here's how it looks:

```
Void gen_and_sort(numels, genstyle)
int numels;
int genstyle;
{
-----Emacs: gen.c                      (C)--Top-----------------------------
cd /work/nutshell/gtools/screens/
make -k
cc     -c gen.c -o gen.o

Compilation finished at Wed Nov  1 13:27:38
--**-Emacs: *compilation*          (Compilation:exit [0])--All-------------
```

Note that the compilation buffer doesn't correspond to any file; if you want to save it, you'll have to specify a filename. Moreover, you won't be warned if you quit Emacs without saving the compilation buffer. (Any buffer whose name begins with an asterisk is considered a scratch buffer that you don't want to save.)

In the preceding short example, the compilation proceeded without error. That's not always the case—and, when something goes wrong, Emacs helps you find the trouble spots. Let's say that our compilation had the following inauspicious result:

```
Void gen_and_sort(numels, genstyle)
int numels;
int genstyle;
{
-----Emacs: gen.c                      (C)--Top-----------------------------
cd /work/nutshell/gtools/screens/
make -k
cc     -c gen.c -o gen.o
"gen.c", line 5: TYPE1 undefined
"gen.c", line 9: syntax error at or near symbol }
--**-Emacs: *compilation*          (Compilation:exit [1])--Top-------------
(No files need saving)
```

The compiler is complaining about errors on lines 5 and 9. Note that we can't even see the line of code that's causing the trouble. But doing so is easy, by typing **C-x `** (that's **C-x** followed by a backward quote). This makes Emacs parse the contents of the compilation buffer, look up the first error message, and position the cursor on the line that the compiler has complained about:

```
int genstyle;
{
■     if (genstyle == TYPE1) {
          init_type1(numels);
-----Emacs: gen.c                      (C)--30%-----------------------------
"gen.c", line 5: TYPE1 undefined
"gen.c", line 9: syntax error at or near symbol }
make: *** [gen.o] Error 1
make: Target `gen' not remade because of errors.

-----Emacs: *compilation*          (Compilation:exit [1])--24%-------------
Parsing error messages...done
```

With a little thought, it's pretty clear what happened: this file does not include the header in which TYPE1 was defined. After fixing this, you can type **C-x `** again to get to the next trouble spot.

A very useful feature of **C-x `** is that it works regardless of where the cursor is and what files are currently visible in buffers. It looks at your compilation buffer, finds the next error, figures out what file the error is in, and displays that file—even if the file is not on the screen. It's even immune to changes to the file. For example, let's say that after looking at the "TYPE1 undeclared" message, you went to the beginning of the file and added a pair of **#include** statements, followed by a blank line. The next time you type **C-x `**, Emacs finds the trouble spot that was originally on line 9 (now line 12).

About the only misfeature of **C-x `** is that it can't work backwards; you can't back up and return to previous error messages, and you can only go through the list of errors once. Emacs complains "No more errors" when you've worked through all the errors from your last compilation.

C-x ` works best when you're using the GNU C (**gcc**) compiler, though it does work with most other UNIX C compilers.

Shell Windows

You can run a UNIX shell within an Emacs editing window by giving the command **ESC x shell**:

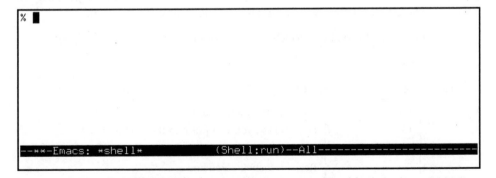

Why would you want to do this? Because you can use Emacs to edit your commands. Shell mode replaces the biggest deficiency of old UNIX shells: minimal command-line editing and an arcane, though powerful, command history facility. It is quite easy to search backwards through a shell window for some arbitrary command you gave ages ago. And, once you've found it, you can copy it and execute it again. If you frequently use commands that give a lot of output (for example, if you're using **diff** to compare two large files), shell mode saves the output, letting you search and inspect it conveniently. There are also times when it's convenient to have a transcript of a shell session; saving your shell window is a lot more convenient than using the rather clumsy UNIX **script** command.

The most obvious problem with a shell window is that common keyboard habits no longer work. For example, you can't type **C-c** to terminate a program, or **C-z** to suspend it; Emacs interprets these keystrokes as commands.

To work around this difficulty, shell mode has a separate set of commands, beginning with the prefix **C-c**. In most cases, you can just stick **C-c** before the command you'd normally use: **C-c C-c** stops the program you're running, while **C-c C-z** pauses it. **C-d** by itself works fine, just as in a regular shell.

The shell also offers a few conveniences. **C-c C-r** moves the cursor to the start of the output from the last shell command. This is convenient if a command produces a lot of output, and you want to find the beginning quickly. **C-c C-y** "yanks" the most recent shell command; it's similar to the C shell's and **bash**'s !! command history.

Shell mode watches for **cd**, **pushd**, and **popd** commands, and changes your default directory (the directory that appears in the minibuffer when you try to open a file) accordingly. The assumption, which is usually pretty good, is that if you have **cd**ed to a directory, you will sooner or later want to edit files in that directory. Many programmers we know find this feature extremely convenient. We confess that we find it annoying and have disabled it—but you're probably better off spending some time playing with it before making your own decision.*

Here's a summary of the shell mode's special commands:

Table 3-4: Emacs

Command	Shell equivalent	Meaning
C-c C-c	C-c	Interrupt (i.e., terminate) job
C-c C-z	C-z	Stop job (so you can put it in the background)
C-c C-r	none	Move cursor to last command's output
C-c C-y	!!	Recall last shell command

---

* If you want to disable it, add the following lines to your *.emacs* file:

```
(setq-default shell-cd-regexp nil)
(setq-default shell-pushd-regexp nil)
(setq-default shell-popd-regexp nil)
```

Tags

Emacs's "tags" facility is similar to the "tags" facility that was built into *vi*. It provides a way to make source-code navigation easier.

The tags commands are based on a "tags" database, which consists of a single file named *TAGS*. This file lists function names, and (optionally) typedefs, and where they appear in the source files. The command **etags** builds the database; execute it in a shell like this:

```
% etags -t list of source files
```

where the *list of source files* is just that: a list of files that you want to be indexed in the database. The –t option tells the command to include typedefs in the database. So to build a *TAGS* file from all the sources in a directory, you'd give the command:

```
% etags -t *.[ch]
```

Once you've built a tag table, you can use it for navigation, with the Emacs command **ESC .**, which lets you specify a string to look for. There are two ways to use the tag table. The more laborious way is to simply type **ESC .**; you'll get a prompt in the minibuffer, asking you which tag you want to find. Type the name of a function or type definition, followed by **Return**. For example, we'll find the function **init_random** in our sample program:

```
void gen_and_sort(numels, genstyle)
int numels;
int genstyle;
{
        if (genstyle == TYPE1) {        /*  \* 
              init_type1(numels);
        } else {
              init_random(numels);
        }
}
-----Emacs: gen.c               (C)--All------------------------------
Find tag: (default init_type1) init_random
```

Type the name of the function you want to look at (**init_random**); when you're done, type **Return.**[*] (Emacs may prompt you for the name of a *TAGS* file; just type **Return** to accept the default, which is the *TAGS* file in the current directory.) You'll see something like this:

---

[*] You don't have to type the entire function name; all you need is a unique substring.

```
/* initialize with random numbers */
void init_random(number)
int number;
{
        int i;
        for (i = 0; i < number; i++) {
                x[i] = random();
        }
}



-----Emacs: initran.c         . (C)--All-------------------------------
Mark set
```

Emacs has found the file in which **init_random** lives and has positioned the cursor on the first line of the function.

There's an even simpler way to use tags. When you type **ESC .**, Emacs generates a "default" tag by reading the name that's under the cursor. So, if you're looking at a call to **init_random**, you can easily jump to the function's definition by putting the cursor on top of the function name and typing **ESC . Return**. The **Return** is really an answer to the "Find tag: " prompt in the minibuffer, accepting the default. Note that the cursor must be on top of the function's name, *not* on top of an argument or something else on the line.

The command **C-x 4 .** is similar to **ESC .**, except that it puts the tag you're looking for in a new window. This feature makes it simple to look at a function call and the function definition simultaneously.

Using Other Tags Files

Emacs can have only one tag file loaded at a time. The first time you use a tag command, Emacs loads a file—by default, the one in the current directory. If you want to switch to another *TAGS* file, use the command **ESC x visit-tags-table**. Emacs prompts you in the minibuffer for the name of a new tag table; type the name, followed by **Return**, and the file is loaded.

Working with multiple tag files can be convenient if you're involved in a very large project that encompasses code in several directories.

Searching and Replacing with Tags

One of the nicest features of tags—and, unfortunately, one we can only touch upon—is that it allows you to do search and replace operations that span a whole set of files, rather than just an individual file. It's particularly nice that these commands work with any string you want to find, not just the function and structure names in the tag database; in this case, the database is only providing a list of files to be searched.

Assume you want to search for a particular use of the variable *number* somewhere in the program. To do so, give the command ESC **x tags-search**. Emacs prompts you for a search string in the minibuffer:

```
/* initialize with random numbers */
void init_random(number)
int number;
{
        int i;
        for (i = 0; i < number; i++) {
                x[i] = random();
        }
}



-----Emacs: initran.c        (C)--All------------------------------
Tags search (regexp): █
```

Type the string you're searching for, followed by **Return**; Emacs finds the next occurrence of your search string. You are not restricted to the current file; Emacs looks through all the files from which the tags database was compiled. Note that this is a "regular expression" search, not an incremental search. To repeat the search (i.e., to find the next occurrence of the same string), type ESC ,.

The command ESC **x tags-query-replace** lets you do a full query-replace through all of the files listed in the tags database. We won't describe its behavior much; it's almost the same as the query-replace (ESC %) that we described earlier. When you reach the end of the file, the search-replace operation terminates—temporarily. You can do any other editing you'd like without leaving the file. At any time, you can continue the search-replace by typing ESC , and continuing with the next file.

Some Other Modes and Commands

Emacs does so many things that a single chapter can give only a sample. However, we'd feel remiss if we didn't provide some sort of summary for what else is available. Emacs's biggest "feature" isn't any single thing that it does, but the huge number of things that it can do together; it's a complete working environment. This summary will be brief, but perhaps enough to get you interested:

- *Text-mode* is pretty basic; it's ideal for editing "normal text" (e.g., documentation, letters). There are also special modes for editing TEX, *troff*, and Scribe input files.

- *Dired-mode*: The command **C-x d** starts a "directory editing" mode, in which Emacs lets you "edit" a UNIX-style directory listing. You can use this mode to delete, rename, and edit files.

- *Mail and Gnus*: Emacs provides modes for reading and writing electronic mail and Usenet news.

- *Picture-mode*: Picture mode lets you create "line-drawings" easily (i.e., drawings composed of stars, underscores, etc.). Line drawings are so archaic that many people wonder why you'd want them; but if you'd like to stick a little flow chart into a comment block, there's no alternative.

- *Lisp-mode* and *Lisp-interaction-mode*: These are special modes for editing Emacs Lisp (and other Lisp) files. Emacs Lisp is the language used for customizing the editor. Lisp-mode is used only for writing Lisp code, while lisp-interaction-mode can execute the code you type with Emacs's built-in Lisp interpreter.

- *spell-buffer* is a built-in spell checker. The command **ESC $** checks the current word; **ESC x spell-buffer** checks the entire buffer you're editing. (There are a few other flavors of the spell command.)

- *abbrev-mode* allows you to define abbreviations for commonly used words and phrases, to save you the trouble of retyping them. Abbreviation mode is often used to check for common misspellings as you're typing.

There's much more: special modes for all sorts of obscure languages, a few games, and more. Don't hesitate to explore.

4

Compiling and Linking with gcc

Now that you can use Emacs to edit a program, you need to be able to compile it. The FSF's compiler is named **gcc**. It does much more than just compile a program: by default, it compiles the source code, assembles the assembly language code the compiler produces, and invokes the UNIX loader, **ld**, to produce an executable file. It also includes a compiler for the C++ language.[*]

Like all the Free Software Foundation tools, **gcc** comes with online documentation that you can view through the **info** command and that can also be ordered in hardcopy form from the FSF. In this case, the book is called *Using and Porting GNU CC*.

C Compilation

Even though the **gcc** compiler does everything behind the scenes, it's worth delineating the steps it has to perform to create an executable binary. Figure 4-1 shows how data flows through the various stages and what files can be created along the way. The stages are:

preprocessing

This step resolves directives like **#define**, **#include**, and **#if**. Like many UNIX systems, **gcc** invokes a separate utility called **cpp** to do the preprocessing.

---

[*] It also includes a compiler for Objective C, another object-oriented C dialect. In the UNIX world to date, Objective C is used widely in the NeXT community, but hasn't attracted a lot of excitement elsewhere. The Objective C compiler isn't supported by Cygnus and won't be discussed further.

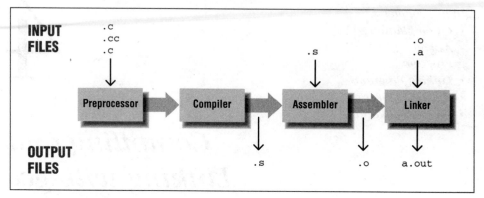

Figure 4–1: Stages of compilation

compilation

This produces assembly language from the input files; since the assembler is usually invoked right away, the output is not normally saved in files.

assembly

This takes the assembly language as input and produces object files with .o extensions. While some compilers build in the assembly capability, **gcc** does it by internally invoking a separate utility called the assembler, **gas**. GNU assemblers aren't available for all architectures; if the GNU assembler isn't available, **gcc** invokes the "native" assembler (**as**).

linking

This is the final stage, where the .o modules are placed in their proper places in the executable file. Library functions that the program refers to are also placed in the file. (Systems with shared libraries use a slightly more complicated method.)

UNIX compilers perform this phase by internally invoking the linker, which is called *ld*.[*] **gcc** also cleans up by deleting any object files that it created from source files (but not any pre-existing object files that you specified on the command line). You can stop **gcc** at each of these stages and do what you want with the output, but before we look at that, let's see what you normally do when compiling.

---

[*] The initials stand for "link editor," but we haven't heard anybody use this term for years. In some early UNIX documentation, **ld** is also called a "loader," which can be confusing because most people think of loading as reading the executable file into memory at run time.

Basic Use of gcc

As an all-in-one processor, **gcc** could be run like this, producing an executable file from a set of C source files:

```
% gcc -o filter filter_driver.c define_stack.c global_var.c site_specific.c
```

The –o filter argument tells **gcc** to name the executable file *filter*. If you don't specify an –o argument, **gcc** chooses the default name *a.out*, which is not particularly informative (and would cause multiple executables to overwrite each other). So everybody uses the –o argument. All the rest of the arguments on this particular command line are source filenames.

But programmers rarely build everything at once; they're more likely to compile each source file to check for errors and to recompile selected ones each time they have to perform maintenance. So a more likely series of commands would be:

```
% gcc -c filter_driver.c
% gcc -c define_stack.c global_var.c
% gcc -c site_specific.c
% gcc -o filter filter_driver.o define_stack.o global_var.o site_specific.o
```

The **-c** option means "compile but do not link." So **gcc** stops after the compilation phase each time, creating the object file *filter_driver.o* from *filter_driver.c* and so on. At the end, all the object files are combined to make the executable file. Since the inputs to the last command are all object files, no compilation or assembly is required: **gcc** just invokes the linker.

Using **gcc** to invoke the linker is vastly preferable to using **ld** separately; **gcc** ensures that the program is linked with the correct libraries and initialization routines.

Defining Constants

A few other options are commonly used. One, the **-D** option, acts like **#define** in the source code: it sets the value of a symbol:

```
% gcc -c -DDOC_FILE=\"info\" -DUSE_POLL filter_driver.c
```

The first **-D** option sets DOC_FILE to the string "info" (because of the backslashes, the quotation marks actually become part of the symbol's definition). This can be useful for controlling which file a program opens. The second **-D** option defines the USE_POLL symbol. (It happens to set it to the value 1, the default, but you probably don't care; your program just uses an **#ifdef** directive to check whether it's set.)

Some symbols—usually those identifying the type of computer system you're compiling on—are automatically defined by the compiler. If you want to suppress one of these symbols, use the –U*name* option. This is equivalent to putting:

```
#undef name
```

at the beginning of each source file.

If you have an include file in a non-standard directory, specify this directory in an –I option. For instance, suppose you have two directories for code, */usr/src* for source files and */usr/headers* for header files. While you're compiling in the */usr/src* directory, you can tell *gcc* where to find the header files through the command:

```
% gcc -c -I../headers filter_driver.c
```

Linking with Libraries

Another common compilation option is –l, which specifies a library. And the option specifies this in a particularly arcane way. First, –l must be specified at the end of the command, after the filenames, while all other options are specified before the filenames. Here's a typical command; the inputs are object files, so the command just runs the linker (that's the time when libraries are read, of course).

```
% gcc -o plot main.o plot_line.o -lm
```

The –l**m** option specifies the math library. Wait till you hear what the **m** stands for! When you specify –l*name*, the system searches for lib*name*.**a** in the directory where the system stores its standard libraries, normally */usr/lib*. So the math library you are looking for is */usr/lib/libm.a*. (Systems that offer shared libraries use a slightly different convention).

Like include files, libraries can sometimes be in non-standard places. Use the –L option to make **gcc** look in a particular directory for libraries. For instance:

```
% gcc -o plot -L/src/local/lib main.o plot_line.o -lm
```

This command tells **gcc** to look for libraries first in */src/local/lib*, then in the standard location. If someone has put a local version of a library in */src/local /lib*, that version is used in preference to the standard version in */usr/lib*.

UNIX linkers search libraries in the order in which they occur on the command line and only resolve the references that are outstanding at the time the library is searched. Therefore, the order of libraries and object modules on the command line can be critical. (This is why we told you to put –l options after the filenames.)

Consider the command:

```
% gcc -lmine file4.c
```

This command searches for the library file *libmine.a* to resolve any function references needed for linking. However, the linker has not yet processed the object module for *file4.o* (created by the **gcc** command and normally deleted if compilation and linking are successful). Therefore, there are no outstanding function references, and the library search has no effect. If the program needs this library, the **gcc** command produces "Undefined symbol" messages during the loading phase, and the linker does not produce an executable file. To perform this compilation correctly, enter the command:

```
% gcc file4.c -lmine
```

Now the loader searches the library file after processing *file4.c* and is able to resolve any references requiring this library.

When compiling a C program, you often don't need to list any libraries explicitly on the command line. **gcc** automatically searches the system call library, I/O library, and run-time initialization routines. If you use any math routines, you'll need to search for the math library (**-lm**); if you're compiling C++ code, you may need to include the C++ libraries (**-lg++**).

How gcc Handles Files

Exactly how the compiler treats any file depends on the file's name. The compiler strips the initial part of the name, then determines how to process the file on the basis of the filename's extension. In each case, the compiler passes the file to the appropriate program for preprocessing, compilation, or assembly, and it links all resulting object modules together to produce an executable file. The following table shows how the compiler recognizes different file types:

Filename	Interpretation	Action
file.c	C source	Preprocessed and compiled by **gcc**
file.C	C++ source	Preprocessed and compiled by **g++**
file.cc	C++ source	Preprocessed and compiled by **g++**
file.i	Preprocessed C source	Compiled by **gcc**
file.ii	Preprocessed C++ source	Compiled by **g++**
file.s	Assembly language source	Assembled by **as**
file.S	Assembly language source	Preprocessed and assembled by **as**
file.o	Compiled object module	Passed to **ld**
file.a	Object module library	Passed to **ld**

All other files, together with options that **gcc** does not recognize, are passed to **ld**, the loader—either the "native" loader supplied by your vendor, or the GNU loader. As a result, almost all loader options are available directly through **gcc**.

In the commands shown earlier in this chapter, the –l and –L options were actually passed to the linker. In general, **gcc** passes on unrecognized options to the linker, so you can specify linker options without having to invoke the linker separately.

If you're writing C++ code, you can use the **g++** command instead of **gcc**. You're actually getting the same compiler; however, when it is invoked as **g++**, the compiler expects C++ instead of regular C source code. Also, **g++** uses different default libraries.

Output Files at Each Stage of Compilation

If you want to preserve the output of **gcc** at some intermediate stage, either for debugging purposes or to manipulate the code directly, you can do so. Here's how, for each stage:

preprocessing

An –E option in **gcc** sends the preprocessed code to the standard output, instead of compiling the program.

compilation

To save the assembly language output, run **gcc** with the –S option. This produces files whose names end with *.s* in place of the source file's *.c*.

assembly

As we have seen, running with –c produces object files whose names end with *.o*.

We have just finished a long discussion of the many kinds of input that the compiler takes and the different kinds of output that it can provide. Pictures are not always worth a thousand words, particularly when it comes to summarizing a lot of disparate information. But it may help you to remember this information if you view the compiler as a kind of "machine" with different inputs and outputs, as outlined earlier in Figure 4-1.

The input file's name determines where it goes into the machine. *.c* and *.C* files go to the preprocessor, *.i* and *.ii* files go straight to the compiler, and so on. Compilation options determine which stage of the machine produces output (i.e., how many stages of the machine you run). –S means that you stop after the assembler and the output filename ends with *.s*. If you keep this picture in mind, the compiler's machinations will not seem so strange; you will stop seeing preprocessing, compilation, assembly, and linking as separate steps and come to see compilation as one big assembly line, for which **gcc** is the production manager.

make and the Compiler

make is one of UNIX's most important tools and one that many programmers don't take advantage of—even programmers who have used UNIX for a long time. It is a program for automating compilations. Once you have created a *makefile* that describes how to build an executable, **make** automatically figures out which object files are out of date, recompiles those files from the most recent source code, and links together a new executable. The GNU version of **make** (often called **gmake**, occasionally **gnumake**) is even more powerful, and well worth your time.

Because **make** is so important, we have devoted a separate chapter to it (Chapter 7, *Automatic Compilation with make*). You can do some simple experiments with **make** without reading that chapter or even without writing a makefile (a description of how to build your executable). For example, to compile the source file *faa.c*, enter the command **make faa.o**. **make** sees that *faa.c* exists and issues the command **gcc -c faa.c**. If *faa.o* is newer than *faa.c*, there is no reason to compile; in this case, **make** does nothing. **make** therefore can save a lot of compilation time. If you work on large applications, using **make** can save you hours. It can also save you many headaches, because you don't have to remember when you last compiled any object module, which libraries you need to compile correctly, and so on.

Compilation Options

The following sections discuss other important options that are available with the **gcc** compiler. For the most part, these are the same options you'd expect to see with the traditional UNIX compilers. There are many, many other options—perhaps several hundred all together—that control various details of compilation and optimization. The chances are that you will never need these, but it won't hurt to familiarize yourself with the complete documentation for **gcc**.

Displaying compiler behavior

The **-v** (verbose) option prints the compiler's version number and complete details about how each pass is executed. This option is particularly useful for finding out exactly which options your program is being linked with.

C language options

We'll start by listing a few options for controlling the warning messages that **gcc** produces. There are many options for controlling warnings; it's possible to request (or inhibit) many warning messages on a per-message basis. We're not sure that's really useful; we'll limit ourselves to a few options that control large groups of messages:

-w

> Suppress all warning messages.

-W

> Produce some additional warning messages about legal (but questionable) coding practices.

-Wall

> Produce even more warning messages about questionable coding practices.

-Wtraditional

> Produce warning messages about code that is legal in both the "Kernighan and Ritchie" and ANSI definitions of the C language, but behaves differently in each case.

-Werror

> Make all warnings into errors; that is, don't attempt to produce an object file if a warning has occurred.

Now, we'll discuss how to control various features of the C and C++ languages. There are basically three options to worry about: **-traditional**, **-ansi**, and **-pedantic**. In most cases, it's fairly easy to tell which you want. Older C code—code that predates the standard—should be compiled with **-traditional**. Newer code that has been written to conform to the ANSI standard should be compiled with **-ansi**. Either option can accept prototypes, where you specify the arguments on the same line as the function name, as in func (char *arg).

Note that the ANSI C standard and "traditional" (Kernighan and Ritchie) C both define the behavior of the preprocessor—either explicitly or implicitly. Therefore, the options listed below affect both **cpp** and **gcc**:

-traditional

> Supports the traditional C language, including lots of questionable, but common, practices. The traditional option also supports all of the FSF's extensions to the C language.

-ansi

> Supports the ANSI C standard, though somewhat loosely. The FSF's extensions are recognized, except for a few that are incompatible with the ANSI standard. Thus, ANSI programs compile correctly, but the compiler doesn't try too hard to reject non-conformant programs, or programs using non-ANSI features.

-pedantic

> Issues all the warning messages that are required by the ANSI C standard. Forbids the use of all the FSF extensions to the C language and considers the use of such extensions errors. It's arguable whether or not anyone wants this degree of conformity to the ANSI standard. The FSF obviously feels that it isn't

really necessary; they write "This option is not intended to be *useful*; it exists only to satisfy pedants." We feel that it's useful to check for ANSI conformity at this level and also that it's useful to disable the FSF's own extensions to the language. We may be pedants, but historically, extensions to a language have typically been used rather cynically to trap developers into dependence on a particular vendor's dialect. This isn't the kind of the behavior the FSF means to, or should, encourage. As the **gcc** manual points out, **-pedantic** is not a complete check for ANSI conformance—it only issues errors that are required by the ANSI standard.

Preprocessor options

The following set of options control the **cpp** preprocessor from the command line:

-M
> Read the source files, figure out which other files they include, and output lists of dependencies for *make*. There is one dependency list for each source file. The dependency lists are sent to standard output, and compilation doesn't proceed past preprocessing (i.e., **-M** implies **-E**). This option can make it much easier to generate correct makefiles.

-C The preprocessor normally deletes all comments from the program. With **-C**, it doesn't. This flag may be useful in conjunction with **-E** when you are trying to make sure that the preprocessor is doing what you intended. In such cases, leaving your comments in may be handy.

> The **-C** option doesn't automatically imply **-E**, but **gcc** won't let you use **-C** on the command line unless **-E** is also present.

Options to specify libraries

The following options are not common, but you may find them useful in particular situations:

-nostartfiles
> Don't use the standard system startup files when linking. This is useful for cross-compilation, or for compiling code for an embedded processor, where you may want to provide your own startup file.

-nostdlib
> Don't use the standard libraries and startup files when linking. Again, this is useful when you want to provide your own libraries, overriding the default libraries.

–static

> Link only to static libraries, not shared libraries.

–shared

> If shared libraries are available, use them wherever possible, rather than static libraries. (This is the default.)

Debugging and profiling options

These options request the compiler to create additional code and an expanded symbol table for the various profilers and debuggers (**dbx**, **prof**, **gprof**, and the branch count profiler). They are extremely helpful for debugging and tuning code under development, but should not be used for production programs.

–p Link the program for profiling with **prof**. When you execute a program compiled with this option, it produces a file named *mon.out* that contains program execution statistics. The profiler **prof** reads this file and produces a table describing your program's execution.

–pg

> Link the program for profiling with **gprof**. Executing a program compiled with this option produces a file named *gmon.out* that includes execution statistics. The profiler **gprof** reads this file and produces detailed information about your program's execution. See Chapter 9, *Program Timing and Profiling*, for more information. For example, the following command compiles the file *program.f*, generating code for profiling with **gprof**:

```
% gcc -pg program.f
```

–g Generate an expanded symbol table for debugging. See Chapter 6, *Debugging C and C++ Programs*, for more information. This is actually a much more complex option than it appears to be, due to the large number of object formats that are around. The **-g** option enables debugging with the GNU debugger, **gdb**. It also enables debugging with "native" debuggers—but, because **-g** puts additional information in the symbol table that most debuggers aren't used to finding, you may have trouble: in some situations, the debugger may refuse to read the file or may crash. If you need to use your system's native debugger, and you have trouble with **-g**, try **-gstabs** for **dbx** on BSD UNIX systems; **-gcoff** for **sdb** under SVR3 and earlier releases of System V; **-gxcoff** for **dbx** on the RS/6000; and **-gdwarf** for SVR4 debuggers. Additional options give even finer control over the debugging information present in an object file.

On many systems, optimization and debugging are incompatible. Many compilers won't allow **-g** and **-O** to appear on the same command line. With **gcc**, optimization and debugging aren't incompatible. The results can be surprising and unintuitive: optimization can change the order in which statements are evaluated, eliminate variables, and even eliminate entire sections of code. However, if you're familiar with the workings of an optimizing compiler, you should be able to figure out what's going on.

Optimization

gcc incorporates a sophisticated optimizing compiler; on most systems, it usually generates faster code than the native compiler. Here are the most commonly used compilation options:

–O Equivalent to –O1.

–O0

No optimization. This is the default. With optimization turned off, **gcc** tries to generate code that is easy to debug—that is, you can set a breakpoint between any two statements and modify variables, and the program will behave exactly as it should. **gcc** also tries to generate code quickly.

–O1

The compiler tries to reduce both the size of the compiled code and the execution time. Compilation is slower than with –O0 and requires more memory.

–O2

Enables more optimizations than **–O1**. Compilation time is even slower; the resulting code should be even faster.

–ffast-math

Make floating-point arithmetic optimizations that violate the ANSI or IEEE standards. Code compiled with this option may yield incorrect results—but it will be slightly faster. Seriously: carefully written code shouldn't run into trouble. But make sure you test it.

–finline-functions

Expand all "simple functions" into their callers. The compiler gets to decide whether any function is "simple" or not. Inline expansion is a two-edged sword; it can make a program faster (by eliminating calling overhead) or slower (by making instruction cache performance worse). You'll have to experiment with this to see whether or not it helps.

–fno-inline

Inhibit all inlining, even inlining that is requested by the `inline` keyword in the source code. **gcc** performs inlining according to statements in the source code with both **–O1** and **–O2**; the keyword is ignored if optimization isn't in effect.[*]

---

[*] The `inline` keyword, used in the declaration or definition of a function, is a **gcc** extension to the C language. It requests inline expansion for the function. If you compile with **–ansi** or **–traditional**, the `inline` keyword is not allowed, but you can use `__inline__` instead.

-funroll-loops

On some architectures, loop unrolling can be a very important optimization. It minimizes loop overhead and creates many opportunities for further optimizations. With the **-funroll-loops** option, **gcc** unrolls all loops that have a fixed iteration count known at the time of compilation. Loop unrolling is another risky optimization; it can improve performance, but it can also penalize performance significantly: the object file becomes larger, which can significantly hurt cache performance. Compile time also increases.

Passing options to the assembler or linker

gcc allows you to pass options directly to the assembler or linker when they are invoked:

-Wa,_option-list_
Pass the *option-list* to the assembler.

-Wl,_option-list_
Pass the *option-list* to the linker.

In both cases, the *option-list* is just a list of options recognized by the assembler or the linker. There must not be any spaces in the list; options in the list are separated by commas.

Here's an example that's both instructive and useful: producing a listing of the assembly language generated, together with C source listings.[*] To do this, we need to pass the **-alh** options to the assembler (generate listings of assembly code and high-level source); we also need to pass the **-L** option to the assembler (retain local labels). And we need **gcc**'s **-g** option (generate additional symbols for debugging; the additional symbols tell the assembler where to find the source code). The resulting command looks like this:

```
% gcc -c -g -Wa,-alh,-L source.c
```

Listings that include both assembly code and source are interesting from two standpoints. You may want to see how your code has been compiled; this is instructive, whether or not you're optimizing and even if you aren't interested in assembly level debugging. What's more important, though, is that you can generate a C/assembly listing for optimized code. This can be very helpful for debugging under optimization. The big problem with debugging optimized code is that there is no longer a simple mapping from your source code into assembly language. With a listing, you can find out exactly what the compiler did to your code and get a much better idea of what the code is doing.

---

[*] This trick doesn't work correctly in all releases of **gcc**. You may get only an assembly language listing.

Assembling a C Program

The GNU assembler is really many assemblers folded into one (or many different programs with the same name, depending on how you'd rather look at it). You can usually ignore the assembler; the compiler invokes it automatically and is usually able to specify everything the assembler needs to know about your environment. In rare cases, you may need to ask for an assembly option explicitly; in these cases, you'll need to run the assembler as a separate program or use **gcc**'s -**Wa** option to pass additional options to the assembler.

In this section, we'll talk a little about what the assembler does. We won't discuss the assembly language itself. The FSF's documentation explains the general syntax of assembly language, but refers you to the vendor's architecture manual for processor-dependent details: overall architecture, instruction set, etc.

The assembler takes a program written in an assembly language and produces an object module. By convention, assembly language programs have the extension *.s*. If no errors occur during assembly and if the object module contains no references to external (imported) symbols, the assembler makes the file executable and names it *a.out*. If the object module includes references to external symbols, *a.out* is not executable. The linker (described later in this chapter) is able to link this object module with other modules to produce an executable program.

Invoking the Assembler

To invoke the assembler, enter the command:

```
% as list-of-options list-of-source-files
```

where *list-of-options* is a series of assembly options and *list-of-source-files* is one or more assembly language files. (Unlike most UNIX assemblers, the GNU assembler can work on several files at a time.) The *list-of-source-files* can contain the special name --, which means "Read standard input for assembly source code."

The assembler has many options; most of them are architecture-specific and are used to describe the target processor more precisely. For example, if you're assembling for the SPARC architecture, -**Av6** says to use "version 6"; -**Asparclite** says to assemble for the "SPARClite" processor. These options will be important to you if you're cross-compiling; check the FSF's manual for more details.

One generally useful set of options controls listings. These options are:

-ah

    Generate a listing of the high-level code only. (Only possible if the object file was compiled with **gcc**'s -**g** option).

-al   Generate a listing of the assembly language code only.

-as

Generate a listing of the symbol table only.

The options may be combined; for example, **-ahls** generates high-level, assembly, and symbol table listings.

Program Segments

The object file that **as** produces is divided into several segments. While you almost never need to worry about these segments, some programming-related activities (like generating statistics on memory use) require you to know what they are:

- The *text segment* contains the executable code (i.e., machine language instructions) itself. It is normally read-only. A read-only text segment allows several processes running the same program to share the same text segment while they are running, conserving memory. This is called *shared text*.

- The *data segment* is used for all static and initialized data.

- The *bss segment* is used for uninitialized data. Rather than generating a huge object file with a giant data segment consisting largely of zeros, the assembler puts initialized data into the data segment; the bss segment then tells the operating system how much room to reserve for uninitialized data at run time.

Linking Programs

The **ld** linker combines several object modules and libraries into a single executable file. It resolves references to external variables, external procedures, and libraries, creating a complete, self-sufficient program. You never need to invoke **ld** explicitly. In most cases, it is simpler to use the **gcc** command to link files, even if you do not have any source files to compile. **gcc** guarantees that certain libraries will be present in the proper order even if they are not listed on the command line. If you use **ld** as a linker, you need to mention these libraries explicitly.

This section does not provide a complete description of all the linker's facilities. For more information, see the entry for **ld** in Section 1 of the *UNIX Programmer's Reference Manual*.

Invoking ld

The rules for invoking **ld**, if you must do so, are the same as for **gcc** or **as**. The basic **ld** command is:

```
% ld list-of-options list-of-files-and-libraries
```

where *list-of-files-and-libraries* is a series of filenames and library specifications. To include a library in this list, use the notation –l*name*, where the name of the library file is either */lib/libname.a* or */usr/lib/libname.a*. The linker processes the *list-of-files-and-libraries* in order. When it reaches a library, it extracts only those modules that it currently needs to resolve external references. Consequently, the position in which libraries appear in this list is important. For example, the command:

```
% ld prog1.o -lm prog2.o
```

results in an "Undefined symbol" message if *prog2.o* refers to any programs in the library */usr/lib/libm.a*—unless you happen to be lucky and *prog2.o* only uses routines that the linker extracted for the sake of *prog1.o*. Note that libraries may refer to other libraries; thus, the command:

```
% ld prog1.o -lat -lfo
```

leads to "Undefined symbol" messages if the *fo* library requires any routines from **at**.

This situation is more complex for a user-generated library. Such a library should contain an index, so that the linker can find each module regardless of its order within the library. Some systems always generate an index when you create or modify the library with the **ar** command (the GNU **ar** does this). On other systems you have to put in the index yourself by using the **ranlib** command.

If you want to create an executable file, the beginning of the first file in the *list-of-files* must be the program's entry point. This is *not* the same as the apparent entry point to your C source program. Before your program begins executing, the computer must execute a standard run-time initialization routine. To ensure that this is in place, */lib/crt0.o* must be the first file in the *list-of-files*. This ensures that this initialization routine is linked to your program.

Alternatively, you can link by using the **gcc** command without any C source files. When **gcc** invokes the linker, it automatically adds *crt0.o* and many other libraries in the proper place. For example, the command **gcc exp.o** generates the following **ld** command:

```
% ld -dc -dp -e start -X o -o a.out /usr/lib/crt0.o exp.o -lc
```

In this command, the run-time initialization module */usr/lib/crt0.o* appears explicitly, in addition to requests to resolve references to the C library (the general run-time library). You can see for yourself what **ld** command is generated when you compile a program on your system, by invoking **gcc** with the –**v** (verbose) option.

Linker Options

The **gcc** compiler passes any options it does not recognize to the linker. The most important options can therefore be placed directly on the **gcc** command line. These options are:

-o *name*

> Instead of naming the executable output file *a.out*, name it *name*.

-l*name*

> Link the program to the library named *libname*.a. The linker looks in the directories */lib* and */usr/lib* to find this library.

-L*dir*

> To find any libraries, look in the directory *dir* before looking in the standard library directories */lib* and */usr/lib*.

-s Remove the symbol table from the executable output file. This makes the output file significantly smaller, but makes debugging almost impossible. Therefore, this option should not be used until the program works successfully. Note that using the program **strip** has the same effect.

-x Remove all local symbols from the output file. Global symbols (subprograms and common block names) remain in the output file. This reduces the object file's size. Ignored unless **-s** is specified.

-n Make the text segment read-only.

-r Create an object file that can be included in further linking runs (i.e., further passes through **ld**). Among other things, this inhibits "Undefined symbol" messages (because the symbols may be defined in a later **ld** pass) and prevents **ld** from creating common storage immediately. If you wish to create common storage at this time, use the **-d** option also.

-e *name*

> Use the symbol *name* as the entry point to the executable program. By default, the entry point is the beginning of the first object module. **gcc** automatically links your object files with a run-time initialization module (*/usr/lib/crt0.o*) that starts your program and provides its initial entry point. If you run the linker separately, you must either put */usr/lib/crt0.o* at the start of your object files, or provide your own entry point.

-M

> Produce a "load map" that shows where each function is located in the resulting object file, where each section begins and ends, and the value of each global symbol.

−b *format*

> Read object modules in the given *format*. To get a list of formats that **ld** understands, give the command **objdump −i**. This can be helpful in some cross-development situations. The −b option applies to all object files and libraries following it on the command line, until another −b option appears. In theory, you can use this feature to link objects from several different formats into a single executable.

−oformat *format*

> Create object modules in the given *format*. Again, **objdump −i** gives you a list of formats that **ld** understands. **ld** is configured to produce "the most reasonable" output format for its target machine. Its assumptions about what is "reasonable" are probably true about 99.99 percent of the time. But there may be special-purpose situations in which you'd want another output format.

Here's an example of a customized **ld** command:

```
% ld -r -o bigofile.o prog1.o prog2.o -lmylib
```

This command links the files *prog1.o* and *prog2.o* and the library file */usr/lib/libmylib.a*. The resulting file is named *bigofile.o*; it can be linked further and may still contain unresolved references.

Note that if you need the −b and −oformat options, you can't use Cygnus's pre-built binaries; it turns out that their customers would rather have smaller executables than the ability to mix-and-match object formats. If you require these options, see Cygnus's installation notes; they describe how to build your own copy of **ld** with multiple-format support included.

Linker Scripts

One advanced feature of the GNU linker is its ability to work from scripts written in its own command language. If you are a true masochist, you might be able to avoid running **gcc** altogether; you might be able to implement your own compiler as a linker script! Seriously, there are probably few situations in which you'd actually need a linker script, but you should be aware that they exist for purposes like:

- Gaining tight control over the format of the output file—perhaps so an embedded application will fit into the smallest possible ROM, perhaps to optimize link order (as discussed in the next section).

- Supporting an object format that **ld** doesn't provide—perhaps an object format of your own design, or an object format for some special-purpose operating system.

Link-Order Optimization

If you've done a lot of development work, you have probably noticed that the order in which you link your files can have a significant effect on performance. By changing the link order, you're changing the way the executable file "lies" in the instruction cache. The cache is a fast area of memory that stores pages of instructions so that the processor doesn't have to go back to slower parts of memory (or even worse, the disk) for every new instruction. Certain link orders minimize instruction-cache miss. The effect usually isn't large, but in pathological cases (i.e., a really bad link order on a machine that's very sensitive to cache miss), link optimization can speed up runtime by 50 percent.

Unfortunately, not much can be said about link-order optimization. There are few rules, if any; and all the rules have many exceptions. In general, it's a good idea to place modules that call each other near each other in the object file—and the easiest way to do this is to place the modules next to each other on the command line. The reasoning behind this heuristic is simple: if function A makes many calls to function B, and both A and B can fit into the cache simultaneously, you won't pay a penalty for cache miss. Your best chance of fitting both functions into the cache simultaneously occurs when they are located next to each other in the object file. The **–M** option, which produces a "load map," shows you how the object file is arranged; it will help you investigate cache performance.

Normally, rearranging the order of the object modules on the command line is sufficient for experimenting with link-order optimization. However, you can get very fine control over your executable file by writing a linker script. If you have a thorough knowledge of your target machine's architecture, you may be able to use this to advantage—though you'll probably reach the point of diminishing returns fairly quickly.

Creating Libraries

The command **ar** creates libraries (or archives) of object modules. They are similar to the UNIX utilities with the same names, except that you don't need a separate **ranlib**. This section gives a brief description of how to use these commands.

To create a new library, use the **ar** command, as follows:

```
% ar rs lib-name list-of-files
```

The option **r** indicates that the command **ar** should add the files named in the *list-of-files* to the library named *lib-name*, creating a new library if necessary. If a file is mentioned twice in the *list-of-files*, **ar** includes it in the archive twice. The **s** option tells **ar** to produce an index for the archive; this is the function that **ranlib** would perform. If you include the **s** option whenever you create or modify a library, you'll never need to use **ranlib**.

To update a library, use the command:

```
% ar rus lib-name list-of-files
```

This compares the dates of any listed files with the version of the file in the library. If the file in *list-of-files* is more recent than the version contained in the library, **ar** substitutes the newer version for the older version. The **s** option updates the library's index.

To delete one or more files from a library, use the command:

```
% ar ds lib-name list-of-files
```

This deletes all the files found in *list-of-files*.

To extract one or more files from a library, use the command:

```
% ar x lib-name list-of-files
```

This does not modify the library file itself. It extracts the files named in the *list-of-files* from the library, regenerating them in the current directory with their original names. Normally, the timestamp of the extracted files is the time at which **ar** recreated them. If you use the option **xo** instead of **x**, **ar** sets the timestamp of the extracted files to the time recorded in the archive.

You can still create an "ordered" (index-less) library with **bar** and invoke **ranlib** as a separate step if you want. However, there's no longer any good reason for doing that. Therefore, we won't discuss **ranlib** further.

Cross-Compilation

The FSF's compilation tools are often used in cross-compilation environments: compiling code on one platform for execution on another. For example, you may want to compile code on a Sun SPARC to run on a 486-based machine. Or—more to the point—you might want to compile code on a SPARC to run on an Intel 960 control processor embedded in some other piece of hardware, like a laser printer or a robot.

Cross-compilation raises a number of problems that you don't have when compiling "native" (i.e., for the system on which the compiler is running) code:

- You may need to build a cross-compiler. You may need to provide a few "extra pieces" needed to build the cross-compiler correctly.

- You may need to find an assembler and a linker for the target architecture.

- You need to find header files for the target architecture and store them where the compiler can find them.

- You may need to find libraries for the target architecture and store them where the compiler can find them. (Some common libraries are provided by the FSF.)

- You may need to find any run-time startup files needed for the target architecture. The FSF provides *crt0.o*, but that won't help if you're not compiling for a UNIX system.

In essence, you have to provide the entire compilation environment yourself. You can't rely on **gcc** to find pieces (library files, header files, startup files) in the "usual places." You can't even assume that the operating system is roughly the same on both machines. If you're compiling for an embedded i960 processor, that processor probably isn't running UNIX; it is probably running a lightweight real-time operating system, either of your own design or someone else's.

Building a Cross-Compiler

The FSF's **gcc** can be built in many cross-compilation configurations. However, the easiest way to get a cross-compiler is to find a pre-built one. Cygnus Support provides pre-compiled binaries for many of these cross-compilation configurations. Unfortunately, we weren't able to include these on the CD because of space limitations. (The CD does contain source code for all cross-compilation configurations.) So you have two choices: either contact Cygnus, or build the cross-compiler yourself.

Table 4-1 shows the cross-compilation configurations that Cygnus currently supports. For an updated list, check their Web site (*http://www.cygnus.com*). If you are interested in other cross-compilers, contact Cygnus; their support plan is based largely on customer demand.

Table 4–1: Supported Cross-Compilers

Standard Embedded Configurations Supported		
Host	Target	Output Formats
SPARC Solaris 2	PowerPC	EABI
	M68K	a.out, COFF, VxWorks
	i960	COFF, VxWorks
	SH	COFF
	H8/300	COFF
	MIPS	ELF, ECOFF

Table 4–1: Supported Cross-Compilers (continued)

SPARC SunOS 4	PowerPC	EABI
	M68K	a.out, COFF, ELF, VxWorks
	i960	COFF, VxWorks
	i386	COFF, ELF
	SH	COFF
	H8/300	COFF
	MIPS	ELF, ECOFF
RS6000 AIX 3	PowerPC	EABI
	M68K	a.out
RS6000 AIX 4	PowerPC	EABI
	M68K	a.out
HPUX 9	PowerPC	EABI
	M68K	a.out, COFF, VxWorks
	i960	VxWorks
	H8/300	COFF
HPUX 10	PowerPC	EABI
DOS/Windows	PowerPC	EABI
	M68K	a.out, COFF
	i386	COFF
	SH	COFF
	H8/300	COFF
	MIPS	ELF, ECOFF
SGI Irix 5	PowerPC	EABI
	SH	COFF
	MIPS	ELF, ECOFF
PowerPC AIX 4	PowerPC	EABI

Non-Standard Embedded Configurations Supported

Host	Target	Output Formats
SPARC Solaris 2	AMD29K	COFF
	M68K	VxWorks 5.1
	i960	VxWorks 5.1
	SPARC	VxWorks
	SPARClite	a.out, COFF
SPARC SunOS 4	AMD29K	COFF, VxWorks
	M68K	VxWorks 5.1
	i960	VxWorks 5.1

Table 4-1: Supported Cross-Compilers (continued)

	i386	a.out
	SPARC	a.out
	SPARClite	a.out, COFF
RS6000 AIX 3	i960	VxWorks 5.1
HPUX 9	AMD29K	COFF
	M68K	VxWorks 5.1
	i960	VxWorks 5.1
DOS/Windows	i386	COFF
	SPARC	a.out
	SPARClite	a.out, COFF
MacOS	SH	COFF
	MIPS	ECOFF
RS6000 AIX 4	i960	VxWorks 5.1

Note that your target architecture really has two components: the machine itself, and the object file format that you want to use. For example, for the SPARClite architecture, you can choose between the traditional BSD UNIX *a.out* format, the COFF format (used on SVR3 and compatible with SVR4), and the "vxworks" format (a third-party real-time operating system).

The correct way to invoke the cross-compiler and other tools depends on how the tools were installed. Cygnus's installation procedure places all compilation tools and other utilities in a common directory, and uses the architecture type as a prefix to the "normal" name. For example, the cross-compiler for the AMD 29000 is **amd-29k-udi-gcc**, the assembler is **amd-29k-udi-as**, the linker is **amd-29k-udi-ld**, and so on. Likewise, tools that generate *a.out* format for the SPARClite processor have the prefix **sparclite-aout**: **sparclite-aout-gcc** and so on. You'll probably want to define aliases that "point to" the appropriate compiler: for example, **a-gcc** for the AMD cross-compiler.

The FSF's installation recommendations are somewhat different—and deserve mention, since the FSF provides many cross-compilers that Cygnus doesn't support. When you build a compiler, you use the shell script **configure** to specify different configuration options and set up the sources and makefiles appropriately. If you're building a cross-compiler, one of these options will be **--build=**TARGET, where TARGET is the name of your target architecture: the machine for which you're compiling. (The FSF's **gcc** documentation specifies, in great detail, how to construct target names.) Tools are then installed in a separate directory for each target architecture; and the command:

```
% gcc -b TARGET other-options
```

selects a specific compiler.

In either case, the compiler should be able to find the other tools it needs (linker, assembler, and so on); you should be able to invoke **gcc** and forget about the specific cross-assembler and cross-linker you're using.

As much as possible, the FSF's cross-compilers provide a standard set of libraries for all compilation environments: *libc.a, libg.a, libg++.a, libm.a,* and *libiberty.a. libm.a,* and so on. However, if you want more exotic libraries (e.g., X Window System libraries), or if your software won't be running on a POSIX-compliant system, you'll have to provide your own libraries and tell the compiler (and linker) where to find them.

Another potential trouble spot for cross-compilation comes in the interface between the library and the operating system. Many library functions are really only "wrappers" that make it more convenient to call the underlying operating system—and, hence, they make assumptions about what services the operating system provides. The assumptions are minimal, but the target system has to do something better than panicking when the program issues a call. This issue will be discussed more in the next chapter.

5

Libraries

If you're at all familiar with UNIX and C programming, the libraries you'll find in a free software development environment shouldn't confuse you. The libraries you expect will all be there: standard I/O, the math library, the strings library, etc. The libraries are ANSI C– and POSIX-compliant. In addition, there are many functions that UNIX programmers expect, but that aren't specified by either of these standards.

UNIX and C have been intertwined since they began. But as they evolved, and as C moved to other platforms and gained the honor of ANSI standardization, libraries have undergone a split.

Some C functions have been standardized and are now found everywhere, So even if you've used C exclusively on a DOS system, you'll recognize *printf, scanf,* and all the other friends when you move to GNU tools. But system calls and math libraries are another story. You'll have to learn these from scratch. In this book we'll help you with two essential system functions: error handling and signals.

After an introduction to error handling and working with time functions, we'll discuss briefly the operating-system support required to use the Cygnus libraries; i.e., we'll discuss the system calls that the libraries rely on. If you're doing native compilation, operating-system support shouldn't be an issue. However, if you're cross-compiling, you may need to find the system call routines yourself.

Then we'll give a very brief introduction to the facilities available in the GNU C++ libraries. We'll close the chapter by revisiting the issue of licensing, which protects free access to GNU tools, but might affect your ability to distribute your software product.

The Free Software Foundation publishes a book on library calls named the *C Library Reference Manual*. But the libraries included on the CD with this book use Cygnus libraries, which are documented in a book from Cygnus Support called *The Cygnus C Support Library*. The C++ library (*libg++*) is described in the *User's Guide to the GNU C++ Library*, available through the **info** command or from Cygnus Support.

Error Handling

UNIX programs always return an exit code. Exit codes usually go unnoticed, but are always present. They are most often used by shell scripts and by **make**, which may take some alternative action if the program doesn't finish correctly.

By convention, most programs return an exit code of zero to indicate normal completion. Nonzero exit codes usually mean that an error has occurred. There are some notable violations of this convention (e.g., **cmp** and **diff**), but we recommend you obey it. C shell users can print exit codes by entering the command:

```
% echo $status
```

If you use the Bourne shell (**sh**) or a derivative like **bash**, you can print the exit code with the command:

```
$ echo $?
```

When you are writing a program, to have it return an error code, call the function *exit*, with the error code as an argument:

```
int code;

exit(code);
```

Although the error code is an int, its value should be between 0 and 255.

Functions aren't that different from programs: their returned value indicates whether they succeeded or failed. If you want to write healthy code, you should always check the value returned from a function. The code below shows one way to test for an error:

```
#include <stdio.h>

/* write to standard output and check for error */
if ( printf(...) == EOF ) exit(1); /* output failed; terminate */
/* normal processing continues */
```

The manual page for *printf* says that it returns the constant EOF if it fails; if it succeeds, it returns the number of bytes transmitted. If you look in *stdio.h*, you'll see that EOF is defined as -1. As a rule, a positive or zero return value indicates success; a negative value indicates failure. However, there are many exceptions to this convention. Check the manual page, and if a symbolic constant (like EOF) is available, use that rather than a hard-wired constant.

If you want more information about what went wrong with your function, you can inspect the errno variable. When a system call fails, it stores an error code in errno. UNIX then terminates the system call, returning a value that indicates something has gone wrong—as we just discussed. Your program can access the error code in errno, figure out what went wrong, and (possibly) recover, as in the example below:

```
#include <stdio.h>
#include <errno.h>

FILE *fd;
int fopen_errno;

main (int argc, char **argv)
{
/* try opening the file passed by the user as an argument */
if ( (fd=fopen (argv[1], "r")) == NULL)
    {
    /* test errno, and see if we can recover */
    fopen_errno = errno; /* save errno */
    if (fopen_errno == ENOENT) /*no such file or directory*/
        {
        /* get a filename from the user and try opening again */
        ...
        }
    /* otherwise, it's an unknown error */
    else
      {
        perror("Invalid input file");
        exit (1);
      }
   }
}
/* normal processing continues */
```

On UNIX systems, the header file *errno.h* defines all possible system error values. Note that this code immediately copies errno to a local variable. This is a good idea, since errno is reset whenever a system call from your process fails, and there's no way to recover its previous value.

Another way to use the error number, without examining it yourself, is to call *perror*, which sends a message describing the error to the standard error I/O stream. It's used like this:

```
#include <stdio.h>

perror("prefix to message");
```

The "prefix to message" given as an argument to *perror* is printed first; then a colon; then the standardized message. For example, if the previous function call failed with the errno ENAMETOOLONG because the user passed a long string of garbage as an argument, the function call `perror("Invalid input file");` would result in the output:

```
Invalid input file: File name too long
```

Signals

UNIX systems send signals to programs to indicate program faults, user-requested interrupts, and other situations. Most generally, signals are a simple interprocess communication—an aspect that's taken much further with the extended signal facilities that POSIX.4 defines. However, for the most part, signals are simply the way in which the operating system informs the process of an action that requires attention—whether it's a memory access violation or an external event.

Many signals are purely informative; others cause the program to change its state in some way. For example, when you enter CTRL-C at the keyboard, you are sending the signal SIGINT to the program, which tells the program to terminate. If the program attempts an illegal memory access, the operating system sends it the signal SIGSEGV.

When a signal arrives, the program takes one of the following actions:

Ignore
> It ignores the signal and keeps running as if nothing happened.

Terminate
> It terminates, possibly leaving a core dump.

Stop
> It stops running, in a way that allows the program to be restarted.

Continue

It resumes running, given that the program is currently stopped.

Execute handler

It executes a signal-handling routine that it has previously installed. (This action is never the default.)

The default action depends on what signal is received and whether or not the program has requested any non-standard action. The signals on any system are defined in the header file *signal.h*. They can vary from system to system, though most UNIX systems have settled on a set of 32 signals. The following six signals—certainly the most important—are available on all systems:

Signal	Default Action	Meaning
SIGABRT	Terminate	Sent when the program calls *abort*
SIGFPE	Terminate	Floating point arithmetic error
SIGILL	Terminate	Illegal instruction
SIGINT	Terminate	Interrupt; sent when user types CTRL-c
SIGSEGV	Terminate	Segmentation violation; illegal memory access
SIGTERM	Terminate	Termination request (sent by software)

It's also worth noting SIGKILL, which is available on virtually all systems, because its behavior is slightly different. SIGKILL is the "terminate with extreme prejudice" signal. The process stops dead in its tracks; it is not allowed to catch or ignore the signal. It's also worth noting that many systems provide SIGUSR1 and SIGUSR2 as user-definable signals that are available to applications.

Two functions are available for dealing with signals: *raise*, which a program can use to send a signal to itself, and *signal*, which a program uses to change the default action for any signal. *raise* is very simple; it has a single argument, which is the name of a signal (i.e., one of the constants defined above). Here's how it is used:

```
#include <signal.h>
int ret;
...
ret=raise(SIGINT);
```

This function call sends the signal SIGINT. The return value, *ret*, is 0 if *raise* is successful; 1 if it fails. However, note that a signal may terminate the process—in which case, *raise* will never return.

If you want to send a signal to an arbitrary process (rather than sending a signal to yourself), you need to call *kill*, which has two arguments: a process ID and a signal name. We won't discuss *kill* here because it's a part of the operating system interface, not the Cygnus C library.

The function *signal* changes the default action that a process takes when it receives a signal. It looks like this:

```
#include <signal.h>
void * res;
...
res = signal(signal, whattodo);
```

where *signal* is the name of a signal (one of the constants defined in *signal.h* and *whattodo* is one of the following:

SIG_IGN

Ignore this signal.

SIG_DFL

Do whatever the default is for this signal.

handler

A pointer to a signal-handling function; in this case, the process executes the signal handler when it receives the specified signal. When the handler is called, it is passed the signal number as an argument. If the handler exits by calling *return*, the program continues executing after receiving the signal. If the handler calls *exit* or *abort*, execution doesn't continue after receiving the signal.

If *signal* succeeds, the returned value, *res*, is the previous action taken for the signal: either SIG_DFL, SIG_IGN, or the address of the signal handler. If *signal* fails, it returns the value SIG_ERR—which, by coincidence, is assigned the value –1.

Here's a very simple program that exercises the signal handler:

```
#include <signal.h>

void inthandler(int signal)
{
    printf("received signal %d\n",signal);
    abort();
}

main()
{
    signal(SIGINT, inthandler);
    sleep(60);
}
```

The program installs the function *inthandler* as an interrupt handler for SIGINT; then it sleeps, waiting for the user to type CTRL-c. When you type CTRL-c, *inthandler* is called; it prints its message, then calls *abort* to terminate execution. Here's how it looks:

```
% a.out
CTRL-creceived signal 2
Abort (core dumped)
%
```

You can install a separate signal handler for each signal that you care about; or you can install a single handler and let it figure out what to do on the basis of the argument passed to it.

Time

Knowing the current time is important in most programs for various reasons. On UNIX systems, the **time** call gets the current time in seconds from the operating system. The time is simply a long integer that contains the number of seconds since an arbitrary moment—midnight at the beginning of January 1, 1970. (Yes, this value will eventually wrap around—sometime in the 21st century for systems that stick to 32-bit longs.)

An integer value should be useful for calculating elapsed time, but most timing you'd want to do—in order to schedule tasks in your program, for instance—requires a finer granularity than one second. Modern operating systems provide calls that give you the time in milliseconds, but these calls are non-standard. Consult the documentation for your operating system.

The **time** call is precise enough for mundane tasks like displaying the date and time to the user, but you have to convert the integer into a more meaningful format. The calls listed below do this. They all require you to include the file *<time.h>*. In the rest of this section, we'll show how to get and display the current time.

char *asctime(struct tm *tm)
> Returns a 26-character string that displays the time indicated by the 11-member *tm* structure. Superseded by *strftime*.

char *ctime(time_t *clock)
> Returns a 26-character string that displays the time indicated by the integer in *clock*.

struct tm *gmtime(time_t *clock)
> Breaks the time reported by *clock* into the 11-member *tm* structure, using UTC (Greenwich Mean time).

```
struct tm *localtime(time_t *clock)
```
Breaks the time reported by *clock* into the 11-member *tm* structure, using the local time zone.

```
int strftime(char *buf, int bufsize, char *fmt, struct tm *tm)
```
Converts the time contained in the *tm* structure to a string of *bufsize* characters and stores it in *buf*, using the format specified by *fmt*.

```
char *strptime(char *buf, char *fmt, struct tm *tm)
```
The converse of *strftime*. Converts the time contained in *buf* to the *tm* structure, parsing *buf* in the format specified by *fmt*.

It would be nice if somebody could provide a single standard call that got the time and formatted it for you, but such is not to be your fate as a UNIX programmer.

From a glance at the previous list of calls, you can probably tell that it's pretty important to understand the *tm* structure. Here it is:

```
struct   tm {
         int     tm_sec;    /* measured from 0 to 59                   */
         int     tm_min;    /* measured from 0 to 59                   */
         int     tm_hour;   /* measured from 0 to 23                   */
         int     tm_mday;   /* day of the month, measured from 1 to 31 */
         int     tm_mon;    /* month, measured from 0 to 12            */
         int     tm_year;   /* year, where zero is 1900                */
         int     tm_wday;   /* day of the week, measured from 0 to 6   */
         int     tm_yday;   /* day of the year, measured from 0 to 365 */
         int     tm_isdst;  /* 1 is daylight saving time, else 0       */
         char    *tm_zone;  /* name of timezone                        */
         long    tm_gmtoff; /* timezone's distance from UTC in seconds */
};
```

Each element of the time that you'd be interested in is contained in a separate member of the structure. Watch those integers! They're not consistent. The day of the month is measured starting at 1, whereas the other integer values start at zero.

Universal coordinated time or UTC [*sic*] used to be known as Greenwich Mean time. It's the worldwide standard for reporting the time, using the local time in Great Britain and not recognizing daylight saving time. If you want to get UTC (we don't know why you would) you can call **gmtime**. For local time, use **localtime**.

Here is some simple code that retrieves the time by calling **time** and passing its return value to **localtime**. Then the code extracts the hour and minute and displays the time. We're doing this the long way, grinding out a format manually, so you'll appreciate being able to use *strftime* later.

```
#include <time.h>
#include <stdio.h>
#include <strings.h>
```

```
struct tm *current_struc;
time_t *current_int;
char for_user[6];
char time_tmp[3];

(void) time( &current_int );
current_struc = localtime( &current_int );

/* Start out for_user with the hour */
sprintf(time_tmp, "%2d", current_struc->tm_hour);
strcpy(for_user, time_tmp);

/* Add a colon */
strcat(for_user, ":");

/* Finish with the minute, always making it two digits */
sprintf(time_tmp, "%2.2d", current_struc->tm_min);
strcat(for_user, time_tmp);

printf("Time is (or was, 7 calls back) %s\n", for_user);
```

Now let's use *strftime* to create a string suitable for display. The first argument is a buffer to put the string in, and the second argument is the size of this buffer. You have to choose a format—here we've chosen hh:mm—and specify it in the third argument. The fourth argument is the *tm* structure.

```
(void) strftime(for_user, sizeof(for_user), "%H:%M", current_struc);

printf("Time is %s\n", for_user);
```

In the format we chose, %H stands for the hour and %M for the minute. We put a colon between them, which comes out literally in the display. You can format your string any way you want, putting in spaces, commas, and special characters like \n for newline.

Now that you see the concept behind the format, you can look at all the available descriptors in Table 5-1. If you don't want to mess with individual descriptors, just use %c and you'll get the date and time in a reasonable format. If you check the %R entry, you'll see that we didn't even have to do all the work that was in the previous example.

Table 5-1: strftime Format Descriptors

Descriptor	Result
%a	Day of the week as a word, abbreviated
%A	Day of the week as a word, spelled out
%b	Month as a word, abbreviated (same as %h)
%B	Month as a word, spelled out
%c	Date and time in the format mm/dd/yy hh:mm:ss

Table 5-1: strftime Format Descriptors (continued)

Descriptor	Result
%C	Date and time using words
%d	Day of the month as an integer that can contain a leading zero to make up two digits, measured from 01 to 31
%D	Date in the format mm/dd/yy
%e	Day of the month as an integer that can contain a leading blank if it is only one digit, measured from 1 to 31
%h	Month as a word, abbreviated (same as %b)
%H	Hour as a two-digit integer on a 24-hour clock, measured from 00 to 23
%I	Hour as a two-digit integer on a 12-hour clock, measured from 00 to 11
%j	Day of the year as a three-digit integer, measured from 001 to 366
%k	Hour as an integer that can start with a blank, on a 24-hour clock measured from 00 to 23
%l	Hour as an integer that can start with a blank, on a 12-hour clock measured from 00 to 11
%m	Month as a two-digit integer, measured from 01 to 12
%M	Minute as a two-digit integer, measured from 00 to 59
%n	Newline
%p	A.M. (morning) or P.M. (afternoon)
%r	Time in the format hh:mm:ss AM
%R	Time in the format hh:mm
%S	Second as a two-digit integer, measured from 00 to 59
%t	Tab
%T	Time in the format hh:mm:ss
%U	Week of the year as a two-digit integer, measured from 01 to 52, where Sunday is the first day of the week
%w	Day of the week, measured from 0 to 6
%W	Week of the year as a two-digit integer, measured from 01 to 52, where Monday is the first day of the week
%x	Date in the format mm/dd/yy
%X	Time in the format hh:mm:ss
%y	Year of the century as a two-digit integer, measured from 00 to 99
%Y	Year, as a four-digit integer
%Z	Time zone
%%	Produces a percent sign (%) in the output

System Interface Issues

The free software libraries don't supply the actual interface between the libraries and the operating system (i.e., functions like *read* and *write*); these can be found in the operating system's C library. The kernel has to have the operations to support the calls. As long as you stick to the functions provided by your system, everything should work.

Cross-compilation (as usual) presents some tricky problems:

- Your compilation target may be able to perform all the functions you need, but you don't have the right libraries available on the system where you're compiling.

- Your target might not be able to do the things you're asking for in your system calls. If you're developing software for some kind of embedded system, your target may not have an "operating system" in any meaningful sense at all—certainly not a POSIX-compliant one.

In the first case, the problem is relatively simple: find the libraries you need, put them on the compilation system, and make sure that **gcc** (and implicitly **gld**) knows how to find them. You might be able to get away with copying the libraries directly from the target system.

The second case is substantially more complicated. If you're compiling for a system that isn't POSIX-compliant (or that isn't even a "system"), you'll need to provide the system interface functions on your own. You might check with your processor vendor to see whether it supplies a library. If not, you have to develop your own. There are any number of approaches, but basically, there are two extremes:

- Develop a library of "stubs" that allows your code to compile correctly and run in some minimal sense. These stubs will return failure whenever the program asks for a system service that isn't available—in the extreme case, this could be just about anything.

- Develop a library containing fully POSIX-compliant versions of all the interface functions you need.

The first approach might be adequate for experimentation, and for temporizing while you're waiting for your vendor to provide something. If you're ever going to release a product, though, you'll eventually need to get real libraries from somewhere.

Let's say you want to write enough functions so that a POSIX-compliant program can compile and link. Your functions may return errors on every call, because the program is asking for things your system cannot do, but at least you can load the program. Table 5-2 shows the interface functions you need to find or develop, and what each one must do to behave in a POSIX-compliant manner.

Table 5-2: POSIX Functions in a Cross-Compilation Environment

Name	Function	Minimal requirements
_exit	Exit without cleanup	None; avoid calling routines that need it: in particular, *exit* and *system*
close	Close a file	Return -1 (error) always
execve	Start new executable	Return -1 and set errno to ENOMEM
fork	Create new process	Return -1 and set errno to EAGAIN
fstat	Get file status	See later in this chapter
getpid	Get process ID	Return 1
isatty	Is I/O descriptor a terminal?	Return 1 (yes)
kill	Send signal	Return -1; set errno to EINVAL
link	Create new filename	Return -1; set errno to EMLINK
lseek	Set position in file	Return 0 (success)
read	Read from file	Return 0 (success)
sbrk	Extend data segment	See later in this chapter
stat	Get file status	See later in this chapter
times	Get timing statistics	Return -1
unlink	Delete directory entry	Return -1; set errno to ENOENT
wait	Wait for child process	Return -1
write	Write to a file	See the following section

That's pretty minimal. However, you may be running in a very minimal environment: for example, your target environment may not support multiple processes at all. In that case, defining *execve* to return failure unconditionally is perfectly reasonable; on such a minimal system, it's hard to imagine any reason (aside from an error) for calling *execve*. Again, though—if your target system does have multiple processes, you'll eventually have to provide a more complete implementation. This minimal library really only proves that your code can link correctly and gives you a chance to see that it can do something somewhat intelligent when it runs.

Stubs for I/O Routines

You need to come up with a way to make *write* work, at least for whatever minimal I/O your processor provides! *write* is used for all output, of any kind, so a stub that does nothing leaves you with a program that's incapable of producing output. Such programs usually aren't good for much.

You certainly don't have to implement an entire filesystem, though. If the only I/O available is through a serial port, you can create a *write* function that sends characters to the serial port. Assuming that you have a function *writechar* that writes one character to the port, you can write the following code, suggested in Cygnus's documentation:

```
int write(int file, char *ptr, int len)
{
    int i;

    for (i=0; i < len; i++) writechar(*ptr++);
    return len;
}
```

Because this implementation of *write* assumes a terminal-like output device, we'll also make *isatty* return 1 (yes) all the time. It's a plausible solution, since that's the only kind of output we have. It's also plausible because, under UNIX, one important property of a terminal device is that you can't perform a *seek*, and our minimalist set of stubs don't implement seeking in any reasonable way.

Finally, Cygnus suggests that *stat* and *fstat* should always tell the caller that a file descriptor is a "character special" device. Again, that's consistent; the only device we have is a terminal, which would be a character special file. *stat* and *fstat* are implemented as:

```
int stat(char * file, struct stat *st)
{
    st -> st_mode = S_IFCHR; return 0;
}
int fstat(int file, struct stat *st)
{
    st -> st_mode = S_IFCHR; return 0;
}
```

The other fields of the *stat* structure are left undefined; we don't know enough to fill them in reasonably.

Stub for sbrk

The *malloc* family assumes that *sbrk* exists; furthermore, calls to *malloc* are scattered throughout many of the libraries (including standard I/O), to say nothing of most programs. Therefore, you'll be lucky if you can get a program to work without at least a minimal *sbrk*, even if your target environment has no concept of memory management.

In this minimal environment, though, it's fairly easy to come up with an implementation that should work. Here's a function suggested in Cygnus's documentation:

```
caddr_t sbrk(int incr)
{
    extern char end; /* defined by gld */
    static char *heap_end;
    char *prev_heap_end;

    if (heap_end == 0) heap_end = &end;
    prev_heap_end = heap_end;
    heap_end += incr;
    return (caddr_t) prev_heap_end;
}
```

This function just extends the data segment (as defined by the symbol *end*, which is generated by the linker). It doesn't do any checking to make sure that additional memory exists, that it's mapped correctly, that it's OK to allocate more memory, etc. So you'll get in trouble using this in any kind of multiprocessing environment, and you'll get in trouble if you ask for memory you don't have. However, in a very simple environment, it might do the trick.

Run-Time Environment

gcc assumes that there's a startup module named *crt0.o*; this module sets up memory, does other initialization tasks, transfers control to your program's *main* routine, and cleans up after *main* returns. If you're working in a native environment, *crt0.o* isn't a problem; Cygnus provides a startup module for you. However, if you're cross-compiling, it may be up to you to provide the startup module yourself. Exactly what you need depends on what you're doing. Some examples are distributed with the Cygnus source code.

If you have to write your own, here's what *crt0.o* is required to do:

- Define the symbol *start*, which is the location of the first instruction to execute.

- Set up the stack pointer. Where to store the stack, and how to manage it, is up to you.

- Set all the memory in the program's BSS (uninitialized data) segment to zero.

- Do any other initialization that's specific to your hardware (and software) environment.

- Call your program's *main* routine.

C++ Classes

The free software development environment includes the C++ class library *libg++.a*. This library is searched whenever you compile with **g++**. It contains many simple, but useful, classes that can keep you from reinventing the wheel: string manipulation, stacks, and so on. Just declare a variable of type String, Stack, or whatever, and then you can perform all the functions provided.

We'll just show some examples using the String class here, to give you a feel for what it's like to use the libg++ classes. You can get more detailed information from the Cygnus/FSF documentation.

Let's suppose you are reading in some filenames and want to look for version IDs. A filename with a version ID always looks something like *file.V1*—the version number is included as a suffix beginning with an uppercase V. Here's a simple program that catches any file ending with the string *.V1*:

```
#include <iostream.h>
#include <String.h>

main()
{
    String user_input;
    cin >> user_input ;
    int start = user_input.index(".V1");
    if (start != -1)
        cout << "found Version ID .V1\n";
}
```

It's really nice not to worry about allocating memory and checking the length of the string constantly. To use String functions, we include the file *String.h*. Now we can declare a String variable named *user_input*, read into it as usual, and invoke the *index* function on it. This function, named after the familiar C library function, accepts a string as an argument and returns the starting point of the first instance of the string. Zero represents the first position in string, and a return value of –1 means that the string wasn't found.

But *index* can do quite a bit more than the C library function. Since we're working in C++, it can be overloaded in several different ways—the arguments that you pass determine which version of the function runs.

Thus, you can give it a starting position to search from. For instance, if we want to see whether there are more occurrences of *.V1* in the name, we can tell it to keep looking. Here we start three characters past the place where the previous *.V1* was found:

```
if (user_input.index(".V1", start+3) != -1)
        cout << "found another Version ID .V1\n";
```

Or, to find the last occurrence, we can tell the function to search backward like the C library functions *rindex* and *strrchar*. A negative second argument means "Start this many characters from the end and search toward the beginning."

```
user_input.index(".V1", -1)
```

But the most powerful feature of the String class is its support for regular expressions. Remember that we're searching for any suffix that consists of an uppercase V followed by a number. If we were looking through a list of files with the **grep** utility, we would construct a regular expression like:

```
\.V[0-9]+$
```

See Figure 5-1 for a breakdown of this expression. The \. matches the period (you need the backslash because otherwise the period has a special meaning). v matches itself. The [0-9] matches any digit, while the plus sign says "one or more must be present." The dollar sign indicates the end of the line—it ensures that we find the string only if it's at the end of the filename.

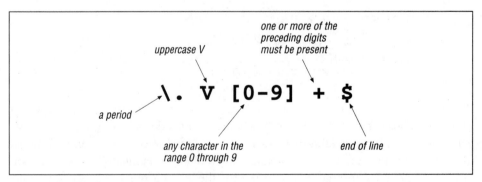

Figure 5–1: Regular expression

Putting this regular expression into a program is trivial. Just declare a variable of type Regex. When the variable is passed as the first argument to *index*, it invokes GNU regular expression functions instead of simple string functions.

Here is a program that finds any suffix containing a version number. Note that we needed to double the backslash when we put the regular expression into a variable—that's required by standard C language parsing.

```
#include <iostream.h>
#include <String.h>

main()
{
    String user_input;
    Regex version_id("\\.V[0-9]+$");

    cin >> user_input ;

    int start = user_input.index(version_id);
    if (start != -1) {
        int rest = user_input.length()-start;
        cout << "found Version ID " <<
            user_input.at(start,rest) << "\n";
    }
}
```

We used the *length* and *at* functions to extract the string that matched. The *length* function simply returns the length of the string. Then we subtracted the starting position from the length to get the length of the substring that matched.

The *at* function returns a substring that starts at the position *start* and extends for *rest* characters. Thus, we displayed the string by printing the return value of *at*.

Since we know our substring is at the end of the string, the String class provides an even simpler way to do the extraction. We can just use the *from* function to return everything from the start of the substring to the end of the container string. Now our program looks like this:

```
#include <iostream.h>
#include <String.h>

main()
{
    String user_input;
    Regex version_id("\\.V[0-9]+$");

    cin >> user_input ;

    String actual_version=user_input.from(version_id);
    if ( actual_version != '\0') {
        cout << "found Version ID " <<
            actual_version << "\n";
    }
}
```

The *from* function finds an embedded substring and grabs everything up to the end of the string, including the embedded substring. Similarly, the *through* function starts at the beginning of the string and grabs everything up to and including the embedded substring.

If you want to exclude the embedded substring from the returned string, use the *before* or *after* function. Thus, the following code changes the suffix of a filename to *.bak*. First it uses the *contains* function, which returns a Boolean value, to check whether the string contains a period. Then it changes everything following the period to bak. The period itself is left alone, because we used the *after* function.

```
if (user_input.contains("."))
        user_input.after(".")="bak";
```

We've cheated a bit here; we've assumed that the string contains only one period. It would be more robust to find the last period in the string:

```
int start = user_input.index(".", -1);
if (start != -1)
    user_input.at(start,user_input.length()-start)=".bak";
```

Note that assignment statements work with String variables. Comparisons can also be made using standard operators:

```
while (user_input != "quit") {
        cin >> user_input ;

    ⋮
```

We certainly haven't conveyed the power of the libg++ classes (not even the full scope of the String class), but hopefully this quick tour has given you a sense of the library's conventions.

Libraries and Licensing

Without stumbling into a discussion of legal issues on which we're admittedly not experts, we'll revisit very briefly the rules surrounding the libraries in the free software development environment.

The FSF originally issued a set of libraries covered by their General Public License. This wasn't acceptable in many commercial applications, since it required library source code to be shipped with the product. In many cases (particularly embedded applications) shipping source code is irrelevant or impossible. Even if you had the source code for the microprocessor in your VCR, what would you do with it?

The FSF created a special version of the GPL for libraries (called the LGPL) which relaxed the source distribution requirement. However, the LGPL created a new, and equally problematic, requirement: that it be possible to replace the libraries with an updated library release. This isn't a problem for system software, but again, it's just not realistic for embedded systems. How would you download the new libraries to your VCR?

6

Debugging C and C++ Programs

This chapter describes the **gdb** debugger, a powerful tool for debugging in C and C++. In some ways, **gdb** has a similar feel to **dbx**, the source debugger for BSD UNIX. But, as is typical with the FSF's tools, **gdb** provides a lot more functionality, including the ability to work with C++ at the source level, and the ability to debug processes that are already running. (The old System V debugger, **sdb**, is a relic of the dark ages; both **gdb** and **dbx** go far beyond its capabilities.)

gdb lets you run a program, stop execution within the program, examine and change variables during execution, call functions, and trace how the program executes. It also has command-line editing and history features similar to those used with **bash** (the GNU shell) and Emacs. This section proceeds by describing **gdb**'s basic features and commands in their simplest terms. At first, we'll make the examples as simple as possible. We will address more difficult issues later.

As with any debugger, some of the breakpoint and execution trace options can make your program run extremely slowly—intolerably slowly for any practical application. These tend to be the most interesting options. Don't despair. There are some workarounds that limit the flexibility of these options, but still give a reasonable (if not stunning) performance. We will point out which debugging features lead to unacceptable debugging performance and how to work around them.

To get full documentation on all **gdb** commands, read the *Debugging with GDB* manual online or order it from the Free Software Foundation.

Compilation for gdb

Before you can use **gdb** to debug a program, compile your code with the **-g** option. This causes the compiler to generate an augmented symbol table. For example, the command:

```
% gcc -g file1.c file2.c file3.o
```

compiles the C source files *file1.c* and *file2.c*, generating an expanded symbol table for use with **gdb**. These files are linked with *file3.o*, an object file that has already been compiled. **gdb** can be used to debug source code in *file1.c* and *file2.c*, but not code from *file3.c*, unless that code was also compiled with the **-g** flag.

The compiler's **-g** and **-O** options are not incompatible; you can optimize and compile for debugging at the same time. Furthermore, unlike many other debuggers, **gdb** even gives you somewhat intelligible results. However, debugging optimized code is difficult since, by nature, optimization changes the program itself. The relationships in your source code may change from under your feet in the executing program. You may find that variables (or even lines of code) have disappeared as a result of optimization, that assignments aren't taking place when you think they are, and so on. Your life will be easier if you debug new programs as thoroughly as possible before trying to optimize them. It is also easiest to debug code that conforms strictly to the ANSI C standard. Programs that play fast and loose with the standard can be hard to debug. On some systems, optimizing such code may reveal bugs that were not previously apparent.

Starting gdb

To debug a compiled program with **gdb**, use the command:

```
% gdb program [ core-dump ]
```

where *program* is the filename of the executable file you want to debug, and *core-dump* is the name of a core-dump file left from an earlier attempt to run your program. By examining the core dump with **gdb**, you can discover where the program failed and the reason for its failure. For example, the following command tells **gdb** to read the executable file *qsort2* and the core dump *core.2957*:

```
% gdb qsort2 core.2957
GDB is free software and you are welcome to distribute copies of it
 under certain conditions; type "show copying" to see the conditions.
There is absolutely no warranty for GDB; type "show warranty" for details.
GDB 4.15.2-96q3 (sparc-sun-solaris2),
Copyright 1996 Free Software Foundation, Inc.
Core was generated by 'qsort2'.
Program terminated with signal 7, Emulator trap.
```

```
#0   0x2734 in qsort2 (l=93643, u=93864, strat=1) at qsort2.c:118
118                       do i++; while (i <= u && x[i] < t);
(gdb) quit
```

The startup is fairly verbose; it tells you which version of **gdb** you're using.[*] Then it tells you how the core file was generated (by the program **qsort2**, which received signal 7, an "emulator trap"), and what the program was doing (executing line 118). The prompt (gdb) tells you that **gdb** is ready for a command. In this case, we'll just quit.

Both the executable file and the core file arguments are optional. You can supply a core file later with the **core** command. In either case, if you provide the name of a file that doesn't exist, or that doesn't have a recognizable format, **gdb** gives you a warning message like this:

```
% gdb nosuchfile

"/home/los/mikel/cuser/nosuchfile": No such file or directory
(gdb)
```

You can request several options when you invoke **gdb**. The most useful are:

-d *dir*

Tell **gdb** to look in *dir* for source files. We'll show you why this is useful later on.

-x *file*

Before accepting any commands, **gdb** reads and executes the commands in *file*. This way you can set up some things you know you want to do every time, like set a breakpoint at a certain statement.[†] You can use multiple **-x** options; the different files are executed in order.

-nx

Don't execute commands from the initialization file (normally *.gdbinit*).

-q   Don't print the introductory and copyright messages upon startup.

-help

Print a help message showing all command-line options and quit.

-batch

Run in batch mode; execute any startup files (unless they're suppressed), followed by any files specified with **-x** options, and then exit with status zero.

---

[*] By default, **gdb** prints the long "free software" message whenever it starts. From now on, we'll omit this message whenever we start. You can suppress the message by giving the command **gdb -q**.

[†] You can also initialize **gdb** by placing start-up commands in the file *.gdbinit* in your home directory.

Basic gdb Commands

With just a few commands, you can get most of your work done in **gdb**. The basic things you have to do are look at your source code, set breakpoints, run programs, and check variables.

If you forget what command to use (or want to check for obscure features) use the built-in help facility. You can request a particular command (like **help print**) or one of the following topics, which print a list of relevant commands:

help aliases
help breakpoints
help data
help files
help internals
help obscure
help running
help stack
help status
help support
help user

Listing a File

To see the contents of the source file from which the executable program was compiled, use the command **list**:

```
% gdb qsort2
(gdb) list
13        void qsort2();
14        void swap();
15        void gen_and_sort();
16        void init_organ();
17        void init_random();
18        void print_array();
19
20        main()
21        {
22                int power=1;
(gdb)
```

When you type **list** without any arguments, **gdb** shows you the lines surrounding the code that has just executed. Since we haven't yet run the program, **gdb** shows us the entry to the *main* function. The numbers on the left side are the line numbers of your source program; you will use these line numbers to issue many debugging commands. As you see, **gdb** numbers all lines, including comments and blank lines.

To print specific lines from the file you are currently debugging, use a **list** command of the form:

(gdb) **list** *line1,line2*

To list the first 10 lines from a particular function, use a **list** command of the following form:

(gdb) **list** *routine-name*

If you repeat the **list** command without any arguments, **gdb** lists the next few lines, and so on until it reaches the end of the file. By default, **gdb** lists 10 lines each time you enter the command. The section "Advanced Features" later in this chapter explains how to change this default setting.

gdb can't take into account changes to the code produced by conditional compilation (**#ifdef**) or file inclusion (**#include** statements). You will see these statements in your listings verbatim; it is your responsibility to know what they did. You have to know how the program was compiled—in particular, what was included and what was omitted.

If **gdb** cannot find the source file required to produce a listing, it prints the message:

Function *name* not defined

In this message, **gdb** says that it can't find the source file for the function *name*.

Executing a Program

To run the program you are debugging, use the **run** command. This may be followed by any arguments you want to pass to the program, including the standard input and output specifiers < and >, and shell wildcards (*, ?, [,]). You can't use C-shell history (!) or pipe (|) commands. The program you're running gets a full shell environment (as determined by the environment variable SHELL); you can also use the commands **set environment** and **unset environment** to define or delete additional environment variables for the program being debugged.

For example, consider running the program **exp** through **gdb**. The following **gdb** command runs **exp** with the argument **-b**, taking the standard input from *invalues* and redirecting standard output to the file *outtable*:

```
% gdb exp
(gdb) run -b < invalues > outtable
```

If you have not set any breakpoints or used any other **gdb** debugging features, **exp** runs until the program terminates, either correctly or incorrectly. When the program terminates, **gdb** prints the message:

```
Program exited with code n.
(gdb)
```

where *n* is the exit code returned by the program. Upon termination, **gdb** prints the prompt (gdb) to show that it is waiting for the next command.

If you give the **run** command without arguments, **gdb** reuses the arguments you gave for the previous **run** command. This is helpful; when you're debugging, you often need to start the program repeatedly. You can change the arguments that are passed to the program with the **set args** command; you can see the default argument list by giving the command **show args**. For example:

```
(gdb) set args -b -x
(gdb) show args
Arguments to give program being debugged when it is started is "-b -x".
(gdb)
```

To terminate a program while it is running under **gdb** control, press CTRL-C. This returns control to **gdb**, which then prompts for a new command; it does not return directly to the shell. To exit **gdb**, enter **quit**:

```
(gdb) run
CTRL-C
Program received signal SIGINT, Interrupt.
qsort2 (l=95136, u=97479, strat=1) at qsort2.c:119
119                     do j--; while (x[j] > t);
(gdb) quit
The program is running.  Quit anyway (and kill it)? (y or n) y
```

If the program you're debugging is currently "runnable" (i.e., it's waiting at a breakpoint, stopped by CTRL-Z, or in any other state where you could continue execution), **gdb** asks you to confirm whether or not you want to quit.

If the program you're debugging terminates abnormally, control returns to **gdb**. You can then use **gdb** commands to find out why the program terminated. The following example shows a program run that caused a segmentation violation by accessing data beyond the end of the program's stack. The **backtrace** command gives a stack backtrace showing exactly what the program was doing when it bombed out:

```
% gdb badref
(gdb) run
Starting program: /home/los/mikel/cuser/badref

0x22c8 in march_to_infinity () at badref.c:16
16                  h |= *p;
```

```
(gdb) backtrace
#0  0x22c8 in march_to_infinity () at badref.c:16
#1  0x2324 in setup () at badref.c:25
#2  0x2340 in main () at badref.c:30
(gdb)
```

backtrace produces a list of all active procedures and the arguments with which they were called, starting with the most recent. So this display shows that the program died in a function named *march_to_infinity*; this function was called by the function *setup*, which in turn was called by the function *main*. The only thing left is to figure out exactly what went wrong in *march_to_infinity*, which we'll do in the following sections.

Printing Data

You can inspect the values of variables by using the **print** command. Let's use it to see exactly what happened in the previous program. First, we'll list some of the code to see what we're dealing with:

```
(gdb) list
8
9               p=&j;
10              /* march off the end of the world*/
11              for ( i = 0; i < VERYBIG; i++)
12              {
13                      h |= *p;
14                      p++;
15              }
16      printf("h: %d\n",h);
17
```

It should already be pretty clear what's happening. **p** is some kind of a pointer; we can test that by using the **whatis** command, which shows us its declaration:

```
(gdb) whatis p
type = int *
(gdb) print p
$1 = (int *) 0xf8000000
(gdb) print *p
$2 = Cannot access memory at address 0xf8000000.
(gdb) print h
$3 = -1
(gdb)
```

When we look at **p**, we see that it's pointing somewhere up in the stratosphere. Of course, there's no *ad hoc* way to know whether this value for *p* is legitimate or not. But we can see if we can read the data *p* points to, just as our program tried to do—and when we give the command **print *p**, we see that it's pointing to inaccessible data.

print is one of **gdb**'s true power features. You can use it to print the value of any expression that's valid in the language you're debugging. In addition to variables from your program, expressions may include:

- Calls to functions within your program; these function calls may have "side-effects" (i.e., they can do things like modify global variables that will be visible when you continue program execution).

      ```
      (gdb) print find_entry(1.0)
      $1 = 3
      ```

- Data structures and other complex objects

      ```
      (gdb) print *table_start
      $8 = {e_reference = '\000' <repeats 79 times>, location = 0x0, next = 0x0}
      ```

- "Value history" elements (which we'll discuss briefly later in this section)

- "Artificial arrays" (to be discussed later in this section)

If you look at our example of printing a pointer, you'll see $1, $2, and $3 after the two print commands. These are value history identifiers; they mean that you can use $1 in future expressions to identify 0xf8000000 and $3 to identify the constant -1. ($2 identifies the long string constant "Cannot access...", which isn't interesting to us.)

Now, why do you care? Well, let's say that it wasn't obvious to you why 0xf8000000 was an error; you need to do some additional calculations on that number. In this case, let's say you want to subtract the size of an *int* from it—and see if it becomes a valid pointer. You could type it by hand, in which case you'll have to type lots of zeros and double-check that you did it right. Or you can use the value history, which guarantees you'll be using the number that **gdb** printed. Here's how:

```
(gdb) print $1-1
$4 = (int *) 0xf7fffffc
(gdb) print *$4
$5 = 0
```

First, we subtracted one from $1, just to see what happens. The result may be a little surprising, but shouldn't be: since $1 was originally a pointer to an *int*, subtracting 1 subtracts the size of an *int*, or four bytes, from its value. **gdb** generally tries to match the way things are done in the C language.

When we try printing the contents at this new location, we get 0—not an access violation. We were able to make our test without having to retype any of the data, which is easier and eliminates a source of error.

Artificial arrays provide a way to print chunks of memory—array sections, or dynamically allocated areas or storage. Earlier debuggers didn't have good ways to turn an arbitrary pointer into an array—for example, **dbx** could print the data at *p*, and successive elements one at a time, but it didn't have any way to treat them as an aggregate. That's where dynamic arrays come in.

Just for the sake of argument, let's look at the ten integers in memory following the variable *h*. The syntax of a dynamic array is:

```
base@length
```

. So, to print the ten elements following *h*, we use **h@10**:

```
(gdb) print h@10
$13 = {-1, 349, 0, 0, 0, 0, 536903697, 32831, 1, -131080192}
(gdb)
```

Note that this artificial array, as a whole, gets its own entry in the value history—so if, later, you want to refer to its seventh element, you can do so with the following:

```
(gdb) print $13[6]
$14 = 536903697
```

(Remember that in C, array subscripts start at zero.) Or, to get the next ten elements, we could do something like:

```
(gdb) print $13[10]@10
$15 = {-131876248, 0, 65545, -131080268, 57344, 64, 2, 0, -134219000, 9020}
(gdb)
```

If you want to list addresses in vertically arranged columns, issue the following command:

```
(gdb) set print array
```

This is one of several **set** commands that may be useful in unusual circumstances; you can check the **gdb** documentation for more.

Breakpoints

Breakpoints let you stop a program temporarily while it is executing. While the program is stopped at a breakpoint, you can examine or modify variables, execute functions, or execute any other **gdb** command. This lets you examine the program's state to determine whether execution is proceeding correctly. You can then resume program execution at the point where it left off.

The **break** command (which you can abbreviate to **b**) sets breakpoints in the program you are debugging. This command has the following four forms:

break *line-number*

Stop the program just before executing the given line.

break *function-name*

Stop the program just before entering the named function.

break *line-or-function* **if** *condition*

If the following *condition* is true, stop the program when it reaches the given line or function.

break *routine-name*

Set a breakpoint at the entrance to the specified routine. When the program is executing, **gdb** temporarily halts the program at the first executable line of the given function.

For an example of the last form, the following **break** command sets a breakpoint at the entrance to the function *init_random*. The **run** command then executes the program until it reaches the beginning of this function. Execution stops at the first executable line within *init_random*, which is a *for* loop beginning on line 155 of the source file:

```
% gdb qsort2
(gdb) break init_random
Breakpoint 1 at 0x28bc: file qsort2.c, line 155.
(gdb) run
Starting program: /home/los/mikel/cuser/qsort2
Tests with RANDOM inputs and FIXED pivot

Breakpoint 1, init_random (number=10) at qsort2.c:155
155             for (i = 0; i < number; i++) {
(gdb)
```

When you set the breakpoint, **gdb** assigns a unique identification number (in this case, 1) and prints some essential information about the breakpoint. Whenever it reaches a breakpoint, **gdb** prints the breakpoint's identification number, the description, and the current line number. If you have several breakpoints set in the program, the identification number tells you which one caused the program to stop. **gdb** then shows you the line at which the program has stopped.

To stop execution when the program reaches a particular source line, use the **break** *line-number* command. For example, the following **break** command sets a breakpoint at line 155 of the program:

```
(gdb) break 155
Note: breakpoint 1 also set at pc 0x28bc.
```

```
Breakpoint 2 at 0x28bc: file qsort2.c, line 155.
(gdb)
```

Since this happens to be the same place as the previous breakpoint, we get a warning—but **gdb** sets the breakpoint anyway. There's no inherent problem with having two breakpoints at the same place. In fact, it has some uses: for instance, you might want to set two breakpoints with different conditions (which we'll get to in just a moment).

If the program is built from many source files, you set breakpoints in files other than the current source file like this:

```
(gdb) break filename:line-number
(gdb) break filename:function-name
```

To set a conditional breakpoint, use the command **break if** as follows:

```
(gdb) break line-or-function if expr
```

where *expr* is a legal **gdb** expression. **gdb** stops the program when the value of *expr* is nonzero (i.e., true) when it reaches the given line or the entrance to the specified function. This is convenient for stopping in the middle of a loop. For example, the command below stops on the second iteration of this rather odd loop:

```
% gdb qsort2
(gdb) list 43,47
43              printf("Tests with RANDOM inputs and FIXED pivot\n");
44              /*random input, factor of 10 bigger each time*/
45              for (testsize = 10; testsize <= MAXSIZE; testsize *= 10){
46                  gen_and_sort(testsize,RANDOM,FIXED);
47              }
(gdb) break 46 if testsize == 100
Breakpoint 1 at 0x2394: file qsort2.c, line 46.
(gdb) run
Starting program: /home/los/mikel/cuser/qsort2
Tests with RANDOM inputs and FIXED pivot
test of 10 elements: user + sys time, ticks: 0

Breakpoint 1, main () at qsort2.c:46
46                  gen_and_sort(testsize,RANDOM,FIXED);
(gdb)
```

gdb supports another kind of breakpoint, called a *watchpoint*. Watchpoints are sort of like the "break-if" breakpoints we just discussed, except they aren't attached to a particular line or function entry. A watchpoint stops the program whenever an expression is true: for example, the command below stops the program whenever the variable *testsize* is greater than 100000.

```
(gdb) watch testsize > 100000
```

Watchpoints are a great idea, but they're hard to use effectively. They're exactly what you want if something is randomly trashing an important variable, and you can't figure out what: the program bombs out, you discover that *mungus* is set to some screwy value, but you know that the code that's supposed to set *mungus* works; it's clearly being corrupted by something else. The problem is that without special hardware support (which exists on only a few workstations), setting a watchpoint slows your program down by a factor of 100 or so. Therefore, if you're really desperate, you can do the following:

1. Use regular breakpoints to get your program as close as possible to the point of failure.

2. Set a watchpoint.

3. Let the program continue execution with the **continue** command.

4. Let your program cook overnight.

It's also worth mentioning the **tbreak** command, which sets "temporary" breakpoints. They're identical to regular breakpoints, except that they are disabled as soon as they stop the program. They aren't deleted, though; you can use the **enable** command to turn a temporary breakpoint back "on."

Continuing execution from a breakpoint

When stopped at a breakpoint, you can continue execution with the **continue** command (which you can abbreviate as **c**):

```
% gdb qsort2
(gdb) break init_random
Breakpoint 1 at 0x28bc: file qsort2.c, line 155.
(gdb) run
Starting program: /home/los/mikel/cuser/qsort2
Tests with RANDOM inputs and FIXED pivot

Breakpoint 1, init_random (number=10) at qsort2.c:155
155             for (i = 0; i < number; i++) {
(gdb) continue
Continuing.
test of 10 elements: user + sys time, ticks: 0

Breakpoint 1, init_random (number=100) at qsort2.c:155
155             for (i = 0; i < number; i++) {
(gdb)
```

Execution continues until the program ends, you reach another breakpoint, or an error occurs.

If you use the **continue** command when there is no program running, **gdb** prints the message:

```
The program is not being run.
```

You will see this message if you have not yet given the **run** command or if the program you are running has terminated, either normally or abnormally.

Rather than typing **continue** repeatedly, you can just type a **Return** to get to the next breakpoint. (As a rule, typing **Return** repeats the previous command—though there are many exceptions.)

You can also type **continue** with a numeric argument, which means "ignore the next *n* breakpoints you run into." For example, **c 5** ignores the next five breakpoints and stops at the sixth.

Managing breakpoints

To delete a breakpoint, you need to know about two commands: **info breakpoints** and **delete**. The **info breakpoints** command lists all the breakpoints and watchpoints you have created in the program. For example:

```
(gdb) info breakpoints
Num Type           Disp Enb Address    What
1   breakpoint     keep y   0x000028bc in init_random at qsort2.c:155
3   breakpoint     keep y   0x0000291c in init_organ at qsort2.c:168
4   breakpoint     keep y   0x00002544 in gen_and_sort at qsort2.c:79
(gdb)
```

This shows that three breakpoints are currently active, with identification numbers 1, 3, and 4. This list shows how each breakpoint is defined: its *disposition* (whether or not it should be deleted when it is next hit); whether or not it is *enabled*; its *memory address*; and its *definition* (function name, filename, and line number).

Once you know the breakpoint's identification number, you can use the **delete** command to get rid of it. For example, the command **delete 1** deletes the breakpoint at line 155 of *qsort2.c*. The same command is also used to delete watchpoints. The command **delete** without any arguments deletes all the breakpoints in your program.

The command **clear** is similar, though probably easier to use. With a line number as an argument, **clear** deletes all the breakpoints on that line. With a function name as an argument, **clear** deletes any breakpoints at the entry to that function. **clear** without arguments deletes any breakpoints on the current line.

gdb also lets you disable and enable breakpoints. If you've taken the trouble to type in a long **breakpoint** command with conditions, you may want to ignore (disable) it for a few passes through the code, but save it so you can reuse (enable) it later. Here are the commands you should know:

disable *number*
> Disable breakpoint *number*; it remains in the list, but it's inactive until enabled. The argument *number* may be a breakpoint number or a list of breakpoint numbers. If you omit *number*, the command applies to all breakpoints.

enable *number*
> Enable the breakpoint, so that it will once again stop execution. The argument *number* may be a breakpoint number or a list of breakpoint numbers. If you omit *number*, the command applies to all breakpoints.

enable once *number*
> Enable the breakpoint temporarily; it stops execution the next time the program reaches it, and the breakpoint is then disabled automatically. The argument *number* may be a breakpoint number or a list of breakpoint numbers.

Before we leave breakpoints, we should mention that **gdb** supports threads on some systems. Threads are parts of a process; they run independently like separate processes do, but they share global data and other resources of a single process. If your system provides a thread library, **gdb** may be able to set a breakpoint within a single thread.

Inspecting and Assigning Values to Variables

While a program is stopped at a breakpoint, you can investigate what has happened during execution. These basic commands manipulate variables:

whatis
> Identify the type of an array or variable.

set variable
> Assign a value to a variable.

print
> In addition to printing the value of a variable, **print** is used to assign values.

To find the type of any variable, use the command:

```
(gdb) whatis variable-name
```

where *variable-name* is the name of an active variable or array. For example:

```
(gdb) where
#0  init_random (number=10) at qsort2.c:156
#1  0x2584 in gen_and_sort (numels=10, genstyle=0, strat=1) at qsort2.c:86
#2  0x23a8 in main () at qsort2.c:46
(gdb) whatis x
type = int [1000000]
```

Here, we find out that x is an integer array of 1000000 elements. You can also use **whatis** to inquire about structures, although the **ptype** command is even more powerful—for example, while **whatis** gives you the name of a structure, **ptype** gives you the definition of the structure. For example:

```
(gdb) whatis s
type = struct tms *
(gdb) ptype s
type = struct tms {
    long tms_utime;
    long tms_stime;
    long tms_cutime;
    long tms_cstime;
} *
(gdb)
```

As we've seen, the **print** *expression* command prints the current value of any variable or expression. Here are two examples:

```
(gdb) print vec(a,1.0)
$4 = 2.2360679774997898
(gdb) print x[2]
$5 = 1027100827
```

The first evaluates the call to *vec*. Since the function is running, in addition to seeing the return value, you are causing any internal side-effects of *vec* to take place. The next command, **print** x[2], prints a value from the initialized array.

The **print** command can also be used for assignment. Let's say that we don't like this particular value for x[2]; we can reassign it as follows:

```
(gdb) print x[2] = 4 + x[1]
$6 = 143302918
```

This prints the value of the expression 4+x[1], and assigns it to x[2]. The feedback you get by seeing the expression's value usually helps you to detect typing errors; however, if you don't want to see the expression's value, you can use **set variable** instead. The following **set** command is equivalent to the **print** command above:

```
(gdb) set variable x[2] = 4 + x[1]
(gdb) print x[2]
$8 = 143302918
```

If the program has been optimized, it may not be possible to print the value of a variable or assign it a value. For example, a variable that is assigned to a register or eliminated from the code entirely is not accessible to **gdb**. It is always possible to use **whatis** to determine a variable's type. You can also use the more advanced command **info address** *name* to find out where data is stored; this tells you whether or not a variable has been assigned to a register.

Single-Step Execution

gdb provides two forms of single-step execution. The **next** command executes an entire function when it encounters a call, while the **step** command enters the function and keeps going one statement at a time. To understand the difference between these two commands, look at their behavior in the context of debugging a simple program. Consider the following example:

```
% gdb qsort2
(gdb) break main
Breakpoint 6 at 0x235c: file qsort2.c, line 40.
(gdb) run
Breakpoint 6, main () at qsort2.c:40
40              int power=1;
(gdb) step
43                      printf("Tests with RANDOM inputs and FIXED pivot\n");
(gdb) step
Tests with RANDOM inputs and FIXED pivot
45                      for (testsize = 10; testsize <= MAXSIZE; testsize *= 10){
(gdb) step
46                          gen_and_sort(testsize,RANDOM,FIXED);
(gdb) step
gen_and_sort (numels=10, genstyle=0, strat=1) at qsort2.c:79
79              s = &start_time;
(gdb)
```

We set a breakpoint at the entry to the *main* function and start single-stepping. After a few steps, we reach the call to *gen_and_sort*. At this point, the *step* command takes us into the function *gen_and_sort*; all of a sudden, we're executing at line 79, rather than 46. Rather than executing *gen_and_sort* in its entirety, it stepped "into" the function.

In contrast, the following sequence of commands executes *gen_and_sort* without stopping:

```
(gdb) run
The program being debugged has been started already.
Start it from the beginning? (y or n) y
Starting program: /home/los/mikel/cuser/qsort2

Breakpoint 7, main () at qsort2.c:40
40              int power=1;
(gdb) next
43                      printf("Tests with RANDOM inputs and FIXED pivot\n");
(gdb) next
```

```
Tests with RANDOM inputs and FIXED pivot
45                  for (testsize = 10; testsize <= MAXSIZE; testsize *= 10){
(gdb) next
46                          gen_and_sort(testsize,RANDOM,FIXED);
(gdb) next
test of 10 elements: user + sys time, ticks: 0
45                  for (testsize = 10; testsize <= MAXSIZE; testsize *= 10){
(gdb)
```

After the **next** command, **gdb** is ready to execute the next sequential line in the source program. It has executed line 46 entirely, including the call to *gen_and_sort*.

Both **step** and **next** work even if the program's source files are not present. The **step** command does not step into built-in functions or library functions.

Calling Functions

The **gdb** debugger lets you execute a single function call. Several commands support work on individual functions:

call *name*
> Call and execute a function.

finish
> Finish executing the current function and print its return value (if any).

return *value*
> Cancel execution of the current function, returning *value* to the caller.

The **call** command executes the named function. It's almost a synonym for *print*, except it won't print the function's return value if it's void. It has the form:

```
(gdb) call function(arguments)
```

For example, the command:

```
(gdb) call gen_and_sort(1234,1,0)
test of 1234 elements: user + sys time, ticks: 3
(gdb)
```

executes the routine *gen_and_sort* with the arguments 1234, 1, and 0. Breakpoints, watchpoints, and any other **gdb** features may be used within the routine. For example:

```
(gdb) break 79
Breakpoint 11 at 0x2544: file qsort2.c, line 79.
(gdb) call gen_and_sort(1234,1,0)

Breakpoint 10, gen_and_sort (numels=1234, genstyle=1, strat=0)
    at qsort2.c:79
79                  s = &start_time;
```

```
The program being debugged stopped while in a function called from GDB.
The expression which contained the function call has been discarded.
Unable to restore previously selected frame.
```

The function stops at a breakpoint; you can then use **continue** to continue the execution, set other breakpoints, etc.

The **finish** command continues execution of the current function, stopping the program automatically when the function returns, and print the function's return value, if any. For example:

```
(gdb) run
Starting program: /home/los/mikel/cuser/qsort2
Tests with RANDOM inputs and FIXED pivot

Breakpoint 11, gen_and_sort (numels=10, genstyle=0, strat=1) at qsort2.c:79
79              s = &start_time;
(gdb) finish
Run till exit from #0   gen_and_sort (numels=10, genstyle=0, strat=1)
    at qsort2.c:79
test of 10 elements: user + sys time, ticks: 0
main () at qsort2.c:45
45                      for (testsize = 10; testsize <= MAXSIZE; testsize *= 10){
(gdb)
```

We hit a breakpoint in the function *gen_and_sort*; then, using **finish**, we continue execution until reaching the end. At this point, the program is stopped at line 45, in the *main* routine. *gen_and_sort* doesn't have a return value, so none is printed. If you are stopped at a breakpoint within a function, the command **return** terminates execution of the function, leaving the program stopped at the point where the function returns. This sounds a lot like **finish**—except that **return** doesn't actually execute the rest of the function. Doing this can be dangerous, of course—by skipping code that may have side-effects, you could change the behavior of the rest of the program. Anyway, the argument of **return** (if any) is returned to the calling function. It's used like this:

```
(gdb) return return-value
```

Automatic Execution of Commands

gdb lets you attach command lists to breakpoints and watchpoints. These can be used for many purposes, from the mundane to the exotic. At the mundane end, they can give you "automatic" output—for example, you may decide that you want to know the values of *i* and *j* whenever you hit a certain breakpoint. You can save typing by using a command list to print these values, rather than giving **print** commands by hand. At the more exotic extreme, you can use them to fix up erroneous data and continue debugging, allowing you to get more information about what is happening without recompiling the program.

Here's the syntax of a command list:

```
(gdb) commands number
...list-of-commands
...list-of-commands
end
```

The list of commands is applied to the breakpoint (or watchpoint) given by *number*. You may omit *number*, in which case the command list is attached to the most recent breakpoint.

For example, let's say that we're suspicious that a timing calculation is being made incorrectly. We set a breakpoint at line 94 of our program, where the code looks like this:

```
(gdb) break 94
Breakpoint 12 at 0x25e4: file qsort2.c, line 94.
(gdb) run
Starting program: /home/los/mikel/cuser/qsort2
Tests with RANDOM inputs and FIXED pivot

Breakpoint 12, gen_and_sort (numels=10, genstyle=0, strat=1) at qsort2.c:94
94              printf("test of %d elements: user + sys time, ticks: %d\n",
(gdb) list
89              times(s);
90              qsort2(0,numels-1,strat); /* do the sort */
91              times(e);
92              begin = ( s->tms_utime + s->tms_stime);
93              end =    ( e->tms_utime + e->tms_stime);
94              printf("test of %d elements: user + sys time, ticks: %d\n",
95                      numels,end-begin);
96      }
97
```

We'd like to check the values *s and *e whenever we hit the breakpoint, so we add the following patch:

```
(gdb) commands 12
Type commands for when breakpoint 12 is hit, one per line.
End with a line saying just "end".
echo value of s (start time) \n
print *s
echo value of e (end time) \n
print *e
end
```

Note that we used the **echo** command to make our breakpoint output more clear. When we continue execution, we see the following:

```
(gdb) continue
Continuing.
test of 1000 elements: user + sys time, ticks: 2
```

```
Breakpoint 12, gen_and_sort (numels=10000, genstyle=0, strat=1)
    at qsort2.c:94
94                  printf("test of %d elements: user + sys time, ticks: %d\n",
value of s (start time)
$28 = {tms_utime = 13, tms_stime = 21, tms_cutime = 0, tms_cstime = 0}
value of e (end time)
$29 = {tms_utime = 37, tms_stime = 21, tms_cutime = 0, tms_cstime = 0}
(gdb)
```

When we hit the breakpoint, we're automatically shown the timing data. You can put any command into a command list; here are a few commands of particular interest:

silent

Tells **gdb** not to "announce" that it has reached the breakpoint; **silent** is only allowed at the beginning of a command list. It's best not to use **silent** unless you add some kind of **print** command within the command list.

continue

The familiar **continue** command can be used at the end of a command list to make execution continue automatically. You get whatever output your breakpoint generates, but the program doesn't actually stop.

It's also worth noting that there's an "automatic display" feature that can be used to evaluate and print an expression whenever the program stops. For example, the following display commands would have a very similar effect to our previous example:

```
(gdb) display *s
1: *s = {tms_utime = 11, tms_stime = 11, tms_cutime = 0, tms_cstime = 0}
(gdb) display *e
2: *e = {tms_utime = 11, tms_stime = 11, tms_cutime = 0, tms_cstime = 0}
```

Each display is assigned a "display number," which is used to identify the display in other commands. The most significant difference between displays and command lists is that displays cause values to be shown whenever the program stops, rather than at any particular breakpoint. (With one important exception: local variables only appear if the variables are defined in the context in which the program stops.)

To delete a display, use the command **undisplay** *number*, where *number* is the identification number assigned when you created the display. To find out what displays are currently in effect, use the command **info display**.

Variable Scope and Context

The next section describes the definitions and conventions that **gdb** uses to refer to variables, functions, and expressions. In most cases, you can use variable and function names directly, as the examples have up to this point. From time to time, however, **gdb** will not do what you expect: it will complain that a variable is "not in the current context," or it may refer to a variable in a different function. The next section explains why these conflicts occur and how to resolve them.

Active and Inactive Variables

At any time, a variable is either *active* or *inactive*. When you are debugging, you can refer only to variables that are available in the current context. If you refer to a variable that isn't defined in the current context, **gdb** responds with a message like the one below:

```
No symbol "i" in current context.
```

The following rules define when a variable is "in context":

- Global variables are always active, whether or not the program is running.

- If the program is not running, all nonglobal variables are inactive. A program is considered "running" after it has started and before it has terminated (e.g., when it is stopped at a breakpoint). A program is no longer running after it has terminated.

- A local variable within any routine is active whenever the routine, or any function called by the routine, is running. For example, the variable *i* in the routine *g1* is active whenever *g1* is executing. It remains active while *g1* and any routines that *g1* calls are executing.

Examining a core dump file left by a program that terminated abnormally is a special case. When you are doing this, **gdb** allows you to examine any variable that was active when the program terminated. **gdb** does not allow you to change the value of the variables in a core file; this would be meaningless, since you may not continue execution after an abnormal termination.

Variable Names and Scope

It's possible to have many static variables in a program that share the same name, because static variables are only known on a "per-file" basis. To resolve ambiguities, **gdb** provides a way to specify precisely which variable you mean.

A full variable name has the form:

```
file-or-function::name
```

where *name* is the name of the variable, and *file-or-function* is the name of the file or function in which the variable is defined. For example, to print the value of *foo* in a function named *trans*, which is defined in the file *trans.c*, you can use either of the following:

```
(gdb) print trans::foo
(gdb) print 'trans.c'::foo
```

Note that we surrounded the filename with single quotes in the second example.

Moving Up and Down the Call Stack

A number of informational commands vary according to where you are in the program; their arguments and output depend on the current frame. Usually, the current frame is the function where you are stopped. But occasionally you want to change this default so you can do something like display a number of variables from another function.

The commands **up** and **down** move you up and down one level in the current call stack. The commands **up** *n* and **down** *n* move you up or down *n* levels in the stack. Down the stack means farther away from the program's *main* function; up means closer to *main*. By using **up** and **down**, you can investigate local variables in any function that's on the stack, including recursive invocations. Naturally, you can't move down until you've moved up first—by default you're in the currently executing function, which is as far down in the stack as you can go.

For example, in *qsort2*, *main* calls *gen_and_sort*, which calls *qsort2*, which calls *swap*. If you're stopped at a breakpoint in *swap*, a **where** command gives you a report like this:

```
(gdb) where
#0  swap (i=3, j=7) at qsort2.c:134
#1  0x278c in qsort2 (l=0, u=9, strat=1) at qsort2.c:121
#2  0x25a8 in gen_and_sort (numels=10, genstyle=0, strat=1) at qsort2.c:90
#3  0x23a8 in main () at qsort2.c:46
(gdb)
```

The **up** command directs **gdb**'s attention to the stack frame for *qsort2*, meaning that you can now examine *qsort2*'s local variables; previously, they were out of context. Another **up** gets you to the stack frame for *gen_and_sort*; the command *down* moves you back towards *swap*. If you forget where you are, the command **frame** summarizes the current stack frame:

```
(gdb) frame
#1  0x278c in qsort2 (l=0, u=9, strat=1) at qsort2.c:121
121                        swap(i,j);
```

In this case, it shows that we're looking at the stack frame for *qsort2*, and currently executing the call to the function *swap*.

Machine Language Facilities

gdb provides a few special commands for working with machine language. First, the **info line** command is used to tell you where the object code for a specific line of source code begins and ends. For example:

```
(gdb) info line 121
Line 121 of "qsort2.c" starts at pc 0x277c and ends at 0x278c.
```

You can then use the **disassemble** command to discover the machine code for this line:

```
(gdb) disassemble 0x260c 0x261c
Dump of assembler code from 0x260c to 0x261c:
0x260c <qsort2>: save  %sp, -120, %sp
0x2610 <qsort2+4>:     st   %i0, [ %fp + 0x44 ]
0x2614 <qsort2+8>:     st   %i1, [ %fp + 0x48 ]
0x2618 <qsort2+12>:    st   %i2, [ %fp + 0x4c ]
End of assembler dump.
```

The arguments to **disassemble** specify a range of addresses to disassemble. If you want to disassemble an entire function, you can give a function name as an argument; for example, **disassemble swap** produces a machine listing for the function **swap**.

The commands **stepi** and **nexti** are equivalent to **step** and **next** but work on the level of machine-language instructions rather than source statements. The **stepi** command executes the next machine-language instruction; the **nexti** command executes the next instruction, unless that instruction calls a function, in which case **nexti** executes the entire function.

The memory inspection command **x** (examine) prints the contents of memory. It can be used in two ways:

```
(gdb) x/nfu addr
(gdb) x addr
```

The first form provides explicit formatting information; the second form accepts the default (which is, generally, whatever format was used for the previous **x** or **print** command—or hexadecimal, if there hasn't been a previous command). *addr* is the address whose contents you want to display.

Formatting information is given by *nfu*, which is a sequence of three items:

- *n* is a repeat count that specifies how many data items to print.
- *f* specifies what format to use for the output.
- *u* specifies the size of the data unit (e.g., byte, word, etc.).

The following list shows the different formats (*f* values) allowed:

Table 6–1: gdb Output Formats

Format code	Output format
x	Hexadecimal
d	Signed decimal
u	Unsigned decimal
o	Octal
t	Binary ("t" stands for "two")
a	Address; prints both as a hex number and as an offset from the nearest preceding symbol
c	Character constant
f	Floating point (interprets the data as a floating-point number)

The size specifier (*u*) can be one of the following:

Table 6–2: Size

Size code	Data size
b	Byte
h	Halfword (two bytes)
w	Word (four bytes)
g	Giant word (two words, eight bytes)

For example, let's investigate **s** in line 79 of our program. **print** shows that it's a pointer to a *struct tms*:

```
79                      s = &start_time;
(gdb) print s
$1 = (struct tms *) 0xf7fffae8
```

The easy way to investigate further would be to use the command **print *s**, which displays the individual fields of the data structure:

```
(gdb) print *s
$2 = {tms_utime = 9, tms_stime = 14, tms_cutime = 0, tms_cstime = 0}
```

For the sake of argument, let's use **x** to examine the data here. The *struct tms* (which is defined in the header file *time.h*) consists of four *int* fields; so we need to print four decimal words. We can do that with the command **x/4dw**, starting at location *s*:

```
(gdb) x/4dw s
0xf7fffae8 <_end+-138321592>:    9      14      0      0
```

The four words starting at location *s* are 9, 14, 0, and 0—which agrees with what **print** shows.

A group of special **gdb** variables lets you inspect and modify the computer's general-purpose registers. **gdb** provides standard names for the four registers that are available on virtually every modern computer:

Table 6–3: Standard Register Names

Name	Register
$pc	Program counter
$fp	Frame pointer (current stack frame)
$sp	Stack pointer
$ps	Processor status

Beyond that, register-naming conventions vary from architecture to architecture. The best way to find out what registers are called on your particular machine is to give the command **info registers**, which dumps the values of all registers. Note that some of the standard names may be abbreviations for longer names; for example, on SPARC machines, the status register may be called either **$ps** or **$psr**. The **info registers** command uses the longer name.

Signals

gdb normally traps most signals that are sent to it. By trapping signals, **gdb** gets to decide what to do with the process you are running. For example, pressing CTRL-C sends the interrupt signal to **gdb**, which would normally terminate it. But you probably don't want to interrupt **gdb**; you really want to interrupt the program that **gdb** is running. Therefore, **gdb** catches the signal and stops the program it is running; this lets you do some debugging.

The command **handle** controls signal handling. It takes two arguments: a signal name and what should be done when the signal arrives. Possibilities are:

nostop

When the signal arrives, don't pass it on to the program and don't stop the program.

stop

When the signal arrives, stop the program, allowing you to debug. Print a message showing that the signal has arrived (unless messages have been disabled).

print

Print a message when the signal arrives.

noprint

Don't print a message when the signal arrives (and, implicitly, don't stop the program).

pass

Pass the signal to the program, allowing your program to handle it, die, or take any other action.

nopass

Stop the program, but don't pass the signal to the program.

For example, let's say that you want to intercept the signal SIGPIPE, preventing the program you're debugging from seeing it. Whenever it arrives, though, you want the program to stop, and you want some notification. To accomplish this, give the command:

```
(gdb) handle SIGPIPE stop print
```

Note that UNIX signal names are always capital letters! You may use signal numbers instead of signal names.

If your program does any signal handling, you need to be able to test the signal handlers—and to do so, you need a convenient way to send the program a signal. That's what the **signal** command does. Its argument is a number or a name such as SIGINT. For example, let's say that your program has set up a special signal handler for SIGINT (keyboard interrupt, or CTRL-C; signal 2) to take some cleanup action. To test this signal handler, you could set a breakpoint and give the command:

```
(gdb) signal 2
Continuing with signal SIGINT (2).
```

The program continues (as if with the **continue** command), but the signal is delivered immediately and your handler runs.

Signals vary from system to system—not even all UNIX systems agree. For a complete list of signals that your operating system makes available, and how **gdb** handles them, give the command **info signals**.

Convenience Variables

The **gdb** debugger lets you define convenience variables, which may be used in expressions and assignments. Convenience variable names have the form $name, where *name* can be anything except a number. The register variables that were introduced earlier are convenience variables; their names—*pc, sr, sp,* and *fp*, together with any architecture-specific names—shouldn't be used for debugging. In contrast, value-history references are numbers (i.e., $1, $2, etc.), rather than convenience variables.

The **set** command defines and assigns values to **gdb** variables. Use it as follows:

```
(gdb) set variable = expression
```

This command assigns the value *expression* to the named *variable*. If = *expression* is omitted, the variable is defined, but not assigned any value.

Convenience variables can be used in expressions, just like any other variable. Therefore, commands like **print $foo++** are legal: it prints the value of $foo, and increments it. In fact, **print** can be used to create and to assign values to convenience variables (for example, **print $bar=123**); set is only necessary if you don't want to print the result.

Working with Source Files

To aid in finding a particular line of source code, **gdb** provides a command for searching through source files. The command **search** *text* prints the next line in the current file that contains the string *text*; likewise, the command **reverse-search** *text* prints the previous line containing *text*. *text* may be any UNIX regular expression. For example, the command **search return** searches for the file's next **return** statement.

Sources for a large development effort are typically located in several different directories. For example, consider a large program called **digest** located in the directory */work/bin* and using additional sources in the directories */work/phase1*, */work/phase2*, and */work/gastro*. You want **gdb** to look for source files in all these directories when displaying code.

By default, **gdb** looks for source files in the current working directory and the executable program's compilation directory (which is recorded in its symbol table). But if you start **gdb** with one or more **-d** options, the specified directories are added to this search list. So in the example just mentioned, you would start **gdb** as follows:

```
% gdb -d /work/phase1 -d /work/phase2 -d /work/gastro digest
```

Within **gdb**, the command **directory** modifies the list of directories through which **gdb** searches. The syntax is:

```
(gdb) directory list-of-directories
```

gdb adds the directories in *list-of-directories* to the head of the search path. For example, consider the command:

```
(gdb) directory /home/src
Source directories searched: /home/src:$cdir:$cwd
```

After you give this command, **gdb** looks through the directory */home/src* prior to searching the current directory.

If given without any arguments, the **directory** command resets the search list to the default, after prompting you for confirmation:

```
(gdb) directory
Reinitialize source path to empty? (y or n) y
Source directories searched: $cdir:$cwd
(gdb)
```

Customizing gdb

Like most Free Software Foundation products, **gdb** is highly customizable. There are fundamentally three ways to add features to **gdb**:

- Write a "user-defined command," using the **define** command.

- Write a "hook" (an addition to a regular **gdb** command), using the **define** command.

- Write a command file (or script) that can be executed using the **source** command.

Whenever **gdb** begins execution, it looks for the file *.gdbinit* in your current working directory; then it looks for the file *.gdbinit* in your home directory.[*] *.gdbinit* can contain a list of **gdb** commands that **gdb** will execute as it starts up and is an ideal place for defining your own commands or hooks. Note that unlike most other utilities, **gdb** looks for two initialization files. In most cases, you'll be doing all your debugging work for any given project in one directory. Therefore, you can neatly divide your initialization commands into "project-specific" initialization (e.g., commands that are useful for working on a particular program) and "general purpose" customization (for your own keyboard preferences, etc.).

---

[*] In some special environments, the initialization file has a different name.

User-defined commands and hooks

User-defined commands are created as follows:

```
(gdb) define command-name
...command...
...command...
end
```

command-name is the name assigned to the new command you're defining; whenever you give this command, **gdb** automatically executes *command1*, *command2*, and so on, until you're finished. User-defined commands can't have arguments. For example, assume that when you're stopped at a breakpoint, you frequently continue execution to the next breakpoint, and then single-step four machine-language instructions. Here's how to automate the process:

```
(gdb) define runstep
Redefine command "runstep"? (y or n) y
Type commands for definition of "runstep".
End with a line saying just "end".
continue
stepi
stepi
stepi
stepi
end
(gdb) runstep
test of 100 elements: user + sys time, ticks: 1

Breakpoint 1, gen_and_sort (numels=1000, genstyle=0, strat=1)
    at qsort2.c:79
79              s = &start_time;
0x2548   79          s = &start_time;
80              e = &end_time;
0x2550   80          e = &end_time;
83              if (genstyle == ORGANPIPE) {
(gdb)
```

User-defined commands can be very complicated; however, they can also be simple "three-liners" that merely define an alias for a commonly used command. **gdb**'s command abbreviations should be so easy to use, though, that you don't really need to use aliases.

In principle, hooks are similar to user-defined commands. A "hook" is a sequence of **gdb** commands that are executed prior to some "regular" command. For example, if you're single-stepping through code, and you want to print the value of *i* before each step, you can do so by writing a command named **hook-step**:

```
(gdb) define hook-step
Type commands for definition of "hook-step".
End with a line saying just "end".
```

```
print i
end
(gdb)
```

Note that this is *exactly* the same as a "regular" user-defined command; in fact, you can even execute **hook-step** as a normal user-defined command. The only thing that makes this command special is the rule that you append the name of the command to the word **hook-**. To see what it does, let's try single-stepping a bit:

```
(gdb) step
$2 = 0
155             for (i = 0; i < number; i++) {
(gdb) step
$3 = 0
156                     x[i] = random();
(gdb) step
$4 = 1
155             for (i = 0; i < number; i++) {
```

You can see **gdb** printing the value of *i* prior to each **step** operation.

Scripts

Scripts are sequences of **gdb** commands that you can execute when you give the command **source** *filename*. Here are two things to watch out for:

- Scripts terminate automatically if a command in the script encounters an error.

- When executed as part of a script, commands that normally prompt you for confirmation won't; they'll do what you say, without asking questions.

For example, let's say that you want to set a group of breakpoints whenever you start debugging a particular program. You might list a series of **break** commands in the file *setbkpts.gdb*; then you can execute it automatically with the command:

```
(gdb) source setbkpts.gdb
```

(In this case, it might be more convenient to place the breakpoint commands in the *.gdbinit* initialization file in the directory where you'll be doing your debugging.)

Interface to UNIX

The **shell** command starts a UNIX shell. When you exit this shell by typing CTRL-D, control returns to **gdb**.

The command **shell** *shell-command* executes the given shell command and returns control to **gdb** immediately. For example:

```
(gdb) shell date
Mon Apr  6 16:51:20 EST 1987
(gdb)
```

These commands let you execute one or more shell commands quickly without leaving the debugger.

By default, **gdb** starts a Bourne shell. To change this default, use the SHELL environment variable to request a different shell. For example, the command:

```
% setenv SHELL /bin/bash
```

requests the GNU project's Bourne Again shell (**bash**).

C++ Programs

If you write in C++ and compile with **g++**, you'll find **gdb** to be a wonderful environment. It completely understands the syntax of the language and how classes extend the concept of C structures. Let's look at a trivial program to see how **gdb** treats classes and constructors.

Although the purpose of the following program isn't really important, we'll explain it just so you have some context for reading the code: it's a tiny piece of a utility that manipulates index entries for documents. Each index entry is stored in the e_text member of the class, and a short unique string that the program uses to refer to the entry is stored in the e_reference member. This program just creates a single index entry:

```
(gdb) list 1,30
1          #include <fstream.h>
2          #include <strings.h>
3          #include <stdio.h>
4
5          const unsigned int REF_SIZE = 80;
6
7          class entry {
8              char *e_text;
9              char e_reference[REF_SIZE];
10         public:
11             entry(const char *text,
12                 const unsigned int length,
13                 const char *ref) {
14                 e_text = new char(length+1);
15                 strncpy(e_text, text, length+1);
16                 strncpy(e_reference, ref, REF_SIZE);
17             }
18         };
```

```
19
20      main(int argc, char *argv[])
21      {
22              char *text_1 = "Finding errors in C++ programs";
23              char *ref_1 = "errc++";
24              entry entry_1(text_1, strlen(text_1), ref_1);
25      }
```

In order to see the program in action; we'll set a breakpoint at the **entry** statement on line 24. This declaration invokes a function, of course—the **entry** constructor.

```
(gdb) b 24
Breakpoint 1 at 0x23e4: file ref.C, line 24.
(gdb) run
Starting program: /home/los/mikel/crossref/ref

Breakpoint 1, main (argc=1, argv=0xefffffd8c) at ref.C:24
24              entry entry_1(text_1, strlen(text_1), ref_1);
```

Now we'll enter the function. We do this through the **step** command, just as when entering a function in C:

```
(gdb) step

entry::entry (this=0xeffffcb8, text=0x2390 "Finding errors in C++ programs",
    length=30, ref=0x23b0 "errc++") at ref.C:14
14                  e_text = new char(length+1);
```

gdb has moved to the first line of the **entry** constructor, showing us the arguments with which the function was invoked. When we return to the main program, we can print the variable **entry_1** just like any other data structure:

```
(gdb) print entry_1
$1 = {e_text = 0x6128 "Finding errors in C++ programs",
  e_reference = "errc++", '\000' <repeats 73 times>}
```

So C++ debugging is just as straightforward as C debugging.

Interface to Emacs

Emacs has a special mode that makes it particularly easy to use **gdb**. To start it, give the command ESC **x gdb**. Emacs prompts you for a filename in the minibuffer:

```
Run gdb (like this): gdb
```

Add the executable's name and press **Return**; Emacs then starts a special window for running **gdb**, where you'll see this:

```
Current directory is /home/los/mikel/cuser/
GDB is free software and you are welcome to distribute copies of it
  under certain conditions; type "show copying" to see the conditions.
There is absolutely no warranty for GDB; type "show warranty" for details.
```

```
GDB 4.16 (sparc-sun-solaris2.4), Copyright 1996 Free Software Foundation, Inc.
(gdb)
```

You can now give all regular **gdb** commands. When you stop at a breakpoint, **gdb** automatically creates a window displaying your source code and marking the point where you have stopped, like this:

```
struct tms end_time, *e;
        int begin, end;

=>      s = &start_time;
        e = &end_time;

        /* initialize x according to the right style */
```

The mark => shows the next line to be executed. Its position is updated whenever **gdb** stops execution—that is, after every single-step, after every **continue**, etc. You may never need to use the built-in **list** command again!

The source-code buffer is a completely normal Emacs buffer; you can edit it, save it, search in it, etc. The mark => only appears on your screen; you don't need to worry about inadvertently adding it to your code.

There are many other conveniences in the Emacs **gdb** interface. For example, you can use the key sequence **C-c C-s** as an abbreviation for **step**. For more information about these command bindings and other features, give the command **C-h m**. While we find it easier to type the "traditional" **gdb** commands, the continually updated source-code display alone makes Emacs's debugger mode well worth using.

Command Completion and Abbreviations

Throughout this chapter, we've used fairly verbose names for commands. **gdb** has two overlapping features for minimizing your typing.

The most commonly used commands have one-letter abbreviations. One such command is **print**, which may be abbreviated **p**. Table 6-4 lists the commands we have covered; it's also a good command summary.

Table 6-4: gdb Command Abbreviations

Abbreviation	Command	Function
b	break	Set a breakpoint.
c	continue	Continue from breakpoint.
d	delete	Delete a breakpoint (or some other object).
f	frame	Print a stack frame.
h	help	Print help for a command.
i	info	Print information about many different things.
l	list	List source code.
n	next	Single step (step over function calls).
p	print	Display variable or expression.
q	quit	Exit gdb.
r	run	Run the program you're debugging.
s	step	Single step (step into function calls).

Command completion is a more general feature. All commands may be abbreviated to their shortest unambiguous prefix. For example, take the **ptype** command. You can abbreviate it to **pt**. You can't abbreviate it to **p**, because that isn't unique, and **p** has been assigned as an abbreviation for **print**, anyway.

If you want to see what command any prefix will expand to, type TAB. **gdb** then fills in the rest of the command (and beeps, to tell you that it's done something), but doesn't execute it. If **gdb** doesn't provide any expansion, there are two possibilities:

- The command is complete as you've typed it; type **Return** to execute it.

- The command is still ambiguous; type TAB again to see a list of all possible completions; then add one or more characters to make the command unique.

Command completion is a very powerful feature. You can use it almost anywhere. For example, instead of typing **info breakpoints**, you can use the command **i b**. **i** is an abbreviation for **info**, and **breakpoints** is the only **info** subcommand beginning with **b**.

You can also use command completion on variable names, function names, and (truthfully) just about anything else that you might want to complete. Completion of variable names, etc., works the same way as command completion; type an unambiguous prefix, followed by TAB to see the rest of the name. (This may take a while if there are a lot of variables in the program.)

Command Editing

Another useful feature is the ability to edit your commands to correct errors in typing. **gdb** provides a subset of the editing commands available in Emacs, letting you move back and forth along the line you're typing. Here are the most important:

Table 6–5: gdb Command Editing

Keystroke	Command
C-b	Move back one character.
C-f	Move forward one character.
C-a	Move to the start of the line.
C-e	Move to the end of the line.
ESC f	Move forward one word.
ESC b	Move backward one word.
DEL	Delete the character to the left of the cursor.
C-d	Delete the character underneath the cursor.
C-_	Undo the last thing you did.
C-l	Clear the screen.

For example, consider the command below:

```
(gdb) stop in gen_and_sort
```

If this doesn't look familiar to you, it shouldn't; it's a **dbx** command. We really meant to type **break gen_and_sort**. To fix this, we can type **C-a**, then type **ESC d** twice, and then type **break**, followed by **Return**, to execute it:

```
(gdb) break gen_and_sort
Breakpoint 1 at 0x2544: file qsort2.c, line 79.
(gdb)
```

Command editing isn't needed when you're running **gdb** within **emacs**.

Command History

gdb also provides the ability to recall previous commands. It's very similar to the C shell's or **bash** shell's history facility. To enable command history, give the command **set history expansion on**.[*] Then, to recall the previous command, type **!!**.

---

[*] Command history is turned "off" by default, because it can interfere with interpretation of C logical operators (! and !=). When command history is enabled, you can minimize trouble by following the ! in any logical expression with a space.

Likewise, type !c to recall the last command beginning with the character *c*. For example, the few lines below exercise the random number generator:

```
(gdb) set history expansion on
(gdb) print random() + random()
$1 = -1537112880
(gdb) !!
print random() + random()
$2 = 14567834598
(gdb) !p
print random() + random()
$3 = 23984783743
```

If you have enabled history expansion, you can also use Emacs-style commands to navigate to previous commands. **C-p** puts the previous command on the **gdb** command line, letting you edit it and execute it. **C-n** puts the "next" command on the command line (assuming that there is one!). Obviously, **C-n** is meaningful only if you've previously moved backwards in the command history.

You may find that command history comes in handy when you're running **gdb** within **emacs**. We find that it's easier to use regular Emacs commands to move backwards, "kill" interesting commands, and "yank" them back when you want them. As in the C shell, **gdb** provides some fairly complicated mechanisms for editing the commands, but we've found that these are too complex to be really useful; if you're interested, consult the FSF's documentation.

Attaching to an Existing Process

One advanced use of **gdb** is to debug a running process such as a server. When you start **gdb**, give it the name of an executable file and a process ID number. This allows it to "attach" to a running program. For example:

```
% gcc -o qsort2 -g qsort2.c
% qsort2 &
% ps | grep qsort2
  2912 p4 R     0:24 qsort2
  2914 p4 S     0:00 grep qsort2
% gdb qsort2 2912
/home/los/mikel/cuser/2912: No such file or directory.
Attaching program '/home/los/mikel/cuser/qsort2', pid 2912
0x2734 in qsort2 (l=673395, u=677356, strat=1) at qsort2.c:119
119                 do j--; while (x[j] > t);
(gdb)
```

First, we see a warning stating that there's no file named 2912. Ignore this; **gdb** always checks first to make sure there's no core file available. When there isn't, it "attaches" to the running process 2912 (which is our invocation of **qsort2**), stops it in its tracks (at line 119), and lets you begin debugging. When you quit, **gdb** "detaches" itself and lets the program continue.

Attaching to a running process requires a good bit of operating-system support. Most full UNIX systems shouldn't have any trouble, but it won't work in many cross-development environments.

You can also use the **attach** command to attach to a process after you start **gdb**. You can reverse the operation and let the process go free with the **detach** command.

If you are running a program on a remote system, such as an embedded system, you can use **gdb** to debug it. Not all **gdb** facilities will be available, as we said before, because the remote system is probably pretty stripped-down. But you can select a device through a command like:

```
(gdb) target remote /dev/device-name
```

and load a program onto the remote system through something like:

```
(gdb) load file
```

Quick Reference

Table 6-6 shows the most important commands in **gdb**. Even though the full names are shown in the table, you can usually invoke a command by entering the first one or two letters. For instance, **b** is a synonym for **breakpoint**.

The **info**, **set**, and **show** commands accept many parameters that haven't been shown in this chapter; check the **gdb** documentation for the more rarely used ones.

Table 6-6: Common gdb Commands

Command	Action
backtrace	Print the current location within the program and a stack trace showing how the current location was reached. (Synonym: **where**.)
breakpoint	Set a breakpoint in the program.
cd	Change the current working directory.
clear	Delete the breakpoint where you just stopped.
commands	List commands to be executed when breakpoint is hit.
continue	Continue execution from a breakpoint.
delete	Delete a breakpoint or a watchpoint; also used in conjunction with other commands.
display	Cause variables or expressions to be displayed when program stops.
down	Move down the stack frame to make another function the current one.
frame	Select a frame for the next **continue** command.

Table 6-6: Common gdb Commands (continued)

Command	Action
info	Show a variety of information about the program. For instance, **info breakpoints** shows all outstanding breakpoints and watchpoints.
jump	Start execution at another point in the source file.
kill	Abort the process running under **gdb**'s control.
list	List the contents of the source file corresponding to the program being executed.
next	Execute the next source line, executing a function in its entirety.
print	Print the value of a variable or expression.
pwd	Show the current working directory.
ptype	Show the contents of a data type, such as a structure or C++ class.
quit	Exit **gdb**.
reverse-search	Search backward for a regular expression in the source file.
run	Execute the program.
search	Search for a regular expression in the source file.
set variable	Assign a value to a variable.
signal	Send a signal to the running process.
step	Execute the next source line, stepping into a function if necessary.
undisplay	Reverse the effect of the **display** command; keep expressions from being displayed.
until	Finish the current loop.
up	Move up the stack frame to make another function the current one.
watch	Set a watchpoint (i.e., a data breakpoint) in the program.
whatis	Print the type of a variable or function.

7

Automatic Compilation with make

The **make** facility is one of UNIX's most useful tools. It is essentially a programming language for automating large compilations. When used properly, **make** significantly reduces the amount of time spent compiling programs, because it eliminates many needless recompilations. Using **make** properly also guarantees that programs are compiled with the correct options and linked to the current version of program modules and libraries.

The idea behind **make** is that you need not recompile a source file if a current object file already exists. An object file is current if it was compiled more recently than the last change to the source file. For example, consider the following situation: We have just modified *program.c* and want to compile and link it to the modules *inputs.c* and *outputs.c*. The command:

```
% gcc program.c inputs.c outputs.c
```

compiles and links all three modules correctly. If the object modules *inputs.o* and *outputs.o* exist, *and* if they are current (i.e., the source files have not been changed since the object modules were last compiled), we could compile *program.c* with the command:

```
% gcc program.c inputs.o outputs.o
```

In this case, **gcc** compiles *program.c* alone and links it to the two object files. Because this command makes a single compilation instead of three, it takes much less time. However, this compilation places more demands on the programmer, who must remember (or check) when *inputs.c* and *outputs.c* were last compiled and determine whether their object modules are current. This introduces potential for confusion: while compiling *program.c* and linking it to pre-existing object modules is faster, it saves work only if the object modules are correct.

make automates this process, reducing the potential for incorrect compilations while minimizing the overall amount of compilation needed. It determines whether the relevant object files exist and whether they are current and then performs the smallest set of compilations needed to create the output file you want. To understand how **make** performs this task, we need to define some terms:

target

A task that needs to be performed. In many cases, the target is the name of the file you want to create; often it is a name assigned to a task (i.e., a target may be a filename, but it does not have to be).

dependency

A relationship between two targets: target A depends on target B if a change in target B produces a change in target A. For example, an object file, *buzz.o*, depends upon its source file, *buzz.c*, and on any other file that is included within its source file during preprocessing (*buzz.h*). A change in either of these sources changes the contents of the object file when it is created.

up to date

A file which is more recent than any of the files on which it depends. For example, if *buzz.o* is more recent than *buzz.c* and *buzz.h*, it is up to date because it reflects the most recent changes to its source files. If *buzz.o* is older than *buzz.c*, then the source code has been modified since the last compilation, and *buzz.o* does not include the latest changes.

makefile

A file describing how to create one or more targets. It lists the files on which the targets depend and gives the rules needed to compile these targets correctly. For most applications, you will want a single makefile in each source directory, describing how to compile the code in that directory. By default, **make** looks first for a makefile named *makefile*, then it looks for *Makefile*.

To use **make**, you need to create a makefile describing how to create one or more programs correctly; then you need to enter the **make** command to execute the makefile. First, we describe how to create a makefile, which is by far the more difficult of the two topics. Second, we describe how to invoke **make**.

Once you finish this chapter, you can get more ideas on how to use **make** from the O'Reilly book *Managing Projects with make*. The particular features of the powerful version supplied on the CD are documented in the *GNU Make* manual, available online through the **info** command or in hard-copy from the Free Software Foundation.

Creating a makefile

Any makefile, no matter how complex, is a set of instructions describing how to
build a number of *targets*. Often the target is a file; however, a target can be any
name describing a task. For example, the following code is a very simple makefile
describing how to build production and debugging versions of *stimulate*:

```
# A very simple makefile.
# Lines beginning with # are comments.
# Targets begin at the left margin, followed by : .
# Shell command lines must begin with a tab.
stimulate:
#         One or more commands to create stimulate
          gcc -o stimulate -O stimulate.c inputs.c outputs.c
stimulate.db:
#         One or more commands to create stimulate.db
          gcc -DDEBUG -g -o stimulate.db stimulate.c inputs.c outputs.c
```

This makefile does nothing more than list the commands required to create the
two different versions of *stimulate*. It says that the command:

```
gcc -o stimulate -O stimulate.c inputs.c outputs.c
```

is sufficient to compile *stimulate* correctly, that optimization is in effect, and that
no additional debugging code is included. Similarly:

```
gcc -DDEBUG -g -o stimulate.db stimulate.c inputs.c outputs.c
```

correctly compiles the debugging version, *stimulate.db*. The symbol DEBUG is
defined for the preprocessor, telling it to include any debugging code present in
the source files. Optimization is disabled, and the compiler will generate the augmented symbol table needed for **gdb** debugging.

This makefile does not use most of **make**'s features. In particular, this makefile
does not eliminate extra compilations, but just executes the simplest (and slowest)
command that will perform a correct compilation.

NOTE   The first character on a command line *must* be the tab character. A
            command line may not begin with a space or a series of spaces.
            Starting with a space is perhaps the most common error in makefiles;
            it is difficult to find because the makefile usually appears correct. If
            you start with a space instead of a tab, the **make** command displays
            the message "Missing separator."

---

make generates a new shell for each UNIX command line that it executes. Consequently, commands that are executed directly by the shell may only be effective

on a single UNIX command line. In particular, the **cd** command only affects the command line on which it appears. For example, consider the following lines:

```
cd ../stimsource
gcc stimsource.c
```

The **cd** command is useless here; it is effective only on the line in which it appears. To change to the directory *stimsource* before compiling *stimsource.c*, use the command:

```
cd ../stimsource; gcc stimsource.c
```

in your makefile. You can use the continuation character (\) to extend a single UNIX command line over several physical lines. If you do this, the \ must not be followed by any further characters, including spaces and tabs.

In general, to invoke **make**, enter:

```
% make target
```

where *target* is the name of one of the targets defined in the makefile. If you omit *target*, **make** generates the first target. For example, our simple makefile can be invoked in three ways:

```
% make stimulate
```

or:

```
% make stimulate.db
```

or:

```
% make
```

The first command executes the commands needed to make the target *stimulate*, the second generates *stimulate.db*, and the third makes the first target listed in the makefile (which happens to be *stimulate*).

Dependencies

As we mentioned earlier, the previous makefile lists only the commands that will build the targets correctly and makes no attempt to minimize the amount of work it needs to do. Dependencies add the idea of conditional execution to a makefile. In the introduction, we said that a target *buzz.o* depends on a file, *buzz.c*, if a change in *buzz.c* results in a change to *buzz.o*. Using this idea, let's analyze the compilation needed to produce the target *stimulate* from the previous makefile.

Note that *stimulate* depends on the source files *stimulate.c*, *inputs.c*, and *outputs.c*. However, this fact is not particularly useful—by itself, it does not let us write an efficient makefile. *stimulate* really depends on the object files *stimulate.o*, *inputs.o*, and *outputs.o*. We could even say that stimulate does not depend on *stimulate.c* at all. A change to *stimulate.c* has no direct effect on *stimulate*; changing *stimulate.c* affects the object file, *stimulate.o*, which in turn affects *stimulate*. The **gcc** command hides this dependency by automatically running the UNIX linker; you must be aware of it when writing makefiles. To use the dependency, we need to rewrite the compilation command to separate compilation and linking:

```
stimulate: stimulate.o inputs.o outputs.o
        gcc -o stimulate stimulate.o inputs.o outputs.o
```

The first line says that the target *stimulate* depends on the object files *stimulate.o*, *inputs.o*, and *outputs.o*. The second line uses the **gcc** command to link these files, assuming that they already exist. Together, these two lines say "The target *stimulate* is out of date if it is older than *stimulate.o*, *inputs.o*, or *outputs.o*. If this is the case, create a new version of *stimulate* by linking these object files." We use **gcc** to do the linking, rather than invoking the linker **ld** directly, even though no compilation is taking place. We could write two similar lines to link the debugging version, *stimulate.db*. In general, a target line looks like this:

```
target-name: list-of-dependencies
```

This line says that *target-name* depends on all the files listed in the *list-of-dependencies*.

However, this does not account for compiling. The object files *stimulate.o*, *inputs.o*, and *outputs.o* have their own dependency relationships: the corresponding source files and any other files (e.g., header files that might be included within the source files). Therefore, if *stimulate.o* is older than *stimulate.c*, we need to compile a new object file before linking everything to create the target *stimulate*. The same logic applies to *inputs.o* and *outputs.o*. To express these secondary dependencies in a makefile, we list all three object files as targets, with their own dependencies, and provide a command to compile an optimized version of each object file:

```
stimulate: stimulate.o inputs.o outputs.o
        gcc -o stimulate stimulate.o inputs.o outputs.o
stimulate.o: stimulate.c
        gcc -c -O stimulate.c
inputs.o: inputs.c headerfile.c
        gcc -c -O inputs.c
outputs.o: outputs.c
        gcc -c -O outputs.c
```

In addition to the simple dependency relationship between the object file *inputs.o* and its source file, we have also stated that *inputs.o* depends on another file, *headerfile.c*. This could be a file providing some important definitions that the #**include** statement inserts into *inputs.c* during compilation. A change to either *headerfile.c* or *inputs.c* requires *inputs.o* to be compiled anew. Remember to include such files as dependencies in your makefiles.

The previous example illustrates a crucial feature of makefiles: any target can depend on a file that is a target in its own right. In this case, **make** proceeds recursively by making the files on which the target depends, guaranteeing that they are up to date, before making the original target. **make** takes the following steps to generate a target:

1. Checks to see if the files on which a target depends are up to date with respect to their own sources

2. Creates a new version of any file that is out of date

3. Checks to see if the target is up to date with respect to the files on which it depends

4. Creates a new version of the target if it is out of date

Because **make** is recursive, it continues checking dependencies until it can guarantee that all the files needed to generate a target are current. For example, if we change the file *outputs.c* and use the previous makefile to generate a new version of the target *stimulate*, **make** takes these steps:

1. Determines whether *stimulate.o*, *inputs.o*, and *outputs.o* are themselves targets

2. Upon discovering that all three are targets, determines whether they are each up to date relative to their sources

3. Determines that *outputs.o* is older than *outputs.c* and compiles a new version

4. Checks *stimulate*'s date relative to *stimulate.o*, *inputs.o*, and the new version of *outputs.o*

5. Determines that *stimulate* is now out of date with respect to *outputs.o*

6. Creates a new version of *stimulate* by linking the object files

By definition, a target is out of date if it does not exist as a file. Therefore, a target that is a task name, rather than a filename, is always out of date. The command **make** *task* always executes the task.

We can easily create a similar set of lines describing how to build the debugging version of *stimulate, stimulate.db*. These will be identical to the production version, except they will specify some different command-line options for the compilation. These lines should be included with the preceding example in the same makefile; one makefile should describe all useful ways of compiling a given project. There is no restriction on the number of targets that can be in a makefile, and you can enter a UNIX command to **make** any target listed in the makefile. For example, the following lines compile *stimulate.db* with the **-DDEBUG** and **-g** options; i.e., define the name DEBUG for the preprocessor and augment the symbol table for **gdb**. This is shown in the following example:

```
stimulate.db: stimulate.do inputs.do outputs.do
        gcc -o stimulate.db stimulate.do inputs.do outputs.do
stimulate.do: stimulate.c
        gcc -o stimulate.do -c -DDEBUG -g stimulate.c
inputs.do: inputs.c headerfile.c
        gcc -o inputs.do -c -DDEBUG -g inputs.c
outputs.do: outputs.c
        gcc -o outputs.do -c -DDEBUG -g outputs.c
```

This generates a separate set of object files for debugging versions of *stimulate.o*, *inputs.o*, and *outputs.o*. Presumably, these files have been compiled with additional debugging code, which the preprocessor has included through conditional compilation.

Here is another feature we might want in the makefile: a special target to delete all of the object modules and start with a clean slate. In other words, when we enter the command **make clean**, we want to delete everything. To write this section of the makefile, we remember that target names that aren't filenames are always out of date. When we enter the command **make clean**, **make** looks for a file named *clean*. If a file doesn't exist (and we'll agree that we'll never put a file with this name in our development directory), **make** executes all of the commands listed for this target. Here is some typical code:

```
clean:
        rm *.o *.do *~ stimulate stimulate.db
```

Targets such as these are very common. It is also common to see a target named **install**, which moves the finished executable to its final home and sets its access modes appropriately.

These are the basics you need to write useful makefiles. Abbreviations, macros, and default compilation rules (discussed in the next section) are advanced features to let you write shorter, simpler makefiles. At this point you should be able to write a correct makefile for a complex development project.

make can eliminate many needless compilations, while guaranteeing that your programs are compiled correctly. It performs bookkeeping you would otherwise have to do yourself. If you use **make** properly, you will not have to worry about when your object files were compiled or when the source code was modified. Once you have described a target's dependencies accurately, **make** automates this task for you.

Abbreviations and Macros

To simplify writing commands, a makefile can define substitution macros and use several predefined abbreviations. Here are two useful abbreviations:

- $@ stands for the full name of the target.

- $* stands for the name of the target with the suffix deleted.

To shorten the previous makefile, use the $@ and $* abbreviations as follows:

```
stimulate: stimulate.o inputs.o outputs.o
        gcc -o $@ $*.o inputs.o outputs.o
stimulate.db: stimulate.do inputs.do outputs.do
        gcc -o $@ $*.do stimulate.do inputs.o outputs.o
inputs.o: inputs.c inputdefs.h
        gcc -c -O $*.c
inputs.do: ... etc. ...
```

When compiling the target *stimulate*, $@ and $* both stand for the string "stimulate". When compiling the target *inputs.o*, $* stands for the string *inputs* and $@ stands for the string *inputs.o*. These abbreviations are useful in many situations; they are particularly important for writing default compilation rules (discussed later in this chapter).

A macro definition begins at the left margin of the makefile and has the form:

```
macro-name = macro-body
```

When **make** is processing the makefile, it substitutes *macro-body* for the string $(*macro-name*). Therefore, we can shorten the preceding makefile even more by defining the macro abbreviations **DEPENDS** and **DBDEPENDS** (i.e., dependencies for the production and debugging versions) as follows:

```
DEPENDS = inputs.o outputs.o stimulate.o
DBDEPENDS = inputs.do outputs.do stimulate.do
stimulate: $(DEPENDS)
        gcc -o $@ $(DEPENDS)
stimulate.db: $(DBDEPENDS)
        gcc -o $@ $(DBDEPENDS)
```

Macros are also useful for defining a set of compilation options. For example, the macro:

```
CFLAGS = -DDEBUG -g
```

contains the two options we've been using for compiling programs for debugging. The makefile line:

```
gcc -c $(CFLAGS) inputs.c
```

therefore compiles *inputs.c* with the **–DDEBUG** and **–g** options. When you invoke a macro, you need to put a dollar sign before it and enclose it either in parentheses or in curly braces—for instance, either $(CFLAGS) or ${CFLAGS}.

Search Directories

Normally, **make** looks for files in the current directory. Adding a **VPATH** line to the makefile allows **make** to find files in directories other than the current directory. A **VPATH** line has the following form:

VPATH=*dir1***:***dir2***:...:***dirn*

That is, **VPATH** should be set equal to a list of directories, which are separated by colons. The previous line means that when **make** looks for a file, it looks first in the current directory, then in *dir1*, then in *dir2*, and so on until it has exhausted the directory list. This feature is useful if the source code for a large program is split among several directories or if many different executable programs use the same source code. In the latter case, the source code can be in a single directory, the object files and makefile for each executable program can be in a separate directory, and each makefile can use a **VPATH** line to point to the source-code directory.

NOTE   Unlike the features discussed so far, **VPATH** does not work in all versions of **make**, and in some versions it behaves oddly. But GNU **make** has a very robust **VPATH**. It can be used to replace targets in other directories, as well as to find the files that targets depend on.

Default Compilation Rules

Makefiles can become even more efficient if you use *default rules* to define how to build targets. With default rules, you do not need to specify how to build a target explicitly. Instead, you define some standard actions that **make** will use in most common situations. **make** actually has its own internal set of rules, so you can carry out common tasks like compiling a C file automatically.

Two methods exist for defining defaults: suffix rules and pattern rules. Suffix rules work on all versions of UNIX (including those that run on MS-DOS), so we'll describe them first. But pattern rules are more flexible and should be used if you plan to stick to the GNU version of **make**.

To use suffix rules, you must define a set of significant suffixes. (Standard UNIX documentation refers to these suffixes as prerequisites. We consider this term obscure and do not use it; however, you should be aware of it.) The appearance of these suffixes in a target line causes **make** to use a suffix rule to generate this target, if an appropriate rule exists. To specify the list of significant suffixes, use the .SUFFIXES: keyword, followed by the list of suffixes that are involved in any default rules. By itself, .SUFFIXES: clears the suffix list. When it is followed by one or more suffixes, a .SUFFIXES: line adds the new suffixes to the list. For example, the lines:

```
# Start by clearing the list of suffixes.
.SUFFIXES:
# We want to specify suffix rules for .c, .o, and
# .do files.
.SUFFIXES: .c .o .do
```

declare that any suffix rules in this makefile involve the suffixes *.c, .o,* and *.do.*

To specify a suffix rule, list the suffix of the file that **make** should search for (.c, for instance) followed by the one that **make** should build (.o or **.do**). Follow these suffixes by a colon and a semicolon, then enter a UNIX command, stated in as general terms as possible. There must be no spaces in the suffix list for a suffix rule. For example, the statement:

```
.c.o:; gcc -c -o $@ -O $*.c
```

supplies a compilation rule that will be used by default whenever **make** has to build an *.o* file. **make** will use the **gcc** compiler to compile the file named *target'*.c with optimization, producing the object file *target'*.o. If you want to override the suffix rule—to add a **-D** option, for instance— you can do so simply by providing an entry that builds a particular .o file in your makefile.

make lets you specify the abbreviation $< for the source file used to build the target. Thus, $< refers to the .c file in the .c.o rule, and the command can be rewritten:

```
.c.o:; gcc -c -o $@ -O $<
```

Similarly, the statement:

```
.c.do:; gcc -c -o $@ $(CFLAGS) $<
```

specifies a suffix rule for compiling debugging versions of object files. Here we assume that you've set CFLAGS to the debugging options, as shown in an earlier section. This compilation rule is used when a target line lists a *.c* file as a dependency for a *.do* file and when no explicit compilation commands appear.

Putting this in context, consider the following makefile:

```
# Start by clearing the list of suffixes.
.SUFFIXES:
# We want to specify suffix rules for .c, .o, and
#  .do files.
.SUFFIXES: .c .o .do
DEBUGFLAGS = -DDEBUG -g
PRODUCTFLAGS = -w -O
PRODUCTOBJS = program.o other.o
DEBUGOBJS = program.do other.do
EXECNAME = product
# A suffix rule to make a "production" .o file.
.c.o:; gcc -c -o $@ $(PRODUCTFLAGS) $<
# A suffix rule to make a .do file (debugging .o module).
.c.do:; gcc -c -o $@ $(DEBUGFLAGS) $<
# Generate executables:
production: $(PRODUCTOBJS)
        gcc -o $(EXECNAME) $(PRODUCTOBJS)
debug: $(DEBUGOBJS)
        gcc -o $(EXECNAME) $(DEBUGOBJS)
# Target line to make some object modules.
program.o: program.c header.h
other.o: other.c
# Target lines to make some debugging object modules.
program.do: program.c header.h
other.do: other.c
clean:
        rm *.o *.do *~
        rm product
```

This is a complete makefile. The command **make program**.o checks the date of *program.c* and, if needed, uses the suffix rule for creating a *.o* file. This suffix rule leads to the compilation:

```
gcc -c -o program.o -w -O program.c
```

which is compilation with optimization and with warning messages suppressed. Similarly, the command **make other.o** invokes the compilation:

```
gcc -c -o other.o -w -O other.c
```

The commands **make other.do** and **make program.do** create debugging versions of these programs, as determined by the preprocessor variable DEBUG, with no optimization and debugging capabilities. The commands **make production** and **make debug** generate production and debugging executable files by linking (and, if necessary, compiling) the appropriate object files. Finally, **make clean** deletes all object modules and executables.

Note that the suffix rules for building *.o* and *.do* files work because they use abbreviations such as $@ heavily. Abbreviations let you write generic compilation commands that can be used for many different compilations.

GNU **make** provides a more general way of specifying defaults, called pattern rules. These look a lot like normal makefile entries, but they contain percent signs as a wildcard. For instance:

```
%.o : %.c
        gcc $(CFLAGS) -c $<
```

indicates that any object file can be built by replacing the .o in the filename with .c and compiling the file with the resulting name.

The makefile:

```
%_xdr.c %_clnt.c %_svc.c %.h : %.x
        rpcgen $<
```

specifies that several types of files depend on a file with a filename ending in **.x**, which is an input file in a special language used by Sun (ONC) RPC. If you have a file named *prog.x*, running **make** executes the **rpcgen** command to produce *prog_xdr.c*, *prog_clnt.c*, *prog_svc.c*, and *prog.h*.

make takes defaults one step further and provides its own default rules for compilation. For example, if you do not specify a default rule for compiling a .c file, **make** supplies its own default rule. Thus, the following is a complete makefile:

```
program.o: program.c
```

With this makefile, the command **make** executes the compilation:

```
cc    -c program.c -o program.o
```

This is fine if the compiler you want is named **cc** on your system. But the GNU C compiler is often called **gcc**, and is loaded from the CD onto your system under that name. You can invoke the GNU compiler by writing your own rule—but there is an easier solution. The default **make** rule doesn't hard-code the compiler name as **cc**, but instead refers to the macro $(CC). You can get it to use **gcc** by redefining the macro in your makefile:

```
CC = gcc
```

make has its own default rules for C, FORTRAN, **lex**, **yacc**, and some other languages.

In the extreme, you can build a program using a null makefile (i.e., a makefile that is 0 bytes long) or no makefile at all. In the absence of a makefile, the command:

```
% make program.o
```

executes the command:

```
cc    -c program.c -o program.o
```

This is supplied completely by **make**'s default rules. However, this is not a particularly good way to use **make**, because these internal default rules do not, and cannot, know anything about the options you want to use for compilation. Consequently, using them sacrifices much of the versatility that UNIX compilers offer.

Invoking make

To use the **make** facility, create a file named *makefile* in the directory where the source code on which you are working resides. After you have written the makefile, enter the command:

```
% make target-name
```

within this directory, where *target-name* is the name of the task you want to perform. In many cases, *target-name* is the name of a file you wish to generate. Often, it is simply the name of a task and does not correspond to any file. When you enter the **make** command, **make** reads the makefile in the current directory and executes whatever commands are needed to successfully create the target you named. If you omit *target-name*, **make** creates the first target described in the makefile.

Normally, there is a single makefile per directory. This makefile should govern all the compilations for the source code within the directory; of course, it may link this code to other modules that reside elsewhere. Ideally, you and your colleagues have coordinated software development in a way that lets you link your module to standard versions of other modules that have been released.

Convenient Flags

This section lists the most useful options for **make**. Other options are described in the *GNU Make Manual* and in *Managing Projects with make*.

−f *filename*

> Normally, the **make** command looks for a makefile within the current directory that is named either *makefile* or *Makefile*. This option tells **make** to use *filename* as a makefile, rather than the standard makefile. For example, the command:
>
> ```
> % make -f othermake.mk target
> ```
>
> looks in a file named *othermake.mk* for instructions describing how to make *target*.

-n Don't execute any commands. Instead, list the commands that would be executed under normal conditions. In other words, **make** lists the commands it
would issue if it were to **make** a target now, without taking any action. This is
useful for debugging. Remember that **make**'s behavior is time-dependent:
since its behavior depends on the last time a file was modified, **make** does not
necessarily take the same actions every time you use it.

-i Normally, **make** terminates immediately if a command returns a nonzero error
code. The –i option forces **make** to ignore these error codes. (Alternatively,
the makefile can include the special target .IGNORE.) This is particularly useful
because some UNIX programs return a nonzero exit code incorrectly when
used with **make**.

-k The -k option is similar to –i, except that **make** does not attempt to build the
target in which the error occurs. It continues to build any other targets
required.

-q Don't execute any commands. Instead, determine whether the target of this
make is up to date. Return a zero status code if the target is up to date and
return a nonzero status code if the target is not.

-s Normally, **make** prints all commands that it executes on the terminal. With this
flag, **make** is silent and does not print any messages. (Equivalently, the makefile can include the special target .SILENT.)

-j Run multiple commands at once. This is described in the next section.

-t Don't execute any commands found within the makefile. Instead, "touch" all
target files that are out of date, bringing them up to date without changing
them.

-d Print information on what targets are being built and what commands are running. Useful for debugging a makefile.

Parallelism

GNU **make** can run multiple commands at once, using the standard multiprocessing capabilities of UNIX. This is a big time-saver on a multiprocessor system. Just
use the –j option to **make**.

Suppose your program depends on eight object files. If you run **make** with –j, it
can start up to eight compilations at once to create the eight object files. When all
the object files have been created, **make** links them together to form the executable—it knows that it cannot issue the link command until all the compilations
are finished.

Be considerate of other users before you start multiple jobs. After all, you are using their computer resources as well as your own.

make and RCS

The RCS source management system, described in the next chapter, lets a team of programmers store and check out source code in a controlled way. However, source files managed by RCS are not available at all times. Before they can be used, you must first check them out. Furthermore, their date reflects the time they were checked out, not the time they were modified. This may cause extra compilations.

Luckily, GNU **make** knows how to find RCS files (as long as you store them in the same directory as your source files or in a subdirectory named *RCS*) and automatically checks them out as part of a build. For instance, suppose that the source file *program.c* does not exist, but that the RCS file *program.c,v* exists in the directory *RCS*. A build of *program.o* invokes the commands:

```
% make program.o
co  RCS/program.c,v program.c
RCS/program.c,v  -->  program.c,v
revision 1.1
done
cc    -c program.c -o program.o
rm program.c
```

make even returns the files to their original state by removing the *program.c* file it checked out.

One problem with the rules used by GNU **make** is that the RCS filename must end with *,v*. Modern versions of RCS allow you to store files without the *,v* suffix, but they will not be found by **make**. For more information about RCS, see Chapter 8, *Source Management with RCS*.

Error Messages

This section lists the most common error messages that GNU **make** produces and their meanings.

No rule to make target '`target`'. Stop.
> The makefile does not contain any rules showing **make** how to construct the given *target* explicitly, and there are no default rules applicable to *target*.
>
> If *target* is something you specified on your **make** command line, the error could be caused by a simple misspelling, or something like being in the

wrong directory. If *target* was not specified on your command line, then **make** has found it on the right side of a colon on a dependency line or is trying to apply a default rule.

"'*target*' is up to date"

The *target* you specified on the command line is already up to date, and, therefore, **make** is taking no action.

missing separator. Stop.

In a makefile, each line following a target (i.e., each line describing how to build the target) must begin with a tab. This message informs you that the associated line should begin with a tab, but doesn't.

This message can also appear if you have a line of junk in the file—for instance, if you forgot to put a # character at the beginning of a comment, or continued a line without putting a backslash at the end of the previous line.

Target *target* not remade because of errors.

This message appears only if you invoke **make** with the **-k** option. It means that an error (i.e., a nonzero exist status code) occurred while **make** was building *target*. As a result, **make** gave up work on that target and continued to the next.

***command*: Command not found**

The *command* does not exist. Usually this is a simple spelling error. If you can issue the command from your shell, there may be some subtle problem—for instance, perhaps the command is really an alias and therefore is found by your shell, but not by **make**.

illegal option -- *option*

You have invoked **make** with a command-line option that it does not recognize. GNU **make** supports some options that contain multiple characters, but you must put two hyphens in front of them. A common error is to specify a two-hyphen option with just one hyphen.

option requires an argument -- *option*

You have invoked **make** with an option such as **-f** that requires an additional argument.

Recursive variable '*macro*' references itself (eventually). Stop.

The makefile contains a macro that it cannot expand because the macro includes itself (e.g., CFLAGS = $(CFLAGS)).

Some Final Notes

This chapter has described some important makefile features. For more information, see the very thorough online documentation published by the Free Software Foundation, which is also available in printed form as the *GNU Make Manual*. More subtleties about the use of **make** can be found in the Nutshell Handbook *Managing Projects with make*.

This chapter has described **make** in terms of automating compilations. It can also be used for maintaining documentation, accounting, or any other task that involves a large number of files. **make** has been used to tailor online documentation to a particular system configuration by running editor scripts to include and delete sections from manuals.

Remember that makefiles are much more than command lists. They are programs with complicated rules for conditional execution, default actions, and other features. In short, **make** is one of UNIX's most versatile tools when used appropriately. The time you can save during compilation is worth the time you invest writing your makefile.

8

Source Management with RCS

RCS (the *Revision Control System*) is a source-code management tool designed to aid program development under UNIX. RCS meets an important need in managing large programming projects. It allows you to automate many of the tasks involved in coordinating a team of programmers. These tasks include maintaining all versions of a program in a recoverable form, preventing several programmers from modifying the same code simultaneously, helping programmers to merge two different development tracks into a single version, ensuring that a single program is not undergoing multiple simultaneous revisions, and maintaining logs for revisions and other changes.

RCS is meant for source files, not binaries. Recent versions do allow binary files to be stored, but this is not an effective use of RCS. The reason is that RCS keeps track of changes to individual lines. (It uses the UNIX **diff** command to see how you have changed a file.) The concept of "line" means nothing in a binary file, and thus, making a trivial change could cause RCS to store complete copies of both the old and the new versions. You might as well just make a back-up copy of the old version and skip using RCS.

Many UNIX versions provide a collection of tools called SCCS (Source Code Control System), which is functionally identical to RCS but requires a license and has a completely different user interface. If your site uses SCCS, this chapter will still be a useful conceptual introduction; however, you will need to learn a different set of commands.

RCS does not come with a book. (It is not a Free Software Foundation or Cygnus product, so they have not written **info** documentation as they have for the other tools on the CD.) But each of the commands has a manpage.

Revision Trees

RCS maintains your revisions in a tree structure. The first version of a file under RCS control is the root of a tree. It is given revision number 1.1. Succeeding versions that descend linearly from this file are the trunk of the tree, and are numbered 1.2, 1.3, etc.

A new development branch can begin at any point on this tree. This branch consists of another chain of descent beginning from another file. RCS gives the first "branch" beginning at Revision 1.3 the number 1.3.1; it numbers the second branch beginning at this point 1.3.2, etc. The first revision along the first branch is 1.3.1.1, the second is 1.3.1.2, etc. Branches can begin at any point, at any time, and they can start from other branches, from the root, etc. Just as the word root refers to the first element in a tree, we will use the word tip to refer to the last version of a file along a branch. Figure 8-1 shows an RCS tree containing eight versions of one file. The trunk of this tree consists of five versions; a branch (another development path) started from Version 1.3.

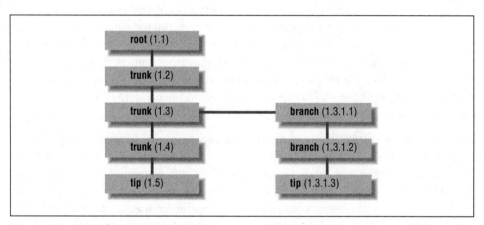

Figure 8-1: A simple RCS revision tree

The tool **rcsmerge** exists to help you merge versions from different branches of development. This tool can be very useful if two developers have been working on different aspects of the same program. One programmer might be fixing bugs in an old release, and another might be adding some new features. **rcsmerge** helps you to integrate both sets of changes painlessly, so that you can produce a new version containing both the bug fixes and the new features.

Basic Operations

The two fundamental commands for using RCS are **ci** and **co**. These commands "check in" and "check out" software that RCS is maintaining. When you check a file in, RCS deletes your source file and creates or modifies a file called *source,v*, where *source* is the name of the original and *,v* is an extension that indicates an RCS file. By deleting *source*, RCS prevents you from doing any further editing without using **co** again. When you check out a file, RCS extracts a version of the file— usually the most recent version—from the corresponding RCS file. To do a simple checkin, use the following command:

```
% ci filename
```

This creates a new RCS version of your file. If the file is not currently managed by RCS, this command places the file under RCS management, gives it the version number 1.1, and prompts you for a description of the file. If the file is already being managed by RCS, this command increments the version number (1.2 follows 1.1) and prompts you for a description of the changes you have made since the last checkin. The following example shows what happens when you check in Revision 1.4 of a file called *test*:

```
% ci test
test,v  <-- test
new revision: 1.4; previous revision: 1.3
enter log message, terminated with single '.' or end of file:
>> fixed a trivial error on the last line
>> .
done
%
```

The prompt ">>" indicates that RCS is waiting for a line of text. Typing a . (period) or pressing CTRL-D on an unused line terminates the log message. At this point, RCS enters the message in its file and prints the word "done".

If you check in a file that is unmodified, RCS uses the old version instead of creating a new version. While this behavior is usually an efficient way to manage the tree, sometimes you want to create a new version without changing the contents of the file. (For instance, you could be starting a new branch of the tree in order to support two different releases of your product.) Force a check-in through the **-f** argument:

```
% ci -f -r1.3.1 test
RCS/test,v  <-- test
new revision: 1.3.1.1; previous revision: 1.3
enter log message, terminated with single '.' or end of file:
>>
```

Used by itself, the command **ci** deletes your working version of the file. If you want to retain a read-only version of the file, enter the command:

```
% ci -u filename
```

In this case, you retain a copy of *filename* for reference. You cannot modify the file, however, because it is no longer checked out.

In order to use a file that has been placed under the control of RCS, use the checkout command, **co**, as follows:

```
% co filename
```

where *filename* is either the name of the file you want to work on or the name of the RCS archive file for *filename* (i.e., the commands **co test** and **co test,v** are identical). This retrieves the latest version of your file from the RCS file in which it has been stored.

By itself, **co** is sufficient if you only want to read, compile, or otherwise use the file without changing it. However, **co** restores your source file with read-only access: you cannot edit it or make changes. If you want to modify the file, use the command:

```
% co -l filename
```

This not only creates a file that you can modify, but also installs a lock. This means that no one else can modify the file until you return it to RCS with **ci**. Other programmers can still use **co**, getting a read-only version of the file. Conversely, if someone else has already locked the file, **co -l** will not let you check it out. If you try to check out a file that someone else has already locked, **co** replies:

```
% co -l lockedfile
co error:  revision n already locked by someone-else
```

where *someone-else* is the username of whoever locked the file. If you see this message, negotiate with the lock's owner to find out when he or she will be finished.

If strict locking (explained below) is in effect, you cannot check in a new version of a file unless you have locked it first: unless you locked the file on check-out, you only have a write-protected version, which you cannot modify and which you don't need to check in. You can always use **co** to check a file out, no matter who has locked it. You can then read it, compile it, and do anything you want *except* change it.

RCS Directories and Files

Before checking a file in or out, RCS always looks for a subdirectory named *RCS* within the current directory. If this directory exists, RCS keeps all the files it creates within that directory, keeping your working directories free from extra clutter.

NOTE   It is possible to circumvent RCS locks by using the UNIX commands
            for changing file access modes, etc. Please don't. If you don't want
            the protection that RCS gives, don't use RCS in the first place. One
            person who refuses to play by the rules can quickly confuse a large
            development effort.

RCS creates a separate RCS file for every file under its management. This file stores a description of the file you are managing, the entire change log, the current version of the file, a list of users who are allowed to access the file, the file's date and time, and a list of changes that lets RCS reproduce any obsolete version of the file at will.

Despite the information they contain, RCS files are not substantially larger than the source files. However, they do grow with time. If you need to reduce your disk requirements, you can use the **rcs** command to eliminate old versions of the file that are no longer needed. Do this with the command:

```
% rcs -orange filename
```

where *range* specifies the revision numbers you want to trim from your file. It can be a single revision number (e.g., **-o1.3** deletes Revision 1.3); two revision numbers separated by a colon (e.g., **-o1.1:1.3** deletes Revisions 1.1, 1.2, and 1.3); a revision number preceded by a colon (e.g., **-o:1.2.4.3** deletes all revisions on branch 1.2.4 up to and including 1.2.4.3); or a revision number followed by a colon (e.g., **-o1.4.3.3:** deletes all revisions from 1.4.3.3 to the tip of branch 1.4.3).

This command also deletes the messages for any discarded versions from the change log. It never deletes the initial description of the file, even if you delete Version 1.1. It never changes version numbering; for example, Version 1.78 remains Version 1.78, even if you delete all previous versions.

The Revision Log

Whenever you check in a file, RCS prompts you for a log message describing the changes you have made since the last revision. This log exists so that you can easily find out who changed the program, when, and why.

The command **rlog** displays the entire log for a file. For example:

```
% rlog test
RCS file:       test,v
Working file:   test
head:           1.2
branch:
locks:
access list:
symbolic names:
comment leader:  <">#  <">
total revisions: 2;    selected revisions: 2
description:
this is a simple test of rcs
to play with it
----------------------------
revision 1.2
date: 86/06/26 10:00:15; author: loukides; state: Exp;  lines added/del: 2/0
another revision to demonstrate the features of a log.
----------------------------
revision 1.1
date: 86/06/26 08:24:14;  author: loukides;  state: Exp;
This is the initial version of the program.
=======================================================
%
```

In addition to the revision number and the log of comments, this display shows the date and time at which each revision was checked in, the author of the modifications, the total number of lines added and deleted in the modification, and the file's current state. Note that RCS considers a modification to a line to be deleting the old line and adding the new line. The state field shows the file's status at each revision. By default, the state field is always **Exp**, which stands for experimental. By using the command:

```
% rcs -s filename
```

you can give any revision any state you wish. This is described in the section called "Other Features" later in this chapter.

Identification Strings

If you wish, RCS can put identification strings into your source code and object files. These strings contain information about the current revision number, the author, and the time the file was last checked in. Here is a typical identification string:

```
$Header: /home/los/mikel/lindecomp.c,v 1.1 1994/06/27 11:28:37 loukides Exp $
```

It shows the filename, the version number, the modification date and time, and the person who made the last modification to this version.

To include an identification string in a file, insert the marker:

```
$Header$
```

To let the program compile correctly, the marker should be within a comment statement. RCS replaces this marker with the identification string whenever you check out the file.

Alternatively, you can place this marker within your source code in such a way that the information gets included in the object file and final executable file; the information can then be viewed by any user through the **what** or **ident** command. Put an initialized character string such as the following in your source file:

```
char rcsid[] = "@(#)$Header$";
```

The name of the variable doesn't matter, only the content. The funny @(#) is a marker that the **what** command looks for. When you check your file into RCS and check it out again, the $Header$ is replaced with information about the file, as we have seen. During compilation, the compiler includes the identification string within the object module. This string is therefore preserved in the resulting object file and in all files to which this file is linked. A user can then determine at a later time which versions were used to produce an executable. Knowing exactly which source code was used to build any release of a program can be essential if you are debugging a large, widely used application.

Several other strings like $Header$ are recognized by RCS; they are all described on the **co** manpage. Thus, RCS replaces the marker Log with the accumulated revision-log messages. Like $Header$, this marker should be contained in a comment.

Other markers with similar functions are $Author$, $Date$, $Locker$, $Revision$, $Source$, and $State$. RCS replaces $Source$ with the complete pathname of the RCS file storing this version. The meanings of the other markers should be self-evident.

The utility program **ident** searches through any file, regardless of its type (i.e., text files, object files, even core dumps) and extracts all identification strings. For example, the command **ident datamasher** prints all the identification strings it finds in the executable file named *datamasher*:

```
% ident datamasher
$Header:lindecomp.c,v 1.3 1994/06/27 11:28:37 mike Exp$
$Header:satman.c,v 1.7 1994/09/21 15:29:38 mike Exp$
$Header:doggies.c,v 1.5 1994/10/20 10:07:38 howard Exp$
```

If you produced *datamasher* by compiling many files under RCS control and linking them, this command summarizes all the modules and revisions from which *datamasher* is built. This can make it easier to discover whether an executable file was linked with the correct versions of all object modules, or it can help you to discover which versions of the source code introduced a particular bug. For example, after reading the previous report, you might remember that Version 1.5 of *doggies.c* had a numeric stability problem that was fixed in Version 1.6. A look at the RCS log for *doggies.c* would confirm this. You could then relink, do some testing, and send your customer a new version of *datamasher*.

Strict Access

By default, RCS is in the strict-access mode. This mode has two important features:

1. No one is allowed to check in a file without locking it first.

2. No one can modify a file unless it was checked out locked.

To take RCS out of the strict-access mode, use the command:

```
% rcs -U filename
```

where *filename* is the name of a particular file under RCS management. It may be either the working filename or the RCS filename (i.e., the name with the *,v* extension). This places RCS in the open-access mode for this file. In this mode, the owner of *filename* can modify the file without locking it first. All other users must still lock a file before modifying it. Use RCS in the "open-access" mode only if you are the only programmer modifying this file. Otherwise, you risk multiple simultaneous modifications by different programmers and thus defeat one of the primary aims of RCS.

Return RCS to strict access with the command:

```
% rcs -L filename
```

More About Checking In

The **ci** command may refuse to let you check in a file, printing the message:

```
ci error: no lock set by your-name
```

This can occur only under two circumstances:

1. If you did not lock the file upon checkout in the strict-access mode

2. If someone locked the file after you checked it out in the open-access mode

ci will not tell you who locked the file. As far as it is concerned, you are the one who is at fault for not locking a file you intended to modify and replace. If this situation occurs, lock the file by using the following command:

```
% rcs -l filename
```

At this point, two things can happen. In the first situation, where no one else locked the file, RCS retroactively locks the file so that you can check in your file normally with the **ci** command. In the second situation, RCS prints the warning:

```
rcs error:  revision n already locked by someone-else
```

where *someone-else* is the username of whoever has locked your file. You need to negotiate with him or her to reach a solution. Presumably, the two of you have been modifying the file at the same time and need to assess any damage. Tools like **rcsdiff** and **rcsmerge** will help you find out the differences between the two files and create a new version that incorporates the modifications to both files.

Neither of these situations should occur unless you or your colleagues are playing "fast and loose" with file access. RCS does not eliminate the need for discipline and coordination. It only makes discipline and coordination easier to live with.

At times, you may want to do a check in, followed immediately by a check out. You may want to install a version reflecting the current state of your program (possibly as a backup), then continue editing immediately. Rather than using two operations, RCS lets you perform both with the command:

```
% ci -l filename
```

This updates the RCS file and gives you a lock without erasing your working file, allowing you to continue editing immediately.

New and Old Generations

At points in the development cycle, you will decide that your program has reached a decisively different stage. You may want your version numbering to reflect this new state: for example, by changing from Version 1.x to Version 2.1. To do this, use the **-r** option when you check in the program, as shown in the following example:

```
% ci -rn filename
```

This assigns the version number n to the most recent version of *filename*. For example, the command:

```
% ci -r2.1 makefile
```

checks in *makefile* with version number 2.1.

If you want to check out an old version of this file, use the **-r** option with **co**. For example:

```
% co -l -r1.4 makefile
```

retrieves Version 1.4 of *makefile*, provided that it has not been declared obsolete. There are several reasons for retrieving an old version: nostalgia and recovering from disastrous modifications are only two of the more likely ones. You may also wish to start a different course of development from a pre-existing software base (e.g., to develop software for two different systems). When you again check in this file, by default RCS creates a new branch for development. It gives the first item in this branch the number $n.1.1$, where n is the number of the version you checked out.

Other Features

RCS can do a lot to tell you what stage your project is in and to help you build programs consistently. The features in this section are management tools for keeping a project on course.

States

You can use the **rcs** command to assign a *state* to any version of a file. A state can be any string of characters, as long as the string has some meaning for you. For example, you can assign the state **Exp** for experimental software, **Stab** for stable software, **Rel** for released software, and **Obs** for obsolete software maintained for archival purposes only. To assign a state to a particular revision of a file, use the command:

```
% rcs -sstate:revision filename
```

where *state* is the state you want to assign and *revision* is a revision number. If you omit *revision*, RCS assigns this state to the latest revision on the main branch of development.

Names

Suppose that you're ready to take a snapshot of your source files. For instance, you want to send a version of the application out to selected customers for beta testing, while you keep on making changes. Later on, someone may ask you for the exact version that you sent out for beta test, and it's going to be a major headache if you have to remember that you used revision 2.2 of one file, revision 2.4 of another, and so on. To help you keep track of random revisions, RCS lets you assign symbolic names.

Use the **-n** option in a **ci** or **rcs** command to assign a name to a revision. This name can be used in place of a revision number in all commands within the RCS system. For example, you can assign the name *betatest* to revision 2.4 of a program with the command:

```
% rcs -nbetatest:2.4 filename
```

After making this assignment, the two commands:

```
% co -rbetatest filename
```

and:

```
% co -r2.4 filename
```

are equivalent. Assign a symbolic name by entering a command of the following form:

```
% rcs -nname:revision filename
```

where *name* is the symbolic name you want to assign, *revision* is the revision number of a specific revision, and *filename* is the name of a file under RCS control. If you omit the revision number, **rcs** deletes the symbolic name.

If you wish, you can assign several different symbolic names to the same revision. But the inverse is not true—you can't assign a single symbolic name to multiple revisions of the same file. If you try, **rcs** prints an error message. For example:

```
% rcs -nworking:1.4 test        Name revision 1.4 "working"
rcs file: test,v
done
% rcs -nworking:1.5 test        Try to name revision 1.5 "working"
rcs file: test,v
rcs error: symbolic name working already bound to 1.4
test,v unchanged.               Error message; nothing happened
%
```

Therefore, to change the name to a different revision number, use the **-N** option. It uses the same syntax as **-n**. For example, the command **rcs -Nworking:1.5 test** removes the name working from revision 1.4 and assigns it to revision 1.5.

You can also check in a file and assign a name at the same time to the revision you are creating. Use **-n** or **-N** on the **ci** command:

```
% ci -nworking test
```

Here you don't specify any revision number, because the **ci** command automatically assigns one.

Changing a File's Description

If you need to change the description associated with a file, use the command:

```
% rcs -t filename
```

This deletes the current description from the RCS file for *filename* and prompts you
for a new description. For example:

```
% rcs -t test
rcs file: test,v
enter description, terminated with single '.' or end of file:
NOTE:  This is NOT the log message!
>> This is a new description for the file.
>> .
done
%
```

This leaves all the logging messages unchanged.

You can do the same thing during checkin by using the **-t** option with the **ci** command. In this case, **ci** will prompt you for a new descriptive message first and then
prompt you for a message for a revision log:

```
% ci -t test
test,v  <--  test
new revision: 1.10; previous revision: 1.9
enter description, terminated with single '.' or end of file:
NOTE:  This is NOT the log message!
>> A new description message
>> .
enter log message, terminated with single '.' or end of file:
>> A new log message
>> .
done
%
```

Access Lists

An *access list* is a list of users who are allowed to use RCS to manipulate a file. In
most cases, RCS refuses to allow anyone not on the access list to lock or otherwise
modify a file. There are only three exceptions to this rule:

- The owner of a file can always access it.

- A superuser can always access any file.

- If the access list is empty, anyone can access the file.

Access lists apply to the RCS revision tree as a whole (i.e., to all revisions of a file).
Either you have access to all versions of a file or you do not have access to any.

When a file is first placed under the control of RCS, it has an empty access list. This means that anyone can access it, provided that it is not locked. To add names to the access list of any file, use the command:

```
% rcs -anames filename
```

where *names* is a list of login names separated by commas. This list cannot contain any spaces. For example, the command:

```
% rcs -aellen,john,james testfile
```

adds the users with login names **ellen**, **john**, and **james** to the file named *testfile*.

If many people are working on the project, it may be simpler to add names in batches, rather than list them individually. Therefore, you may want to copy all the names from one file access list to another. For example, you may wish to create an RCS file, then give it the same access list as other files in the same project. To do this, use the following **rcs** command:

```
% ci newfile            Put newfile under RCS management
% rcs -Aoldfile newfile Give newfile the access list from oldfile
```

To delete names from a file access list, use the command:

```
% rcs -enames filename
```

Again, *names* is a list of names separated by commas; it may not contain spaces. For example, the command:

```
% rcs -eellen,john,james testfile
```

removes the names **ellen**, **john**, and **james** from the access list for *testfile*. Anyone who is allowed to access a file is allowed to edit its access list.

Any user can check out a read-only version of the file, regardless of whether they are on the access list. If you try to lock a file and are not on the access list, RCS replies with the following error message:

```
co error: user yourname not on access list
```

The Next Step

If you use RCS in a large group of programmers trying to get a lot of things done at once, you'll notice some extra things you wish you could do easily. For instance, it can be hard to make changes to multiple branches at the same time or create a personal area for testing bug fixes. Some people use another piece of free software, CVS (which stands for the original name *Concurrent Version System*) to provide additional power. While we don't discuss CVS in this book, it is included with the RCS packages on the CD, and you can read its documentation and try it out. Some sites also add their own scripts to automate common activities; this technique is described in the O'Reilly book *Applying RCS and SCCS*.

9

Program Timing and Profiling

Most programs run in a time-critical environment, so it is important to minimize execution time. However, varying system load and other conditions make it difficult to measure program execution time accurately. It is even more difficult to pinpoint the portions of a program that are performance problems. UNIX provides a group of timing and profiling utilities to help maximize the performance your programs achieve.

There are many aspects of performance: total "wall clock" time, CPU time, the number of times any routine or code segment was executed, the percentage of the total time performing I/O, etc. Therefore, there are many different kinds of profilers, each adapted to a particular purpose. These profilers fall into two major classes:

Simple timers

> Simple timers measure the total time that the system spent executing a program, together with other statistics about the system's CPU usage. The results apply to the program as a whole; they are not broken down in any way. Two simple timers are available:

> **time**
>> A timer built into the UNIX C shell.

> **/bin/time**
>> Another version of **time** that is not built into the C shell.

In addition, timing routines may be called from within the program itself.

Report-generating profilers

Report-generating profilers produce a rather lengthy report analyzing program performance on a routine-by-routine basis. They help you discover which routines account for most of the program's execution time, helping you to direct your tuning efforts to the most important parts of the code.

An early UNIX profiling program was called **prof**. It created a flat profile, showing simply how many calls the program made to each function and how much time was spent in each. Later, Berkeley released a program called **gprof** that did that and much more. The profiler distributed with this book, also called **gprof**, is very close to the Berkeley program. Maybe the **g** in **gprof** stands for GNU now, but it didn't originally; it stood for **graph**.

In addition to the flat profile, **gprof** creates a long listing known as a call graph. It shows how the functions call each other, how much time each function spends on behalf of each of its callers, etc.

Simple Timings

The **time** program provides simple timings. Its information is highly accurate, because no profiling overhead distorts the program's performance. It does not provide any analysis on the routine or trace level. It reports the total execution time, some other global statistics, and nothing more. You can use it on any program without special compilation options.

To get a simple program timing, enter **time** followed by the command you would normally use to execute the program. For example, to time a program named **analyze**, enter the following command:

```
% time analyze inputdata outputfile
       22.3 real         7.1 user          4.5 sys
```

This was entered in the **bash** shell, so the **/bin/time** utility was used. It indicates that 22.3 seconds elapsed during the execution of the command, that 7.1 seconds were spent by the CPU in user space, and that 4.5 seconds were spent executing system calls (part of that time it was idle). Essentially, the code is executing in user space, except when the kernel has to execute a system call for you.

Elapsed time is the wall-clock time from the moment you enter the command until it terminates, including time spent waiting for other users, I/O time, etc. By definition, the elapsed time is greater than or equal to your total CPU time and can even be several times larger.

If the same command were executed under the C shell, the output would look like this:

```
% time analyze inputdata outputfile
9.0u 6.7s 0:30 18% 23+24k 285+148io 625pf+0w
```

This indicates that the program spent 9.0 seconds on behalf of the user (user time), 6.7 seconds on behalf of the system, and a total of 30 seconds elapsed time.

This example also shows the CPU time as a percentage of the elapsed time (18 percent). The remaining data report virtual memory management and I/O statistics. They are the amount of shared memory used, the amount of nonshared memory used (**k**), the number of block input and output operations (**io**), and the number of page faults plus the number of swaps (**pf** and **w**). The memory management figures are unreliable in many implementations, so take them with a grain of salt.

Introduction to Profiling

Now that we have discussed simple timings, we can move to the **gprof** profiler. It provides timing information for individual routines within the program. First, we need to introduce some terminology.

If routine *A* calls routine *B*, we call *A* the parent of *B* and we call *B* the child of *A*. We refer to all the routines that routine *C* calls directly as the children of *C*, and we refer to all routines that *C* calls, directly or indirectly, as the descendants of *C*. For example, consider the routines *A*, *B1*, *B2*, *C1*, *C2*, *C3*, and *D*. *A* calls *B1* and *B2*; *B1* calls *C1*, *C2*, and *C3*; and *D* calls *B2*. Figure 9-1 represents this graphically.

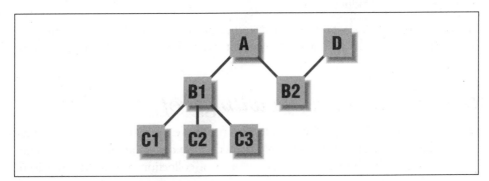

Figure 9-1: A simple call graph

B1 and *B2* are the children of *A*, and *B2* is the only child of *D*. *C1*, *C2*, and *C3* are all descendants of *A*, along with *B1* and *B2*. *A* is the only parent of *B1*, and both *A* and *D* are parents of *B2*.

gprof produces two distinct kinds of output. A flat profile shows the total time that the program spent executing each routine, and an extensive call graph profile analyzes execution time in terms of each routine's parents and children. For example, a flat profile for the previous routines shows the total time spent in *A, B1, B2,* and so on. The call graph profile provides more detail by splitting up the total execution time for each routine into several constituent parts. It shows how much of the total time spent executing any routine can be attributed to calls from each of its parents. It also shows how much of the total time spent executing any routine was spent executing each of the routine's children. This detailed information lets you determine which portions of the program are used heavily and, in addition, why they are used heavily: not just which procedure requires the most execution time, but which calls to this procedure (and which calls within the procedure) account for this time.

An ordinary executable file cannot be profiled. Before you can profile a program, you must enable profiling. To do this, recompile and relink the program's object modules with the **–pg** option. For example:

```
% gcc -pg -o myfile f1.c f2.c...
```

The **–pg** option affects both the compiler and the linker. For the compiler, it inserts code that keeps track of time and the number of calls to each function. For the linker, it causes the necessary initialization and profiling routines to be included in the program.

Programs run significantly slower (roughly 30 percent) when profiling is enabled. Therefore, you should disable profiling (by recompiling and relinking without **–pg**) before releasing a production version.

In addition to the information provided in this chapter, you can find out quite a bit by reading the **info** documentation for **gprof**. We have not found it in hard-copy form.

Generating a Profile with gprof

Once you have enabled profiling with **–pg**, run the executable file with any reasonable input data. This produces a file named *gmon.out*, in addition to any other output produced by your program. *gmon.out* is a collection of statistics in a form that is not readable by humans.

Now you can use the **gprof** utility to interpret these statistics and present them in a usable form. **gprof** produces useful data from one or more *gmon.out* files. To create this table, use **gprof** as follows:

```
% gprof list-of-options executable-file stat-files > output
```

where *executable-file* is the name of the executable file that you are profiling and *stat-files* is a list of *gmon* files that have resulted from executing the program. This feature lets you generate a profile from several different program runs. If you want to generate the profile from a single file named *gmon.out*, you can omit *stat-files*. Similarly, you can omit *executable-file* if the name of the executable file is *a.out*. The output from **gprof** is sent to standard output, which is normally connected to your terminal. Because the output tables are much too large to be viewed on a terminal, you should redirect standard output to a file.

list-of-options is a list of valid **gprof** options. The most common options are:

-b As part of its report, **gprof** normally prints several pages explaining the entries in the profile tables. This option suppresses these explanations.

-e *name*

Do not include the routine *name* in the call graph profile. Similarly, do not include any of *name*'s descendants, unless these routines are called via routines other than *name*. Time spent executing these routines is included in the totals. This option does not affect the flat profile, which includes all routines. The command line may contain any number of **-e** options. For example:

-e sub1 -e sub2

leaves the routines *sub1* and *sub2* out of the call graph.

-E *name*

This is similar to **-e**, but time spent executing the omitted routines is not included in the totals.

-f *name*

Print the call graph profile for *name* and its descendants only. The report includes time from all routines in its totals, whether or not these routines appear in the profile. More than one **-f** option may be used. For example:

-f sub1 -f sub2

prints the call graph for the routines *sub1* and *sub2* and their descendants but omits entries for all other routines.

-F *name*

Similar to **-f**; however, it includes only the times attributable to *name* and its descendants in total time and percentage computations.

-s Merge all listed *stat-files* into a single file, named *gmon.sum*. This file has the same format as other *stat-files* and, therefore, can be used in future **gprof** runs. It is a convenient way to collect data from many runs of an executable file.

-z With this option, **gprof** generates a list of routines that are never called.

For example, the command:

```
% gprof -s myprog statrun1 statrun2 statrun3 > profout
```

produces a profile that combines the data contained in the files *statrun1*, *statrun2*, and *statrun3*. Each of these files was produced by an independent run of the program **myprog**. The profile is placed in the file *profout*. Furthermore, the -s option tells **gprof** to merge the contents of *statrun1*, *statrun2*, and *statrun3* into a file named *gmon.sum*. *gmon.sum* can then be used to merge these data into future program runs.

The purpose of the -e, -E, -f, and -F options may be a little hard to understand, but you'll find them to be your friends once you try profiling a large program. Any program calls a lot of functions you're not interested in, including system calls. Using these options, you can eliminate the noise generated by these functions.

Structure of a gprof Profile

The output from **gprof** consists of three sections. **gprof** first displays the flat profile, which simply lists the total time spent executing each routine. This is followed by the call graph profile, which analyzes the execution time for each routine in terms of its parents and children. Finally, **gprof** includes an index that lists all profiled routines in alphabetical order and assigns an index number to each. (All uppercase letters precede all lowercase letters. Periods and underscores appear first in the collating sequence.) This index number will help you cross-reference routines in the call graph profile.

Both the call graph profile and the flat profile have a single entry per routine. Some routines are from your program and some are library or system calls. Some you will not even recognize, but you can assume that they are called internally by system calls.

To generate the examples in this chapter, we chose a program that tests the popular "quick sort" algorithm. This is not because we're fascinated by the algorithm, but because the program can easily be scaled to run a long time and therefore produce some meaningful figures. The routines in this program are:

main

This barely shows up in the profile, because all it does is set up a signal handler, print a few messages, and invoke *sort_driver*.

sort_driver

> Another trivial routine. *sort_driver* calls either *array_type_organpipe* or *array_type_random* to initialize a large array, and then it calls *qsort* to perform the sort.

qsort

> Here is the central routine. It calls itself recursively, which has an interesting effect on the call graph, and also calls *swap_elem* and *choose_pivot*.

array_type_organpipe

> One initialization routine, invoking the library call *rand* to generate random numbers.

array_type_random

> Another initialization routine, which also calls *rand*.

choose_pivot

> A routine called from *qsort*, and which in turn calls *rand*.

swap_elem

> A basic routine to switch two elements of an array.

signal_handler

> A simple routine we threw in to show what the call graph does with signal handlers.

The Flat Profile

The *flat profile* provides a one-dimensional view of where your program is spending its time. It tells you how much of the program's total time was spent in each function, the average amount of time each function took per call, etc. There is no information about the interaction between functions. Often, you don't need this kind of information; it is usually good enough to know that your program spends 70 percent of its time executing the function *runfast*. If this is all you need to know, you are better off looking at a simple flat report than the voluminous output produced by the call graph profiler.

There is a one-line entry for each function. These entries are sorted according to the amount of time spent executing the function itself, not counting time spent executing the function's descendants. Thus, the routine that took up the most time appears first. Each entry in the flat profile contains the following information:

%time

> Percentage of the program's total execution time spent executing this function. **gprof** does not include time spent executing the function's descendants in this figure.

cumulative *seconds*

>   Total number of seconds spent executing this function and all the functions appearing before it in the flat profile.

self *seconds*

>   Total number of seconds spent executing this function, not including time spent executing the function's descendants

calls

>   Total number of calls to this function that occurred while the program was executing. This figure is not printed for profiler routines.

self *ms/call*

>   Average amount of time in milliseconds spent executing this function each time it was called. For example, a function that contributed 1000 seconds to the program's total execution time and was called 10,000 times averaged 100 milliseconds (0.1 seconds) per call. This figure counts only the time spent executing the function itself and excludes any time spent executing any of the function's descendants.

total *ms/call*

>   Average amount of time in milliseconds spent executing this function and its children each time it was called. For example, if *qsort* averages 2 milliseconds per call, but calls other functions in a way that averages 27 milliseconds per call, the total ms/call for *qsort* is 29, and the self ms/call for *qsort* is 2.

name

>   Name of the function.

For example, here are a few lines from the output of a typical **gprof** flat profile:

```
Each sample counts as 0.01 seconds.
  %   cumulative   self              self     total
 time   seconds   seconds    calls  ms/call  ms/call  name
38.88    24.20     24.20         6  4033.33  4033.33  array_type_organpipe
38.28    48.03     23.83         6  3971.67  3972.64  array_type_random
15.20    57.49      9.46        12   788.33  1181.16  qsort
 7.44    62.12      4.63      1598     2.90     2.92   choose_pivot
 0.06    62.16      0.04       918     0.04     0.04   write
 0.06    62.20      0.04                                mcount
 0.03    62.22      0.02     11715     0.00     0.00   swap_elem
             .
             .
             .
 0.00    62.25      0.00         1     0.00     0.00   sigvec
```

The last line shows that the program required a total of 62.25 seconds of execution time. This includes 0.04 seconds from **mcount**, which is a routine inserted by the **-pg** compiler option to do the profiling. Note that the profiler omits some fields for **mcount**, because you wouldn't be interested in statistics for it.

The first line shows that the profiler collected statistics once every 0.01 seconds; this is a pretty fine resolution. Still, the majority of routines show zero in some of the time fields, because they just ran too quickly to be counted. In addition, you can't trust the timings for routines that were sampled only a few times—routines that ran for less than 0.1 seconds, perhaps.

The most heavily used function in the program is the first one, *array_type_organpipe*; it accounted for more than 24.20 seconds of execution time (38.88 percent of the total) even though it was called only six times. The *array_type_random* routine took almost as much time. Since together they accounted for 48.03 seconds out of the program's 62.25, all your efforts at optimizing are best spent here.

If a program spends only 5 percent of its time executing a given function, you can improve the program's performance by at most 5 percent by modifying the function. This may be a lot of work for very little return.

The *choose_pivot* routine presents an interesting lesson. It's probably not worth worrying about, since it requires only 4.63 seconds, but suppose you did have a reason to reduce this time. Each call to *choose_pivot* must be very short (as the call graph will show us later). The reason it accounts for so much time is that it is called 1598 times. So your strategy should be to look at the ancestors of *choose_pivot* and try to reduce the number of times it is called.

In general, the most important function calls (the calls in which the program spends most of its time) appear at the top of the flat listing. Three strategies are available for improving the performance of the program by looking at these functions:

1. Improve the algorithms used in these functions so they execute more quickly.

2. Improve the calling routine, so the functions are not called as often.

3. Eliminate the routines most often called by rewriting their callers to call them less often.

The last strategy is called inline substitution. It can be very effective for functions that are called many times and do virtually no work (i.e., routines for which the procedure call overhead is large compared to the actual computation they perform).

The Call Graph Profile

In some situations, the one-dimensional information provided by a flat profile is not enough. You need a two-dimensional display that shows why every routine was called: which routines called it, which routines it called, and what the total running time comprised. If several parts of the program call the same routine, you may want to know which calls account for most of the routine's time. Maybe some calls have worst-case arguments that could be better served by a different kind of function, or maybe one part of the program is calling the routine many times when it isn't really necessary. This is the kind of information that a call graph profile provides.

The call graph profile has a complex multiline entry for each routine. Different entries are separated by dashed lines. The column labeled **name**, toward the right side of the report, shows the routine under analysis in each section.

gprof lists the routine's parents above and to the right of the routine's name; it lists the routine's children below and to the right of the routine's name. Each name is followed by the index number that **gprof** assigned, which may make it easier to find your way through the call graph. The index number is enclosed in [] (square brackets). Thus, a function named *again* may be listed as *again [43]*, where the number 43 is the index number assigned to the routine.

Here is an entry for the *sort_driver* routine in our quick sort program:

```
index % time    self  children    called     name
-------------------------------------------------
                0.00   62.21       12/12          main [2]
[3]     100.0   0.00   62.21       12         sort_driver [3]
               24.20    0.00        6/6             array_type_organpipe [4]
               23.83    0.01        6/6             array_type_random [5]
                9.46    4.71       12/12            qsort [6]
-------------------------------------------------
```

Note that *sort_driver* stands out because it is farther to the left than the other routines. Since *main* is above *sort_driver*, *main* is the parent of *sort_driver*. The three routines below *sort_driver* are its children.

Because so much time is spent in *sort_driver*, its % **time** column shows that it uses 100% of the program's time. We already know that this time is actually spent in the children, and this graph reflects that fact in the **self** column. We see that *sort_driver* takes so little time that it is listed as having zero seconds. On the other hand, *array_type_organpipe* takes 24.20 seconds (as the flat profile also told us).

The **children** column shows how much time was spent in all the descendants of the function. Another part of our graph helps to show what this means:

```
index % time    self  children    called     name
-------------------------------------------------
                            5782              qsort [6]
                9.46    4.71       12/12           sort_driver [3]
[6]      22.8   9.46    4.71       12+5782    qsort [6]
                4.63    0.04     1598/1598         choose_pivot [7]
```

```
        0.00    0.03    1173/1824      _flsbuf [10]
        0.02    0.00    11715/11715    swap_elem [12]
                        5782           qsort [6]
-----------------------------------------------------
```

This part of the graph focuses on *qsort*. Essentially, its own code ran for only 9.46 seconds, while it spent 4.71 seconds calling its children.

While we've been focusing on the amount of time spent in each function, the **called** column lists the number of times each function was called. Because we used large arrays for the test program, and each element of the array had to be initialized with the *rand* routine, the graph reports many calls to that routine.

```
index % time    self  children    called       name
-----------------------------------------------------
                0.00    0.00    1598/3818      choose_pivot [7]
                0.01    0.00    2220/3818      array_type_random [5]
[13]     0.0    0.01    0.00    3818         rand [13]
                0.00    0.00    3818/3818      .mul [20]
-----------------------------------------------------
```

For parents and children, the **called** column includes two numbers separated by a slash. The entry 1598/3818 in the *choose_pivot* row means "1598 out of a total of 3818." In other words, *rand* was called 1598 times by *choose_pivot*, and 3818 times in the whole program. Similarly, *rand* called *.mul* 3818 times, and that was all the calls made to *.mul* in the program—no other function called it.

The entry for *qsort*, displayed earlier, shows what happens to recursive routines. The **called** column shows two numbers separated by a plus sign, 12+5782. This means that *qsort* was called 12 times by another routine (the row above shows that this routine was *sort_driver*—it made all 12 of the calls). In addition, *qsort* called itself 5782 times.

Two types of routines are not called from any other routine. One is the *start* routine, which the linker adds to the program to call *main*. The other is a signal handler. As the following part of the call graph shows, the string <spontaneous> is inserted to show that the function has no parent:

```
        -----------------------------------------------
                                              <spontaneous>
[18]     0.0    0.00    0.00                 _sigtramp [18]
                0.00    0.00      1/1          signal_handler [17]
        -----------------------------------------------
```

Tips on Interpreting the Call Graph

Parsing the information in the call graph is difficult already. Using it to improve your program is yet another step. Here are some guidelines to making use of the information.

- When a function's **self** column is higher than its **children** column, it is a prime candidate for optimization. Look for ways to improve its code.

- When a function's **children** column is higher than its **self** column, don't spend much time improving the function's own code. Either reduce the number of calls it makes or work on the children that hog the most time.

- When a function takes up a lot of time, but you don't think you can improve its code (possibly because it is in a library that you don't have control over), look at the parents that have the highest values in the **called** column. Try to reduce the number of times these parents call the function, by doing such things as reducing the number of passes through loops.

- When an expensive child has a high value in the **called** column, focus on reducing the number of times it is called. When it has a low value in ·the **called** column, try to optimize its code.

What Is Cygnus Support?

Cygnus Support is a recognized leader in the software development industry. Cygnus specializes in maintaining and distributing the Cygnus Developer's Kit, based on GNU development tools, by adding stability, portability, and customizibility to the widely used GNU toolset.

Cygnus Support is a major contributor to "Net" GNU, contributing greater than 50 percent of the enhancements to much of the GNU toolset. However, Cygnus does not sell or support "raw" GNU technology directly off the Internet. While Net GNU is an invaluable resource to many developers, for some, it simply lacks the process and controls necessary to deliver commercial-quality software and service as guaranteed by Cygnus Support.

Cygnus has developed a commercial release process that enables the company to deliver high-quality, stable commercial releases and upgrades every three months. This quarterly release cycle improves Cygnus customers' time to market, provides rapid deployment of new features, and allows Cygnus customers to address emerging and niche markets faster and more easily than other software providers.

In conjunction with the Cygnus Developer's Kit, Cygnus offers a range of world-class support and custom development services. These include guaranteed problem response times as short as one day, custom compiler enhancements and optimizations, and the development of complete custom tool chains.

The Cygnus Developer's Kit includes the GNU C/C++ compilers (**gcc** and **g++**), a source-level debugger with GUI interface (**gdb**), a macro-assembler, and a linker; all with source code, released quarterly. Cygnus also provides custom development for hosts and target processors not currently supported by Cygnus.

Cygnus supports and maintains GNU development tools on over 70 platform configurations.

Cygnus has developed strong strategic relationships with many leaders in the semiconductor, computer, and software industries. Current strategic partners include Hitachi, IBM, and Mentor Graphics.

B

Building GNU Software from Sources

If the CD in this book doesn't have executables for your system, don't worry—you may be able to generate them yourself from the sources. The Free Software Foundation and Cygnus Support have created a very nice configuration process that has been tested on most of the systems out there. Basically, all you should have to do is go to the top-level directory named *src* under each tool and issue the commands:

```
$ ./configure
$ make
```

(Why the `./` before `configure`? Because if you leave it off, the shell might not find the command in the current directory—it all depends on what your PATH is.) If you don't see any error messages, you can proceed to install the binaries as described in the previous section.

But when building software, you can never be absolutely sure what will happen. Your system may not be handled quite right by the automatic configuration procedure. In this chapter, we'll explain how the procedure works.

Actually, there are so many messages from these commands that you need a little explanation to know what's an error message and what isn't. Furthermore, you should have a little background about the magic these commands are carrying out, so you'll be able to start troubleshooting when something does go wrong. That will be the subject of the next few sections.

Table B-1 lists the major packages on the CD. Not all of these packages are utilities. It is worthwhile to understand that the GNU project is designing a whole operating system, not just a few tools. Many supporting libraries have been written, and the build process tries to use some of them whenever possible.

Table B-1: Software Packages on the CD-ROM

Package	Description
binutils	Various utilities for dealing with programs and executable files, including the **gas** assembler and **ld** linker
byacc	A free version of the **yacc** parser generator, discussed in the O'Reilly book *lex & yacc*
diffutils	The GNU version of **diff** and related utilities
emacs	The Emacs text editor, discussed in Chapter 3, *Editing Source Code with Emacs*
flex	A free version of the **lex** lexical analyzer, discussed in the O'Reilly book *lex & yacc*
gcc	The GNU C compiler, discussed in Chapter 4, *Compiling and Linking with gcc*
gdb	The GNU symbolic debugger, discussed in Chapter 6, *Debugging C and C++ Programs*
gprof	Profiler, discussed in Chapter 9, *Program Timing and Profiling*
libg++	The GNU C++ library
make	The GNU version of this build utility, discussed in Chapter 7, *Automatic Compilation with make*
rcs	A free source control package, discussed in Chapter 8, *Source Management with RCS*
readline	A library of advanced terminal input functions
texinfo	A set of TEX macros that produce online **info** documentation and hardcopy versions of Free Software Foundation and Cygnus manuals. (To produce hardcopies, you need to get TEX separately.)

A Little History About Build Procedures

As soon as someone wants to offer a piece of software on two different systems—whether the difference is in hardware or in software—problems in building arise. Minor or major changes have to be made to the code, and along with these changes go accommodations to let the same source files be used on both systems. The traditional way to solve this problem is to include both sets of statements in the source file, with **#ifdef** or **#ifndef** directives to tell the compiler which set to use:

```
#ifndef SUNOS_5
        channel = open (<">/dev/kmem<">, 0);
        if (channel >= 0)
           getloadavg_initialized = 1;
#else /* SUNOS_5 */
        /* We pass 0 for the kernel, corefile, and swapfile names
           to use the currently running kernel.  */
```

```
      kd = kvm_open (0, 0, 0, O_RDONLY, 0);
      if (kd != 0)
        {
          /* nlist the currently running kernel.  */
          kvm_nlist (kd, nl);
          offset = nl[0].n_value;
          getloadavg_initialized = 1;
        }
#endif /* SUNOS_5 */
```

The preceding snippet from the GNU **make** source code reflects an enhancement that Sun added to SunOS version 5. Most versions of UNIX let you get information about currently running processes by reading directly from memory through a pseudo-device named */dev/kmem*. Sun decided to provide a layer of library calls to return the same information. Consequently, conditional directives for SUNOS_5 crop up throughout this section of the source code.

UNIX has a bad reputation for coming in too many different versions. But other systems have versions too, although the divergence is less spectacular. If you use Windows, for instance, you are likely to upgrade regularly, so that you can run new programs that require new features from the system. You don't have to worry about building the binaries for the proper version, of course, because the vendor does that for you—but you pay for the service.

System Differences in the Source Files

The differences in hardware and UNIX systems are reflected by program **#ifdef**s in two ways. One, as we've already seen, is to name the hardware or operating system right in the **#ifdef**. But this can lead to problems. Lots of systems are based on System V (or BSD, or whatever) and are pretty close to System V, but store a couple of libraries in a different place or leave out a few calls that System V is supposed to have. On these systems, a directive like **#ifdef** SYSV sometimes does exactly the right thing and sometimes bombs.

The **#ifndef** for SUNOS_5 we saw earlier is the result of such a mismatch; it had to be defined earlier in the source file as follows. The programmer hoped that everything new about version 5 could be captured by combining the features for Sun systems and the features in System V Release 4.

```
#if defined(sun) && defined(SVR4)
#define SUNOS_5
#endif
```

Because guessing the behavior of each operating system is a dangerous business, many programmers define their **#ifdef**s more precisely. They use descriptive strings like TARGET_IS_BIG_ENDIAN_P or HAVE_SYS_SIGLIST. Both of these examples happen to come from GNU software. The first refers to the byte order within a word, a subject discussed in Appendix C, *Data Representations*. The second refers to a character array that many systems define in order to provide text descriptions of signals. By using potentially dozens of different #ifdefs, a programmer can build the software to meet the precise requirements of each system.

What happens when you want to compile such a program on *your* system? You have to know precisely where your system falls concerning each issue where UNIX systems differ. If the programmer uses system names in #ifdefs, you need to be alert to where your system diverges from the standards. If the programmer uses descriptive strings, you need to do research on each one. In either case, if no further help is forthcoming, you have to step through the code and look at each section within each #ifdef. You have turned from a user into a collaborator.

Now, some people like to explore all the tools they port. But this is not appealing to a student or researcher who has many other tasks to get done. And you probably expected to start your study of UNIX by *using* the tools, not by reading their source code. So the programmer really needs to provide another layer of option processing to help you.

System Differences in makefiles

Enter the *makefile*. This is a description of how to build a program. It is read by a utility called **make**, which is described in Chapter 7, *Automatic Compilation with make*. By consolidating definitions in the *makefile*, most programmers make things easier for the person trying to move the software to a different platform. Typical comments look like this:

```
# To use your system malloc, uncomment MMALLOC_DISABLE.
#MMALLOC_DISABLE = -DNO_MMALLOC
# To use mmalloc but disable corruption checking, uncomment MMALLOC_CHECK
#MMALLOC_CHECK = -DNO_MMALLOC_CHECK
```

These lines come from the **gdb** *makefile*, and are present because the GNU project developed an enhanced version of the standard **malloc** library call. Their version cannot be compiled on all systems, so they have made its use optional.

A pound sign (#) in a makefile is a comment symbol; it causes **make** to ignore everything that follows. So if, after reading the discussion in the makefile (and perhaps other documentation provided with the GNU tools) you decide not to use the GNU **malloc** package, take the pound sign away from the second line so it looks like:

```
MMALLOC_DISABLE = -DNO_MMALLOC
```

The string after the equal sign is a **-D** compiler option. Through a sequence of makefile variables like MMALLOC_DISABLE, this option is eventually passed to the compiler command that builds **gdb**. Within the **gdb** source code, the NO_MMALLOC symbol is tested as described earlier to control which form of **malloc** is used.

RCS is the only tool on your CD that you have to configure by editing the makefile. Proper configuration requires careful study of the *read.me* file in the *src* directory and quite possibly some experimentation. In the makefile, you find lots of choices like this:

```
RCSDIR = /usr/local/bin
#RCSDIR = /bin
#RCSDIR = /usr/bin
```

The makefile uses RCSDIR as the directory in which it installs the RCS binaries. Since the first line in the preceding example has no pound sign at the beginning, */usr/local/bin* is currently the value chosen for RCSDIR. You can change this default by putting a pound sign before it, though, and taking the pound sign away from one of the other lines—or just write whatever value you want after the equal sign.

Using makefile variables is significantly easier for the person porting a program than reading through the source code. At least all the choices are in one place. Still, the makefiles can become several hundred lines long, and you have to consider several dozen different options, each requiring some research. So most large projects have added yet another layer of configuration, in an ongoing attempt to make porting as easy as possible.

Configure Scripts

UNIX developers have spent years searching for ways to simplify building programs so that the lessons learned by the first person to carry out a port can be preserved for all future users. The programmers would like a way for you to say to the software package, "I have a Sun running SunOS 5; please build the right binary for me." The solutions create a customized makefile that works for your system.

The best known solution is **imake**, which is used by the X Window System releases. It reads files in a special language specifying what files should be used and what options should be passed to the compiler, then builds a makefile. Other solutions use shell scripts (programs written in the shell command language) that ask you questions about your system, or they use options learned from previous ports.

One of the cleverest solutions is GNU **configure**, which is used by the tools in this book. It is a long and complicated shell script that dynamically determines what is on your system. It checks directories for the locations of libraries, looks in header files, and even compiles and runs little programs to test features of the system. You don't have to do any research on your own—that's all done by the script.

A typical run of the *configure* script produces messages like this, as it checks for a slew of different features:

```
$ ./configure
checking for a BSD compatible install
checking for ranlib
checking how to run the C preprocessor
checking for AIX
checking for POSIXized ISC
          .
          .
          .
```

Configuration Options for GNU Tools

Sometimes the defaults used by the *configure* script are not right for you. Read the first few lines of the script to find the command-line options that let you change defaults. Note that all these options begin with two hyphens. A couple of the most important are:

--exec-prefix

> This tells the makefile where to put binaries when you issue the **make install** command. By default, the script installs files in */usr/local*. If you want something different, such as */fsftool*, enter the command:

```
$ ./configure --exec-prefix=/fsftool
```

--host

> Use this if you find that the *configure* script doesn't guess your host correctly. (You can also build binaries for a different system—in other words, cross-compile the program—but that is more complicated.) The hostname is rather complicated: you have to specify both the hardware and the operating system. A typical option is:

```
$ ./configure --host=sparc--sunos4
```

After *configure* is finished, you should have a file named *Makefile* that is just right for you. Test it out by issuing:

```
$ make
$ make install
```

While Emacs uses a *configure* script like other GNU software, it has some unique features worth mentioning. The most interesting is the option --with-x=no. If you don't have an X terminal, you can use this option to dispense with all the code supporting X.

While you're thinking about what to put in your Emacs executable, be aware that you also get to write some Lisp code. Some Emacs interfaces to other tools (notably mail and Net news) require the definition of some variables. (You can find out what to define by reading the beginning of the *.el* file for each package.) You can then create a file named *site-init.el* in the *lisp* subdirectory of the Emacs source tree. Here is a sample *site-init.el* file, for a hypothetical system in the domain *mysite.com*:

```
(setq news-path "/usr/spool/news/")
(setq rmail-spool-directory "/usr/spool/mail/")
(setq news-inews-program "/usr/local/bin/inews")
(setq gnus-default-nntp-server "news.mysite.com")
(setq gnus-nntp-service "nntp")
(setq gnus-local-domain "mysite.com")
(setq gnus-local-organization "Burgeoning Concepts, Inc.")
(setq sendmail-program "/usr/lib/sendmail")
```

Problems with Builds

By now you may have noted that you need tools in order to build tools. Besides the shell (which is truly essential; you can't even log in without one), every build uses a C compiler and **make**. Virtually all vendors include these tools on the systems they sell to you, but if you don't have them you are stuck with a bootstrapping problem.

The GNU **make** package includes a shell script you can run to build **make**, in case you don't have a version of **make** yet. All you have to do is enter:

```
$ sh build.sh
```

But if you don't have a C compiler, you really can't get anywhere. Your only hope in this case is ask around among your friends, or post a message to a friendly Usenet group, to get a binary of a compiler.

Even when the vendor does provide all the tools you need, the tools sometimes don't work the way the package expects. The Free Software Foundation has done their best to use general constructs that all compilers and versions of **make** recognize, but there is no perfect lowest common denominator—your tool might just do something different. This is just one of many problems you can encounter when porting software.

Problems rarely occur when you run the *configure* script. Most of the time they come up during execution of the compiler commands that run when you enter the **make** command. **make** prints out each command before executing it. If anything goes wrong with a command, you will see a message with the word "error" in it, like:

```
cc -DHAVE_CONFIG_H -DLIBDIR=\"/home/mikel/bin/lib\" \
    -DINCLUDEDIR=\"/usr/local/include\" -c -I. -I. -I./glob \
    -I./../include -g main.c -o main.o
main.c: 25: Can't find include file getopt.h
make: *** [main.o] Error 2
```

What this particular message says is that the preceding **cc** command failed. The reason is that *getopt.h* is not where the source code expected it to be. Since this error occurred during a real build, clearly there are times when the process fails. The *configure* script cannot anticipate everything. (In this case, the **make** package simply didn't contain the header file.)

At this point, you have left the realm where novices can play and entered the adventure of porting. We can't pick out a few simple things to tell you; your problems could stem from a number of areas. There is another O'Reilly book that is all about this problem: *Porting UNIX Software* by Greg Lehey. Perhaps with that book, or with the help of a local expert, you can complete your build and start to enjoy your new software.

Data Representations

Properly speaking, data representation is neither a compiler issue nor a UNIX issue. Data representation is defined by the hardware. However, because programmers are often vitally concerned with the details of data representation and because data representations are gradually standardizing, we will devote some time to data representation issues.

Storage Layout

Like Gulliver's Lilliputia, the computer world is divided into two factions: systems that place the most significant byte of any quantity at the lowest address in memory and systems that place the least significant byte at the lowest address. Borrowing Swift's nomenclature, these are often referred to as *Big-endian* and *Little-endian* systems. The split goes something like this:

Little Endian (Least significant bit at lowest address)	Big Endian (Most significant bit at lowest address)
DEC (VAX and Alpha series)	IBM (370 series and successors)
Intel (8086 series systems)	Motorola (68000- and 88000-series systems)
	Sun Sparc
	SGI
	RS6000

Some processors (in particular, the MIPS R2000 series) have a "mode bit" so they can handle both formats. However, that doesn't concern you. Users usually don't have access to this configuration bit. If you are using this kind of processor, it is set up to work in one mode or the other.

Regardless of the byte ordering, manufacturers generally refer to the least significant bit as bit 0. The most significant bit is therefore bit 7, 15, or 31 (depending on whether you are referring to a byte, a half-word, or a word).

Integer Representation

Integer quantities are usually represented as signed, two's complement numbers of two or four sequential bytes, respectively. The most significant bit of this number (bit 15 or 31) is the sign. For example, the hexadecimal number FFFFFFFF represents -1 if used as a 32-bit int.

You can always depend on char to represent eight bits (capable of storing values from −128 to 127). On a few very, very old systems, a short int would also be eight bits, and a long int would be 16 bits (storing values from -32768 and 32767). But on nearly all systems nowadays, a short int is 16 bits and a long int is 32 bits (storing values from -2147483648 to 2147483647).

Floating-Point Numbers

Until a few years ago, every manufacturer had its own way of representing floating-point numbers. This presented tremendous problems when moving programs from one system to another: porting any but the simplest algorithm to another system generally introduced problems with numerical stability and round-off error. In the last few years, the IEEE standard for floating-point representation (IEEE 754) has come a long way toward eliminating these problems. This standard is particularly widespread in the UNIX world; most manufacturers of UNIX systems adhere to it.

Single Precision

A value that you declare as float, in the IEEE 754 representation, is a 32-bit (single-word) quantity in which bit 31 is the *sign*, bits 30 through 23 are the *biased exponent*, and bits 22 through bit 0 are the *fraction*. That is, the exponent field is 8 bits wide and the fraction field is 23 bits wide, as shown below.

31	30 23	22 0
Sign	Biased Exponent	Fractional Part
1 bit	8 bits	23 bits

The sign is 0 for a positive number, 1 for a negative number.

The biased exponent is the number's binary exponent plus a bias of 127. The bias guarantees that all exponents are positive, simplifying the problem of representing negative exponents. The binary exponent may have any value between -126 and +127 (1 <= biased exponent <= 254). The values 127 and +128 are reserved for exception handling.

The fraction represents the fractional part of the mantissa of a floating-point number. The integer part of this mantissa is always one and is not represented.

The value of any single-precision floating-point number is therefore:

$$(-1)^{**}sign * (1+fraction) * 2^{**}(biased\_exponent–127)$$

float numbers can have values in the range of -3e38 < x < 3e38. (We are using here the floating-point notation where "e38" indicates an exponent of 38; in other words, the preceding number is shifted left 38 decimal places.) The minimum magnitude of the number is 1.2e-38.

Double Precision

In the IEEE 754 representation, a double is a 64-bit (eight-byte) quantity in which bit 63 is the sign, bits 62 through 52 are the biased exponent, and bits 51 through bit 0 are the fraction. That is, the exponent field is 11 bits wide and the fraction field is 52 bits wide, as shown below.

63	62　　　　　　　　52	51　　　　　　　　　　　0
Sign	Biased Exponent	Fractional Part
1 bit	11 bits	52 bits

The sign is 0 for a positive number, 1 for a negative number.

The biased exponent is the number's binary exponent plus a bias of 1023. The bias guarantees that all exponents are positive, simplifying the problem of representing negative exponents. The binary exponent may have any value between -1022 and 1023 (1 <= biased exponent <= 2055). The values -1023 and +1024 are reserved for exception handling.

The fraction represents the fractional part of the mantissa of a floating-point number. The integer part of this mantissa is always one and is not represented.

The value of any double-precision floating-point number is therefore:

$$(-1)^{**}sign * (1+fraction) * 2^{**}(biased\_exponent–1023)$$

double numbers can represent values in the range –1.7e308 < x < 1.7e308. The minimum magnitude of the number is 2.3e-308.

Error Conditions

The IEEE 754 floating-point representation introduced three new quantities to floating-point arithmetic: positive and negative infinity (written Inf and -Inf) and "not-a-number" (written NaN). The infinities represent positive or negative overflow. NaN represents an indeterminate or impossible result. For example, **arccos(1.3)** is NaN; it is neither an overflow nor an underflow, but an impossible result.

A computation that produces an infinity or an NaN may generate an arithmetic exception. Equivalently, a function may return an error code and set the **errno** variable to **EDOM** or **ERANGE**. The details of exception handling are subtle and depend heavily upon the system's implementation. There are many situations in which operations involving infinities or even NaNs are legal; the design of IEEE 754 explicitly allows programs to propagate infinities and NaNs through further calculations, if desired. When infinities and NaNs appear in computations, they behave the way you would expect them to. An infinity plus, minus, or times any nonzero finite number is still an infinity; infinity minus infinity is NaN (indeterminate); infinity times zero is NaN; any operation on an NaN produces another NaN; etc.

D

The GNU General Public License

This appendix covers an important document that you should be familiar with: the GNU General Public License. The General Public License defines the terms under which GNU Emacs, other Free Software Foundation products, and many privately written programs (such as RCS) are distributed. In fact, practically every utility described in this book, except basic UNIX commands, such as we describe in Chapter 2, *Introduction to the UNIX Operating System*, falls under the GPL. We print the license in its entirety.

GNU General Public License

GNU GENERAL PUBLIC LICENSE Version 2, June 1991

Copyright © 1989, 1991 Free Software Foundation, Inc. 675 Mass Ave, Cambridge, MA 02139, USA

Everyone is permitted to copy and distribute verbatim copies of this license document, but changing it is not allowed.

Preamble

The licenses for most software are designed to take away your freedom to share and change it. By contrast, the GNU General Public License is intended to guarantee your freedom to share and change free software—to make sure the software is free for all its users. This General Public License applies to most of the Free Software Foundation's software and to any other program whose authors commit to using it. (Some other Free Software Foundation software is covered by the GNU Library General Public License instead.) You can apply it to your programs, too.

When we speak of free software, we are referring to freedom, not price. Our General Public Licenses are designed to make sure that you have the freedom to distribute copies of free software (and charge for this service if you wish), that you receive source code or can get it if you want it, that you can change the software or use pieces of it in new free programs and that you know you can do these things.

To protect your rights, we need to make restrictions that forbid anyone to deny you these rights or to ask you to surrender the rights. These restrictions translate to certain responsibilities for you if you distribute copies of the software, or if you modify it.

For example, if you distribute copies of such a program, whether gratis or for a fee, you must give the recipients all the rights that you have. You must make sure that they, too, receive or can get the source code. And you must show them these terms so they know their rights.

We protect your rights with two steps: (1) copyright the software, and (2) offer you this license which gives you legal permission to copy, distribute and/or modify the software.

Also, for each author's protection and ours, we want to make certain that everyone understands that there is no warranty for this free software. If the software is modified by someone else and passed on, we want its recipients to know that what they have is not the original, so that any problems introduced by others will not reflect on the original authors' reputations.

Finally, any free program is threatened constantly by software patents. We wish to avoid the danger that redistributors of a free program will individually obtain patent licenses, in effect making the program proprietary. To prevent this, we have made it clear that any patent must be licensed for everyone's free use or not licensed at all.

The precise terms and conditions for copying, distribution, and modification follow.

GNU GENERAL PUBLIC LICENSE

TERMS AND CONDITIONS FOR COPYING, DISTRIBUTION, AND MODIFICATION

0. This License applies to any program or other work which contains a notice placed by the copyright holder saying it may be distributed under the terms of this General Public License. The "Program," below, refers to any such program or work, and a "work based on the Program" means either the Program or any

derivative work under copyright law: that is to say, a work containing the Program or a portion of it, either verbatim or with modifications and/or translated into another language. (Hereinafter, translation is included without limitation in the term "modification".) Each licensee is addressed as "you."

Activities other than copying, distribution, and modification are not covered by this License; they are outside its scope. The act of running the Program is not restricted, and the output from the Program is covered only if its contents constitute a work based on the Program (independent of having been made by running the Program). Whether that is true depends on what the Program does.

1. You may copy and distribute verbatim copies of the Program's source code as you receive it, in any medium, provided that you conspicuously and appropriately publish on each copy an appropriate copyright notice and disclaimer of warranty; keep intact all the notices that refer to this License and to the absence of any warranty; and give any other recipients of the Program a copy of this License along with the Program.

You may charge a fee for the physical act of transferring a copy, and you may at your option offer warranty protection in exchange for a fee.

2. You may modify your copy or copies of the Program or any portion of it, thus forming a work based on the Program, and copy and distribute such modifications or work under the terms of Section 1 above, provided that you also meet all of these conditions:

- You must cause the modified files to carry prominent notices stating that you changed the files and the date of any change.

- You must cause any work that you distribute or publish, that in whole or in part contains or is derived from the Program or any part thereof, to be licensed as a whole at no charge to all third parties under the terms of this License.

- If the modified program normally reads commands interactively when run, you must cause it, when started running for such interactive use in the most ordinary way, to print or display an announcement including an appropriate copyright notice and a notice that there is no warranty (or else, saying that you provide a warranty) and that users may redistribute the program under these conditions, and telling the user how to view a copy of this License. (Exception: if the Program itself is interactive but does not normally print such an announcement, your work based on the Program is not required to print an announcement.)

These requirements apply to the modified work as a whole. If identifiable sections of that work are not derived from the Program, and can be reasonably considered independent and separate works in themselves, then this License, and its terms, do not apply to those sections when you distribute them as separate works. But when you distribute the same sections as part of a whole which is a work based on the Program, the distribution of the whole must be on the terms of this License, whose permissions for other licensees extend to the entire whole, and thus to each and every part regardless of who wrote it.

Thus, it is not the intent of this section to claim rights or contest your rights to work written entirely by you; rather, the intent is to exercise the right to control the distribution of derivative or collective works based on the Program.

In addition, mere aggregation of another work not based on the Program with the Program (or with a work based on the Program) on a volume of a storage or distribution medium does not bring the other work under the scope of this License.

3. You may copy and distribute the Program (or a work based on it, under Section 2) in object code or executable form under the terms of Sections 1 and 2 above provided that you also do one of the following:

- Accompany it with the complete corresponding machine readable source code, which must be distributed under the terms of Sections 1 and 2 above on a medium customarily used for software interchange; or,

- Accompany it with a written offer, valid for at least three years, to give any third party, for a charge no more than your cost of physically performing source distribution, a complete machine-readable copy of the corresponding source code, to be distributed under the terms of Sections 1 and 2 above on a medium customarily used for software interchange; or,

- Accompany it with the information you received as to the offer to distribute corresponding source code. (This alternative is allowed only for noncommercial distribution and only if you received the program in object code or executable form with such an offer, in accord with Subsection b above.)

The source code for a work means the preferred form of the work for making modifications to it. For an executable work, complete source code means all the source code for all modules it contains, plus any associated interface definition files, plus the scripts used to control compilation and installation of the executable. However, as a special exception, the source code distributed need not include anything that is normally distributed (in either source or binary form) with the major components (compiler, kernel, and so on) of the operating system on which the executable runs, unless that component itself accompanies the executable.

If distribution of executable or object code is made by offering access to copy from a designated place, then offering equivalent access to copy the source code from the same place counts as distribution of the source code, even though third parties are not compelled to copy the source along with the object code.

4. You may not copy, modify, sublicense, or distribute the Program except as expressly provided under this License. Any attempt otherwise to copy, modify, sublicense, or distribute the Program is void, and will automatically terminate your rights under this License. However, parties who have received copies, or rights, from you under this License will not have their licenses terminated so long as such parties remain in full compliance.

5. You are not required to accept this License, since you have not signed it. However, nothing else grants you permission to modify or distribute the Program or its derivative works. These actions are prohibited by law if you do not accept this License. Therefore, by modifying or distributing the Program (or any work based on the Program), you indicate your acceptance of this License to do so, and all its terms and conditions for copying, distributing, or modifying the Program or works based on it.

6. Each time you redistribute the Program (or any work based on the Program), the recipient automatically receives a license from the original licensor to copy, distribute, or modify the Program subject to these terms and conditions. You may not impose any further restrictions on the recipients' exercise of the rights granted herein. You are not responsible for enforcing compliance by third parties to this License.

7. If, as a consequence of a court judgment or allegation of patent infringement or for any other reason (not limited to patent issues), conditions are imposed on you (whether by court order, agreement, or otherwise) that contradict the conditions of this License, they do not excuse you from the conditions of this License. If you cannot distribute so as to satisfy simultaneously your obligations under this License and any other pertinent obligations, then as a consequence, you may not distribute the Program at all. For example, if a patent license would not permit royalty-free redistribution of the Program by all those who receive copies directly or indirectly through you, then the only way you could satisfy both it and this License would be to refrain entirely from distribution of the Program.

If any portion of this section is held invalid or unenforceable under any particular circumstance, the balance of the section is intended to apply and the section as a whole is intended to apply in other circumstances.

It is not the purpose of this section to induce you to infringe any patents or other property right claims or to contest validity of any such claims; this section has the sole purpose of protecting the integrity of the free software distribution system, which is implemented by public license practices. Many people have made generous contributions to the wide range of software distributed through that system in reliance on consistent application of that system; it is up to the author/donor to decide if he or she is willing to distribute software through any other system and a licensee cannot impose that choice.

This section is intended to make thoroughly clear what is believed to be a consequence of the rest of this License.

8. If the distribution and/or use of the Program is restricted in certain countries either by patents or by copyrighted interfaces, the original copyright holder who places the Program under this License may add an explicit geographical distribution limitation excluding those countries, so that distribution is permitted only in or among countries not thus excluded. In such case, this License incorporates the limitation as if written in the body of this License.

9. The Free Software Foundation may publish revised and/or new versions of the General Public License from time to time. Such new versions will be similar in spirit to the present version, but may differ in detail to address new problems or concerns.

Each version is given a distinguishing version number. If the Program specifies a version number of this License which applies to it and "any later version," you have the option of following the terms and conditions either of that version or of any later version published by the Free Software Foundation. If the Program does not specify a version number of this License, you may choose any version ever published by the Free Software Foundation.

10. If you wish to incorporate parts of the Program into other free programs whose distribution conditions are different, write to the author to ask for permission. For software which is copyrighted by the Free Software Foundation, write to the Free Software Foundation; we sometimes make exceptions for this. Our decision will be guided by the two goals of preserving the free status of all derivatives of our free software and of promoting the sharing and reuse of software generally.

11. BECAUSE THE PROGRAM IS LICENSED FREE OF CHARGE, THERE IS NO WARRANTY FOR THE PROGRAM, TO THE EXTENT PERMITTED BY APPLICABLE LAW. EXCEPT WHEN OTHERWISE STATED IN WRITING THE COPYRIGHT HOLDERS AND/OR OTHER PARTIES PROVIDE THE PROGRAM "AS IS" WITHOUT WARRANTY OF ANY KIND, EITHER EXPRESSED OR IMPLIED, INCLUDING, BUT NOT LIMITED TO, THE IMPLIED

WARRANTIES OF MERCHANTABILITY AND FITNESS FOR A PARTICULAR PURPOSE. THE ENTIRE RISK AS TO THE QUALITY AND PERFORMANCE OF THE PROGRAM IS WITH YOU. SHOULD THE PROGRAM PROVE DEFECTIVE, YOU ASSUME THE COST OF ALL NECESSARY SERVICING, REPAIR, OR CORRECTION.

12. IN NO EVENT UNLESS REQUIRED BY APPLICABLE LAW OR AGREED TO IN WRITING WILL ANY COPYRIGHT HOLDER, OR ANY OTHER PARTY WHO MAY MODIFY AND/OR REDISTRIBUTE THE PROGRAM AS PERMITTED ABOVE, BE LIABLE TO YOU FOR DAMAGES, INCLUDING ANY GENERAL, SPECIAL, INCIDENTAL, OR CONSEQUENTIAL DAMAGES ARISING OUT OF THE USE OR INABILITY TO USE THE PROGRAM (INCLUDING BUT NOT LIMITED TO LOSS OF DATA OR DATA BEING RENDERED INACCURATE OR LOSSES SUSTAINED BY YOU OR THIRD PARTIES OR A FAILURE OF THE PROGRAM TO OPERATE WITH ANY OTHER PROGRAMS), EVEN IF SUCH HOLDER OR OTHER PARTY HAS BEEN ADVISED OF THE POSSIBILITY OF SUCH DAMAGES.

Appendix

HOW TO APPLY THESE TERMS TO YOUR NEW PROGRAMS

If you develop a new program, and you want it to be of the greatest possible use to the public, the best way to achieve this is to make it free software which everyone can redistribute and change under these terms.

To do so, attach the following notices to the program. It is safest to attach them to the start of each source file to most effectively convey the exclusion of warranty; and each file should have at least the "copyright" line and a pointer to where the full notice is found.

```
<one line to give the program's name and a brief idea of what it does.>
Copyright (C) 19yy <name of author>
This program is free software; you can redistribute it and/or modify
it under the terms of the GNU General Public License as
published by the Free Software Foundation; either version 2 of the License,
or (at your option) any later version.
This program is distributed in the hope that it will be useful,
but WITHOUT ANY WARRANTY; without even the implied warranty of
MERCHANTABILITY or FITNESS FOR A PARTICULAR PURPOSE. See the
GNU General Public License for more details.
You should have received a copy of the GNU General Public
License along with this program; if not, write to the Free Software
Foundation, Inc., 675 Mass Ave, Cambridge, MA 02139, USA.
```

Also add information on how to contact you by electronic and paper mail.

If the program is interactive, make it output a short notice like this when it starts in an interactive mode:

```
Gnomovision version 69, Copyright © 19yy name of author
Gnomovision comes with ABSOLUTELY NO WARRANTY; for details type 'show w'.
This is free software, and you are welcome to redistribute it
under certain conditions; type 'show c' for details.
```

The hypothetical commands 'show w' and 'show c' should show the appropriate parts of the General Public License. Of course, the commands you use may be called something other than 'show w' and 'show c'; they could even be mouse-clicks or menu items—whatever suits your program.

You should also get your employer (if you work as a programmer) or your school, if any, to sign a "copyright disclaimer" for the program, if necessary. Here is a sample; alter the names:

```
Yoyodyne, Inc., hereby disclaims all copyright interest in the program
'Gnomovision' (which makes passes at compilers) written by James Hacker.
<signature of Ty Coon>, 1 April 1989
Ty Coon, President of Vice
```

This General Public License does not permit incorporating your program into pro-prietary programs. If your program is a subroutine library, you may consider it more useful to permit linking proprietary applications with the library. If this is what you want to do, use the GNU Library General Public License instead of this License.

Index

About the Authors

Mike Loukides is a senior editor at O'Reilly & Associates. His current technical focus includes Java programming and networking topics. He is the author of two other O'Reilly books, *System Performance Tuning* and *UNIX for FORTRAN Programmers*. Mike previously worked at Multiflow Computer, where he created all of Multiflow's documentation on programming languages.

In addition to Java and networks, Mike's technical interests include programming languages, system administration, and computer architecture. He is also a passable pianist—in fact, one of the few amateur pianists who even tries to play music by Olivier Messiaen. He lives in Connecticut with his wife, Judy, and their daughter, Alexandra.

Over a ten-year career in computer documentation **Andy Oram** evolved from a proponent of the congenial user-oriented approach to a fanatic on the subject of explaining models and internal operations so as to empower computer users. He was not prepared by his education (which included music and social work) for the philosophical and pedagogical demands of this role, but seems to have fallen into it.

His technical writing career encompassed several computer manufacturers, including Honeywell Information Systems (now Bull) and MASSCOMP (eventually merged with a couple of other companies). During this stint he wrote articles and delivered workshops on making user documentation verifiable through the same quality-assurance process used on other components of a computer system. Eventually giving up on the organizations that make software, he joined O'Reilly & Associates to write and edit the types of books he likes.

Andy has also been a member of Computer Professionals for Social Responsibility for many years and moderates their Cyber Rights mailing list, among other activies. Details can be found at *http://www.ora.com/people/staff/andyo*.

Colophon

Our look is the result of reader comments, our own experimentation, and distribution channels. Distinctive covers complement our distinctive approach to technical topics, breathing personality and life into potentially dry subjects. UNIX and its attendant programs can be unruly beasts. Nutshell Handbooks help you tame them.

A black swan is featured on the cover of *Programming with GNU Tools.* Swans are large aquatic birds that, along with ducks and geese, belong to the family Anatidae. There are seven species of swan distributed through all of the continents except Antarctica. The black swan is a native of Australia, but is now distributed throughout the world.

Unlike most species of Anatidae, female and male black swans share the duty of incubating the eggs. The gray chicks are able to swim almost immediately after hatching, but often hitch rides on their parents' back when tired. Black swans are also almost alone in not adapting their breeding season to the climate they live in. That means that their young hatch during the warmest time of the year in Australia, but in winter in Europe and North America, the hardest time of year for them to survive.

Because of their arching necks and graceful beauty, and because they mate for life, people have long held a romantic fascination with swans. They are the subject of numerous fairytales, legends, and works of art. Swans were once believed to hold special powers because, being animals of the water, air, and land, they were believed to live between all three of these worlds.

Edie Freedman designed this cover and the entire UNIX bestiary that appears on Nutshell Handbooks, using a 19th-century engraving from the Dover Pictorial Archive. The cover layout was produced with Quark XPress 3.3 using the ITC Garamond font. The CD design was created by Hanna Dyer.

The inside layout was designed by Nancy Priest. Text was prepared by Erik Ray in SGML DocBook 2.4 DTD. The print version of this book was created by translating the SGML source into a set of gtroff macros using a filter developed at ORA by Norman Walsh. Steve Talbott designed and wrote the underlying macro set on the basis of the GNU troff -gs macros; Lenny Muellner adapted them to SGML and implemented the book design. The GNU groff text formatter version 1.09 was used to generate PostScript output. The text and heading fonts are ITC Garamond Light and Garamond Book. The illustrations that appear in the book were created in Macromedia Freehand 5.5 by Chris Reilley.

Other Titles Available from O'Reilly

Scripting Languages

Programming Python, 2nd Edition

By Mark Lutz
2nd Edition March 2001
1256 pages, Includes CD-ROM
ISBN 0-596-00085-5

Programming Python, 2nd Edition, focuses on advanced applications of Python, an increasingly popular object-oriented scripting language. Endorsed by Python creator Guido van Rossum, it demonstrates advanced Python programming techniques, and addresses software design issues such as reusability and object-oriented programming. The enclosed platform-neutral CD-ROM has book examples and various Python-related packages, including the full Python Version 2.0 source code distribution.

Learning Python

By Mark Lutz & David Ascher
1st Edition April 1999
384 pages, ISBN 1-56592-464-9

Learning Python is an introduction to the increasingly popular Python programming language—an interpreted, interactive, object-oriented, and portable scripting language. This book thoroughly introduces the elements of Python: types, operators, statements, classes, functions, modules, and exceptions. It also demonstrates how to perform common programming tasks and write real applications.

Python in a Nutshell

By Alex Martelli
1st Edition November 2002 (est.)
400 pages (est.), ISBN 0-596-00188-6

This book offers Python programmers one place to look when you need help remembering or deciphering the most important tools and modules of this open source language. The book deals with the most frequently used parts of the standard library, and the most popular and important third party extensions. Python is an easy scripting language with a huge library that is enormously rich. *Python in a Nutshell* presents the highlights of all modules and functions, which cover well over 90% of a programmer's practical needs.

Python Cookbook

David Ascher & Alex Martelli, Editors
1st Edition July 2002
608 pages, ISBN 0-596-00167-3

The *Python Cookbook* is a collection of problems, solutions, and practical examples written by Python programmers in the style of the popular *Perl Cookbook*. Its potential audience includes both Python programmers and experienced programmers who are new to Python and want to evaluate whether or not the language is suitable for their intended applications. Anyone interested in Python programming will want this wealth of practical advice, snippets of code, and patterns of program design that can be directly lifted out of the book and applied to everyday programming problems.

Exploring Expect

By Don Libes
1st Edition December 1994
602 pages, ISBN 1-56592-090-2

Written by the author of Expect, this is the first book to explain how this part of the Unix toolbox can be used to automate Telnet, FTP, passwd, rlogin, and hundreds of other interactive applications. Based on Tcl (Tool Command Language), Expect lets you automate interactive applications that have previously been extremely difficult to handle with any scripting language.

Jython Essentials

By Noel Rappin & Samuele Pedroni
1st Edition March 2002
300 pages, ISBN 0-596-00247-5

Jython is an implementation of the Python programming language written in Java, allowing Python programs to integrate seamlessly with any Java code. The secret to Jython's popularity lies in the combination of Java's libraries and tools with Python's rapid development capabilities. *Jython Essentials* provides a solid introduction to the language, numerous examples of Jython/Java interaction, and valuable reference material on modules and libraries of use to Jython programmers.

O'REILLY®

To order: 800-998-9938 • order@oreilly.com • www.oreilly.com
Online editions of most O'Reilly titles are available by subscription at safari.oreilly.com
Also available at most retail and online bookstores.

Scripting Languages

Ruby in a Nutshell

By Yukihiro Matsumoto
With translated text by
David L. Reynolds Jr.
1st Edition November 2001
218 pages, ISBN 0-59600-214-9

Written by Yukihiro Matsumoto
("Matz"), creator of the language, *Ruby in a Nutshell* is a practical reference
guide covering everything from Ruby syntax to the
specifications of its standard class libraries. The book is
based on Ruby 1.6, and is applicable to development versions 1.7 and the next planned stable version 1.8. As part
of the successful "in a Nutshell" series *Ruby in a Nutshell* is for readers who want a single desktop reference
for all their needs.

Python Pocket Reference, 2nd Edition

By Mark Lutz
2nd Edition November 2001
128 pages, ISBN 0-596-00189-4

This book is a companion volume to
two O'Reilly animal guides: *Programming Python* and *Learning Python*. It
summarizes Python statements and
types, built-in functions, commonly
used library modules, and other
prominent Python language features.

Programming PHP

By Rasmus Lerdorf & Kevin Tatroe
1st Edition March 2002
528 pages, ISBN 1-56592-610-2

Programming PHP is a comprehensive
guide to PHP, a simple yet powerful
language for creating dynamic web
content. Filled with the unique knowledge of the creator of PHP, Rasmus Lerdorf, this book is
a detailed reference to the language and its applications,
including such topics as form processing, sessions, databases, XML, and graphics. Covers PHP 4, the latest version
of the language.

Python & XML

By Christopher A. Jones & Fred Drake
1st Edition December 2001
378 pages, ISBN 0-596-00128-2

This book has two objectives: to provide a comprehensive reference on
using XML with Python and to illustrate the practical applications of these
technologies (often coupled with cross-platform tools)
in an enterprise environment. Loaded with practical
examples, it also shows how to use Python to create
scalable XML connections between popular distributed
applications such as databases and web servers. Covers
XML flow analysis and details ways to transport XML
through a network.

Python Standard Library

By Fredrik Lundh
1st Edition May 2001
300 pages, ISBN 0-596-00096-0

Python Standard Library, an essential
guide for serious Python programmers, delivers accurate, author-tested
documentation of all the modules in
the Python Standard Library, along with over 300 annotated example scripts using the modules. This version of
the book covers all the new modules and related information for Python 2.0, the first major release of Python
in four years.

PHP Pocket Reference, 2nd Edition

By Rasmus Lerdorf
1st Edition November 2002 (est.)
96 pages (est.), ISBN 0-596-00402-8

Written by the founder of the PHP
Project, this valuable little book is
both a handy introduction to PHP
syntax and structure, and a quick reference to the vast array of functions
provided by PHP. Thoroughly updated
to include the specifics of PHP 4, the language's latest
version, the second edition provides an authoritative
overview of PHP packed into a pocket-sized guide that's
easy to take anywhere. This handbook acts as a perfect
tutorial for learning the basics of developing PHP-based
web applications, and is the ideal companion for O'Reilly's *Programming PHP*.

O'REILLY®

To order: *800-998-9938* • *order@oreilly.com* • *www.oreilly.com*
Online editions of most O'Reilly titles are available by subscription at *safari.oreilly.com*
Also available at most retail and online bookstores.

Unix Basics

Learning the UNIX Operating System, 5th Edition

By Jerry Peek, Grace Todino &
John Strang
5th Edition November 2001
176 pages, ISBN 0-596-00261-0

Learning the UNIX Operating System is the most effective introduction to Unix in print. The fifth edition covers Internet usage for email, file transfers, and web browsing. It's perfect for those who are just starting with Unix or Linux, as well as anyone who encounters a Unix system on the Internet. Complete with a quick-reference card to pull out and keep handy, it's an ideal primer for Mac and PC users of the Internet who need to know a little bit about Unix on the systems they visit.

Learning the Korn Shell, 2nd Edition

By Bill Rosenblatt, Arnold Robbins
2nd Edition April 2002
432 pages, ISBN 0-596-00195-9

Learning the Korn Shell is the key to gaining control of the Korn shell and becoming adept at using it as an interactive command and scripting language. Readers will learn how to write many applications more easily and quickly than with other high-level languages. A solid offering for many years, this newly revised title inherits a long tradition of trust among computer professionals who want to learn or refine an essential skill.

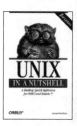

UNIX in a Nutshell: System V Edition, 3rd Edition

By Arnold Robbins
3rd Edition September 1999
616 pages, ISBN 1-56592-427-4

The bestselling, most informative Unix reference book is now more complete and up-to-date. Not a scaled-down quick reference of common commands, *UNIX in a Nutshell* is a complete reference containing all commands and options, with descriptions and examples that put the commands in context. For all but the thorniest Unix problems, this one reference should be all you need. Covers System V Release 4 and Solaris 7.

Using csh and tcsh

By Paul DuBois
1st Edition August 1995
242 pages, ISBN 1-56592-132-1

Using csh and tcsh describes from the beginning how to use these shells interactively to get your work done faster with less typing. You'll learn how to make your prompt tell you where you are (no more pwd); use what you've typed before (history); type long command lines with few keystrokes (command and filename completion); remind yourself of filenames when in the middle of typing a command; and edit a botched command without retyping it.

Learning GNU Emacs, 2nd Edition

By Debra Cameron, Bill Rosenblatt &
Eric Raymond
2nd Edition September 1996
560 pages, ISBN 1-56592-152-6

Learning GNU Emacs is an introduction to Version 19.30 of the GNU Emacs editor, one of the most widely used and powerful editors available under Unix. It provides a solid introduction to basic editing, a look at several important "editing modes" (special Emacs features for editing specific types of documents, including email, Usenet News, and the World Wide Web), and a brief introduction to customization and Emacs LISP programming. The book is aimed at new Emacs users, whether or not they are programmers. Includes quick-reference card.

Learning the vi Editor, 6th Edition

By Linda Lamb & Arnold Robbins
6th Edition October 1998
348 pages, ISBN 1-56592-426-6

This completely updated guide to editing with vi, the editor available on nearly every Unix system, now covers four popular vi clones and includes command summaries for easy reference. It starts with the basics, followed by more advanced editing tools, such as ex commands, global search and replacement, and a new feature, multi-screen editing.

O'REILLY®

To order: *800-998-9938* • *order@oreilly.com* • *www.oreilly.com*
Online editions of most O'Reilly titles are available by subscription at *safari.oreilly.com*
Also available at most retail and online bookstores.

How to stay in touch with O'Reilly

1. Visit our award-winning web site

http://www.oreilly.com/

★ "Top 100 Sites on the Web"—PC Magazine
★ CIO Magazine's Web Business 50 Awards

Our web site contains a library of comprehensive product information (including book excerpts and tables of contents), downloadable software, background articles, interviews with technology leaders, links to relevant sites, book cover art, and more. File us in your bookmarks or favorites!

2. Join our email mailing lists

Sign up to get email announcements of new books and conferences, special offers, and O'Reilly Network technology newsletters at:

http://www.elists.oreilly.com

It's easy to customize your free elists subscription so you'll get exactly the O'Reilly news you want.

3. Get examples from our books

To find example files for a book, go to:

http://www.oreilly.com/catalog

select the book, and follow the "Examples" link.

4. Work with us

Check out our web site for current employment opportunities:

http://jobs.oreilly.com/

5. Register your book

Register your book at:

http://register.oreilly.com

6. Contact us

O'Reilly & Associates, Inc.
1005 Gravenstein Hwy North
Sebastopol, CA 95472 USA
TEL: 707-827-7000 or 800-998-9938
          (6am to 5pm PST)
FAX: 707-829-0104

order@oreilly.com
For answers to problems regarding your order or our products. To place a book order online visit:

http://www.oreilly.com/order_new/

catalog@oreilly.com
To request a copy of our latest catalog.

booktech@oreilly.com
For book content technical questions or corrections.

corporate@oreilly.com
For educational, library, and corporate sales.

proposals@oreilly.com
To submit new book proposals to our editors and product managers.

international@oreilly.com
For information about our international distributors or translation queries. For a list of our distributors outside of North America check out:

http://international.oreilly.com/distributors.html

O'REILLY®